THE CONSTITUTION AND
CIVIL RIGHTS

By Milton R. Konvitz *,1908-*

IN LITTERIS
LIBERTAS

1754·1893

COLUMBIA UNIVERSITY PRESS

NEW YORK · 1947

APR 26 1948

JK
1726
.K6

*This book has been made possible by a grant from the
Rockefeller Foundation and the Cornell Research in Civil
Liberties. The author is deeply grateful for this assistance.*

Copyright 1947 by Columbia University Press

First printing January, 1947
Second printing December, 1947

Published in Great Britain and India by Geoffrey Cumberlege,
Oxford University Press, London and Bombay

MANUFACTURED IN THE UNITED STATES OF AMERICA

Apr. 29, 1948

FOR MY FATHER AND MY BROTHER BENZION

*You as a lump of salt have been thrown
into water and have become into water
and cannot be taken out again: and, whenever
I taste the water, it is salt.*

857426

Preface

THIS BOOK does not treat of political rights, such as the right to vote. Nor does it treat of civil liberties, such as those mentioned in the Bill of Rights (freedom of speech, freedom of the press, freedom of assembly, religious freedom, the right to bear arms, the right to security against unreasonable searches and seizures, security against double-jeopardy and excessive bail, the right to trial by jury, security against self-incrimination, and so on). The scope of this book is defined by its title: *The Constitution and Civil Rights*. In its more technical, limited sense, the term civil rights, as distinguished from political rights and civil liberties, refers to the rights of persons to employment, and to accommodations in hotels, restaurants, common carriers, and other places of public accommodation and resort. The term contemplates the rights enumerated in the federal Civil Rights Act of 1875 and the various acts against discrimination found on the statute books of eighteen states.

For the reason that some of the federal civil rights acts speak of privileges and immunities, as well as rights, it is necessary to consider the constitutional meaning of the term "privileges and immunities." The book, therefore, deals with both civil rights and the privileges and immunities of citizens.

It will be seen that, as the Constitution and statutes have been construed by the Supreme Court, very narrow scope has been given to the meaning of these terms. In so far as the Constitution is concerned, the civil rights, privileges, and immunities can be counted on one hand. This will surely come as a surprise to all readers except the rare specialist. The widespread, well-nigh universal, ignorance of this subject is in part due to the fact that so very little attention has been given to it by political scientists and other scholars. How is the layman to be blamed for his ignorance when attempts have not been made to bring pertinent information to his attention? As far as I know, this is the first time an attempt has been made to deal with this subject in a monograph.

It is hoped that the reader will share the view that the subject is of importance not only to the Negro, the Asiatic, the Catholic, the Jew, and other minority groups, but to the average American citizen who claims devotion to the ideals of democracy, a belief in equality, and dedication to the principles of freedom. In thirty American states there are no civil rights acts; the scope of the federal civil rights acts is extremely narrow. Much new ground remains to be broken. The job has hardly been begun. It is doubtful if many of the thirty states will move in the direction of a broader freedom. When the federal law on civil rights was expressed by the Supreme Court, the issue of states' rights was still very prominent. But today that issue can have little appeal to a free intelligence.

Freedom comes only from the law; but not all law gives freedom. In many of our states there are laws which compel people to wear the badges of slavery; but the Supreme Court, deciding cases on the issue of states' rights, has held such laws to be constitutional. Government by law, said Mr. Willkie, must be substituted for government by caprice and unlimited discretions. But the law itself must also be freed from caprice. The desired result will not be achieved if the states are left to their own devices. It can be achieved only through effective congressional legislation, national in scope, and rooted in the soil from which have come the Declaration of Independence, the Bill of Rights, the Fourteenth Amendment. It can be achieved only through the Supreme Court overruling earlier precedents which were decided on the basis of states' rights instead of human rights and the rights of citizens in a free community. There should be no place in the Constitution for a distinction between citizens as first class and second class.

M. R. K.

School of Industrial and Labor Relations
Cornell University
Ithaca, New York
July 27, 1946

Contents

PART ONE: FEDERAL CIVIL RIGHTS

PART TWO: STATE CIVIL RIGHTS

APPENDICES

Federal Civil Rights

The ultimate aim of government is not to rule, nor to restrain by fear, nor to exact obedience, but contrariwise, to free every man from fear, that he may live in all possible security; in other words, to strengthen his natural right to exist and to work without injury to himself or others. No, the object of government is not to change men from rational beings into beasts or puppets, but to enable them to develop their minds and bodies in security, and to employ their reason unshackled; neither showing hatred, anger, or deceit, nor watched with the eyes of jealousy and injustice. In fact, the true aim of government is liberty.

—BARUCH SPINOZA

CHAPTER 1

Federal Legislation, 1866–1875

O N DECEMBER 18, 1865, the Thirteenth Amendment, abolishing slavery, was ratified. Shortly thereafter, on March 14, 1866, Congress passed a Civil Rights Bill. Two weeks later the bill was vetoed by President Johnson, who feared that, under the terms of the bill, Chinese, Indians, and gypsies, as well as Negroes, might be made citizens. Furthermore, he questioned the wisdom of making citizens of former Negro slaves: "Four million of them have just emerged from slavery into freedom. Can it be reasonably supposed that they possess the requisite qualifications to entitle them to all the privileges and equalities of citizens of the United States?" If intelligent foreigners are required to wait five years before qualifying for citizenship, why should ignorant Negroes be made citizens without delay and without proof of good moral character? Moreover, if Congress can grant civil rights to the Negro, why not also the suffrage and the right to hold office? The bill, Johnson continued, interfered with the natural tendency of capital and labor to become mutually adjusted. If left to their own devices, labor (represented by the former slaves) and capital (represented by the former masters) would work out their problems satisfactorily. But the bill "frustrates this adjustment," by injecting the government between them to protect one against the other—and to discriminate against one in favor of the other; for, Johnson maintained, it discriminated against the white race. The bill also was an interference with states' rights, and was likely to serve as a vicious precedent: if Congress may guarantee to Negroes equal civil rights, may it not grant them the right to vote, the right to hold public office, and the right to marry white persons? [1]

[1] W. E. B. Du Bois, *Black Reconstruction* (1935), pp. 282 ff. Cf. Edward

On April 9, 1866, the bill became law over the veto of the President.

Let us look at this law, the first Civil Rights Act.[2] It declared all persons born in the United States, excluding Indians not taxed, to be citizens of the United States; that such citizens, without regard to race, color, or previous condition of servitude, shall have the same right: to make and enforce contracts, sue, be parties, give evidence; to inherit, purchase, lease, sell, hold, and convey real and personal property; to the full and equal benefit of all laws and proceedings for the security of person and property as is enjoyed by white citizens; to be subject to like punishment, pains, and penalties.

The act provided also that any person who, under color of any law, statute, ordinance, regulation, or custom, shall subject, or caused to be subjected, any inhabitant of any state or territory, to the deprivation of any right secured or protected by this act, or to different punishment, pains, or penalties, on account of such person's race, color, or previous condition of servitude, than is prescribed for the punishment of white persons, shall be guilty of a misdemeanor. Courts of the United States were granted jurisdiction of offenses under the act; federal officers were given the right to proceed against all persons violating the law, and were directed to afford "protection to all persons in their constitutional rights of equality before the law, without distinction of race or color, or previous condition of slavery or involuntary servitude."

In some respects, as will have been noticed, the act anticipated the provisions of the Fourteenth Amendment. That amendment was passed on June 13, 1866—only about two months after the act was passed over the veto—and was submitted to the states for ratification. In view of the existence of the Civil Rights Act, what was the need of the amendment? The answer is that, although the act was upheld by the federal circuit court in two

---

McPherson, *A Political History of the United States during Reconstruction* (1875), pp. 78 ff.
[2] 14 Stat. 39 (1866).

cases in 1866 and 1867,[3] its constitutionality was doubtful; at any rate, it was thought safer to place the substance of the act beyond the reach of the Supreme Court and the Congress of a later time.

The Fourteenth Amendment was ratified on July 28, 1868. The Fifteenth Amendment, providing against discrimination in suffrage on account of race, color, or previous condition of servitude, was passed by Congress in February of 1869 and was ratified on March 30, 1870. Two months later, on May 31, 1870, Congress enacted a new Civil Rights Act [4] under the last two amendments to the Constitution.

The provisions of the 1870 act were as follows: (1) It reenacted the 1866 Civil Rights Act. (2) It provided that all citizens, otherwise qualified by law to vote at any election in any state or subdivision thereof, shall be allowed to vote without distinction as to race, color, or previous condition of servitude. (3) It provided that if two or more persons shall conspire together, or go in disguise, with intent to violate any provision of the act; or to injure, oppress, threaten, or intimidate any citizen, with intent to prevent or hinder his free exercise and enjoyment of any right or privilege granted or secured to him by the Constitution or laws of the United States, or because of his having exercised the same, shall be guilty of a felony. (4) In addition to reenacting the 1866 act, the new statute provided that any person who, under color of any law, statute, ordinance, regulation, or custom, shall subject any inhabitant to the deprivation of any right to make and enforce contracts, sue, be parties, give evidence, and to the full and equal benefit of all laws and proceedings for the security of person and property as is enjoyed by white citizens, or to different punishment, pains, or penalties on account of such person being an alien, or by reason of his color or race, than is prescribed for the punishment of citizens, shall be guilty of a misdemeanor. (5) The act implemented the right

[3] U.S. v. Rhodes, Fed. Case 16,151 (1866); Matter of Turner, Fed. Case 14,247 (1867). See A. C. McLaughlin, *Constitutional History of the United States* (1935), 654–655.
[4] 18 Stat. L. 140 (1870).

of free suffrage, without distinction as to race, color, or previous condition of servitude, by many detailed provisions.

On March 1, 1875, Congress passed "An Act to Protect All Citizens in Their Civil and Legal Rights." [5] The preamble stated that Congress deemed it essential to just government that "we recognize the equality of all men before the law, and hold that it is the duty of government in all its dealings with the people to mete out equal and exact justice to all, of whatever nativity, race, color, or persuasion, religious or political," and that it is "the appropriate object of legislation to enact great fundamental principles into law." The new act provided that "all persons within the jurisdiction of the United States shall be entitled to the full and equal enjoyment of the accommodations, advantages, facilities, and privileges of inns, public conveyances on land or water, theaters, and other places of public amusement; subject only to the conditions and limitations established by law, and applicable alike to citizens of every race and color, regardless of any previous condition of servitude." The person aggrieved by a violation could recover $500, and the offender was also to be guilty of a misdemeanor. Federal courts were given exclusive jurisdiction. (The original bill as adopted by the Senate included schools and cemeteries, but the House substituted a bill from which these were omitted, it was the House bill that became the Civil Rights Act of 1875.) [6]

After the South lost the Civil War it continued its efforts to keep the Negro "in his place." Four states flatly refused to accept the Thirteenth Amendment. South Carolina, Alabama, and Florida ratified the amendment subject to important provisos affecting the political and civil rights of the Negro.[7] All of the Southern and Border states refused to ratify the Fourteenth Amendment.[8] The South opposed freedom, but freedom was achieved notwithstanding; then the South determined that freedom meant only the absence of slavery as it had been known before Emancipation: no political or civil rights. The North felt,

[5] 18 Stat. L. 335 (1875).   [6] Du Bois, *Black Reconstruction*, p. 594.
[7] *Ibid.*, p. 329.   [8] *Ibid.*, p. 321.

on the other hand, that freedom without these rights was only
an illusion and a snare; that a civil rights law was required to
override the effect of the Black Codes which the Southern states
adopted as soon as the North relaxed its vigilance: codes which
fixed on the Negro all the badges of servitude.[9] It was to meet
this situation that Congress passed the various civil rights laws,
culminating in the act of 1875.[10]

[9] See Paul Lewinson, *Race, Class, and Party* (1932), *passim;* C. G. Woodson,
The Negro in Our History (rev. ed., 1945); W. E. B. Du Bois, *Black Folk,
Then and Now* (1939); Charles E. Russell, *Blaine of Maine* (1931). Horace
E. Flack, *Adoption of the Fourteenth Amendment* (1908); Paul S. Peirce, *The
Freedmen's Bureau* (1904); E. B. Callendar, *Thaddeus Stevens, Commoner*
(1882); F. W. Seward, *Story of the Life of William H. Seward* (1891);
Moorfield Storey, *Charles Sumner* (1900); A. A. Taylor, *The Negro in the
Reconstruction of Virginia* (1926) and *The Negro in South Carolina during
Reconstruction* (1924).
[10] For a short history of federal civil rights legislation, see Francis Biddle,
"Civil Rights and the Federal Law," in *Safeguarding Civil Liberty Today*
(Edward L. Bernays Lectures, Cornell University, 1945), pp. 109–144.

CHAPTER 2

The Civil Rights Cases, 1883

ABOUT EIGHT YEARS AFTER the adoption of the 1875 Civil Rights Act, the Supreme Court was called upon to pass on the constitutionality of that statute. The court considered together seven cases: two were indictments for denying to Negroes accommodations and privileges of an inn or a hotel; two cases were actions for denying to individuals privileges and accommodations of a theater; one action was for refusing a Negro a seat in the dress circle in a San Francisco theater; one was for denying to a person full enjoyment of accommodations in the New York Grand Opera House; and the last was an action to recover the statutory penalty from a railway company because of the refusal of the conductor to allow the complainant's wife to ride in the ladies' car because she was a Negro.

The decision and opinions in the *Civil Rights Cases* [1] are of such far-reaching importance that a full analysis of them is necessary. The civil rights legislation adopted by Congress in the years 1866 to 1875 created a new concept of equality: that in the absence of slavery, no man should be subject to the incidents of slavery; that where the reality or substance of slavery is gone, its visible form or appearance should not be seen. The legislation was probably the first attempt in the history of mankind to destroy the branches of slavery after its root had been destroyed. What did the Supreme Court do with this legislation?

It is to be noted at the outset that up to 1883 the Supreme Court had declared only two acts of Congress unconstitutional; namely, in *Marbury v. Madison* (1803),[2] and in the notorious *Dred Scott* case (1857).[3] In 1883, in the *Civil Rights Cases*, it

[1] 109 U.S. 3 (1883). [2] 1 Cranch (U.S.) 137 (1803).
[3] 19 How. (U.S.) 393 (1857).

added a third instance. In the history of the people of the United States the *Civil Rights Cases* have played almost as tragic a role as has the *Dred Scott* case.

In his opinion for the majority of the court Mr. Justice Bradley stated that the purpose of the 1875 law was to declare that in the enjoyment of accommodations and privileges of inns, public conveyances, theaters, and other places of public accommodation, no distinction shall be made between citizens of different races or color, or between those who have and those who have not been slaves.

CONSTITUTIONALITY UNDER THE FOURTEENTH AMENDMENT

The first section of the Fourteenth Amendment, said Bradley, is prohibitory upon *states* only; *state action* of a particular character is prohibited; but the invasion of rights by an *individual* is not covered by the amendment. The legislative power of Congress is only to nullify state action which violates the prohibition. While Congress may adopt legislation to meet the exigency of state action adverse to the rights of citizens as secured by the amendment, such "legislation cannot properly cover the whole domain of rights appertaining to life, liberty and property, defining them and providing for their vindication." Congress is authorized by the amendment to adopt only corrective, not general, legislation; it may counteract only state action.

Said Bradley,

If this legislation is appropriate for enforcing the prohibition of the amendment, it is difficult to see where it is to stop. Why may not Congress with equal show of authority enact a code of laws for the enforcement and vindication of all rights of life, liberty, and property?

The statute, he continued, is repugnant to the Tenth Amendment, which reserves to the people and the states the powers not delegated to the United States. In other words, laws for the "enforcement and vindication of all rights of life, liberty, and property" are within the province of the states exclusively.

The court held that the 1866 and 1870 civil rights acts were to be distinguished from the objectionable 1875 act, for the

earlier laws were limitations on the states only; they were corrective in character, intended to counteract and furnish redress
against state laws and proceedings, and against customs having
the force of law; the penal part of the laws referred to state
action only.

As to the civil rights guaranteed by the Constitution, the Court
held that the wrongful acts of an individual, unsupported by state
authority in the shape of laws, customs, judicial or executive proceedings, are "simply a private wrong, or a crime of that individual"; the person wronged must look for vindication or redress to the laws of the state.

The case is different, said Bradley, from the situation in which
Congress is clothed with direct and plenary powers of legislation
over a whole subject, accompanied by express or implied denial
of such power to the states; for example, in the regulation of foreign or interstate commerce, or commerce with Indian tribes, or
the coinage of money, or the establishment of post offices and
post roads, or declaring war.

In these cases Congress has power to pass laws for regulating the
subjects specified in every detail, and the conduct and transactions of
individuals in respect thereof. But where a subject is not submitted
to the general legislative power of Congress, but is only submitted
thereto for the purpose of rendering effective some prohibition against
particular state legislation or state action in reference to that subject,
the power given is limited to its object, and any legislation by Congress in the matter must necessarily be corrective in its character,
adapted to counteract and redress the operation of such prohibited
state laws or proceedings of state officers.

Here the legislation, said Bradley, was not corrective but primary and direct.

Up to this point the court had discussed the question presented by the act on the assumption that a right to enjoy equal
accommodations and privileges in all inns, public conveyances,
and places of public amusement is one of the essential rights of
the citizen which no state can abridge or interfere with. The
court construed the law as unconstitutional because it was in-

tended not as a restraint on state action but only on individual action; the court said, therefore, that it was unnecessary to examine its initial assumption.

Congress has plenary power as to territories and the District of Columbia; the cases considered, however, arose within the states. Therefore the constitutionality of the act as limited to territories and the District of Columbia was not presented; nor did the cases present the question of the power of Congress under the commerce clause to pass laws regulating rights in public conveyances passing from state to state.

CONSTITUTIONALITY UNDER THE THIRTEENTH AMENDMENT

Under this amendment primary and direct legislation may be enacted, as the amendment is not a limitation on state action only. It was argued on behalf of the Negroes that Congress has the power to pass all laws necessary and proper for abolishing all badges and incidents of slavery in the United States, and that under this power the law in question is constitutional; for a denial of equal accommodations and privileges is, in itself, a subjection to a species of servitude within the meaning of the Thirteenth Amendment. Assuming that Congress has the power to outlaw badges and incidents of servitude, the question is whether, under the Thirteenth Amendment, denial to a person of admission to the accommodations and privileges of an inn, a public conveyance, or a theater, does subject that person to any form of servitude, or tend to fasten upon him any badge of slavery.

Is there any similarity, asked the court, between servitudes outlawed by the amendment and a denial by the owner of an inn, a public conveyance, or a theater, of its accommodations and privileges to an individual, even though the denial be founded on the race or color of that individual? Bradley asked: "Where does any slavery or servitude, or badge of either, arise from such an act of denial? . . . What has it to do with the question of slavery?"

While it was true that when slavery prevailed proprietors of inns and public conveyances were forbidden by the Black Codes of the states to receive persons of the African race, the purpose, said the court, was to prevent escapes from the control of masters; it "was no part of the servitude itself."

Does slavery have any inseparable incidents? Yes, said the court, and named the following:

compulsory work;
restraints of movements;
disability to hold property;
disability to make contracts;
disability to have standing in court;
disability to act as a witness against a white person;
severer punishments;
"and such like burdens and incapacities."

The 1866 Civil Rights Act, passed under the Thirteenth Amendment and before the adoption of the Fourteenth, undertook to wipe out these incidents of slavery, "constituting its substance and visible form." This legislation—certainly since its reenactment under the Fourteenth Amendment—is constitutional; and the following are fundamental rights which are the essence of civil freedom:

right to make and enforce contracts;
right to sue;
right to be parties;
right to give evidence;
right to inherit property;
right to purchase, sell, lease, and convey property.

These rights constitute the essential distinction between freedom and slavery.

Altogether different is the 1875 act, said the court; for this law covers "social rights of men and races in the community."

The Thirteenth Amendment has not outlawed race, class, or color distinctions. While these may be outlawed by the Fourteenth Amendment when created by state actions, they are not outlawed by the Thirteenth Amendment.

Can the act of a mere individual, the owner of the inn, the public conveyance or place of amusement, refusing the accommodation, be justly regarded as imposing any badge of slavery or servitude upon the applicant, or only as inflicting an ordinary civil injury, properly cognizable by the laws of the state, and presumably subject to redress by those laws until the contrary appears?

Such an act of refusal, said the court, has nothing to do with slavery or involuntary servitude.

It would be running the slavery argument into the ground to make it apply to every act of discrimination which a person may see fit to make as to the guests he will entertain, or as to the people he will take into his coach or cab or car, or admit to his concert or theatre, deal with in other matters of intercourse or business.

However, if state laws themselves were to make any unjust discrimination, Congress would have the power under the Fourteenth Amendment to afford a remedy.

In slavery days there were thousands of free Negroes who enjoyed all the essential rights of life, liberty, and property, the same as white citizens;

yet no one, at that time, thought that it was any invasion of his personal status as a freeman because he was not admitted to all the privileges enjoyed by white citizens, or because he was subjected to discriminations in the enjoyment of accommodations in inns, public conveyances and places of amusement. Mere discriminations on account of race or color were not regarded as badges of slavery. If, since that time, the enjoyment of equal rights in all these respects has become established by constitutional enactment, it is not by force of the Thirteenth Amendment (which merely abolishes slavery), but by force of the Thirteenth and Fifteenth Amendments.

DISSENT BY MR. JUSTICE HARLAN

Mr. Justice Harlan was the lone dissenter; his forty-page opinion deserves a high place among the writings of American statesmen marking progress in the development of democratic thought. We shall give here a close analysis of his statement.

He opened his dissent with the remark that the opinion for the majority of the court proceeded upon grounds

entirely too narrow and artificial. I cannot resist the conclusion that the substance and spirit of the recent amendments of the Constitution have been sacrificed by a subtle and ingenious verbal criticism. Constitutional provisions, adopted in the interest of liberty, and for the purpose of securing, through national legislation, if need be, rights inhering in a state of freedom, and belonging to American citizenship, have be'n so construed as to defeat the ends the people desired to accomp h, and which they supposed they had accomplished by change their fundamental law.

The pose of Section 1 of the 1875 act was to prevent *race* discrim tion in respect of accommodations and facilities of inns, pu conveyances and places of public amusement, said Harlan; d Section 2 merely provides a penalty against any one deny or aiding or inciting a denial, to a citizen of that equality o ght given by Section 1.

Harlan ed attention to the well-established principle that in doubtful ses the question of the constitutionality of legislation should decided in the affirmative. There must be a clear and strong c viction of the incompatibility of the Constitution with the legi tive act for the latter to be declared void · the case must be clear one.

Harlan inte tingly contrasted the decision of the majority under the ame...ments with three Supreme Court precedents involving the rights of masters over their slaves.

1. *Prigg v. Pennsylvania.*[4] In Section 2 of Article IV of the Constitution it was provided that "no person held to service or labor in one state, under the laws thereof, escaping into another, shall, in consequence of any law or regulation therein, be discharged from such service or labor, but shall be delivered up on claim of the party to whom such service or labor may be due." Under the authority of this clause Congress in 1793 passed a Fugitive Slave Law, establishing a mode for the recovery of

[4] 16 Pet. (U.S.) (1842).

fugitive slaves and prescribing a penalty against the person who should obstruct or hinder the master in recovering the fugitive slave.

Pennsylvania argued that the obligation to surrender fugitive slaves rested upon the states, subject to the restriction that they should not pass laws liberating such fugitives; that the Constitution did not take from the states the right to determine the status of all persons within their jurisdiction; that it was for the state in which the alleged fugitive was found to determine whether he was in fact a freeman or a fugitive slave; that the only power of the Federal government was, by judicial instrumentality, to restrain and correct, but not to prevent or forbid, in the absence of hostile state action. Pennsylvania argued, in other words, that the 1793 law was unconstitutional, for Article IV of the Constitution was intended *as a restraint only on state legislative action, but not on individual action; while the act passed by Congress was directed against individuals.*

But the court turned a deaf ear to such suggestions and held that Congress was authorized by the Constitution to adopt primary legislation to enforce the master's right. The court held that the clause of the Constitution conferring a right should not be so construed as to make the right a shadowy one, or leave citizens without remedial power adequate for its protection, when another construction of the clause would enforce and protect the right granted. Congress is not restricted to legislation for the execution of its expressly granted powers: for the protection of rights guaranteed by the Constitution, Congress may employ such means as are necessary and proper, or appropriate, to attain the proposed ends. Since the right of the master to have his slave delivered to him was guaranteed by the Constitution, the fair implication was that the national government was clothed with appropriate authority and functions to enforce that right. The court said:

It would be a strange anomaly and forced construction to suppose that the national government meant to rely for the due fulfilment of its own proper duties, and the rights which it intended to secure, upon state legislation, and not upon that of the Union.

The 1793 act was upheld as constitutional.

2. *Ableman v. Booth.*[5] The provisions of the Fugitive Slave Act of 1850 were far in advance of previous legislation. The act placed at the disposal of the master seeking to recover his fugitive slave substantially the whole power of the nation: "Congress omitted from it [the act] nothing which the utmost ingenuity could suggest as essential to the successful enforcement of the master's claim to recover his fugitive slave." The court held the act to be "in all of its provisions fully authorized by the Constitution of the United States."

3. *Dred Scott v. Sanford.*[6] The case was instituted by Scott, who claimed to be a citizen of Missouri. The defendant was a citizen of another state. The object of the case was to assert the title of Scott and his family to freedom. The defendant pleaded in abatement that Scott, being a Negro whose ancestors were brought into this country and sold as slaves, was not a citizen. The only issue, according to the court, was whether emancipated Negroes, or Negroes born of parents who had become free before the birth of their children, were citizens of a state in the sense in which the word "citizen" is used in the United States Constitution.

The court considered the question who were citizens of the states when the Constitution was adopted; and who, at that time, were recognized as "the people" whose rights and liberties had been violated by the British government.

In his opinion for the court, Chief Justice Taney said that neither slaves nor their descendants, whether free or not, were then considered a part of the people;

they had for more than a century before been regarded as beings of an inferior race, and altogether unfit to associate with the white race, either in social or political relations, and so far inferior that they had no rights which the white man was bound to respect, and that the Negro might justly and lawfully be reduced to slavery for his benefit.

[5] 21 How. (U.S.) 506 (1859).   [6] 19 How. (U.S.) 393 (1857).

The judgment of the court was that "people of the United States" and "citizens" mean the same thing; that *free Negroes were not part of the people and not citizens;* that they could claim none of the rights and privileges which the Constitution provides for and secures to citizens of the United States; that, whether slaves or freemen, Negroes were subject to the authority of white persons, "and had no rights or privileges but such as those who held the power the government might choose to grant them."

It was in the light of these cases, said Harlan, that the amendments were adopted.

THE STATUTE UNDER THE THIRTEENTH AMENDMENT

The Thirteenth Amendment, he said, wiped out slavery; it was followed by the 1866 act which conferred national citizenship on Negroes. Negroes were citizens, therefore, before the Fourteenth Amendment was adopted. While the power of Congress to enforce the master's right to have his slave delivered up on claim was implied from the recognition of that right in the Constitution, the power conferred by the Thirteenth Amendment does not rest upon implication or inference; the power to enforce the amendment by appropriate legislation was expressly granted. The court had uniformly held that the national government has the power, whether expressly given or not, to secure and protect the rights conferred or guaranteed by the Constitution. "That doctrine," said Harlan,

ought not now to be abandoned when the inquiry is not as to an implied power to protect the master's rights, but what may Congress, under power expressly granted, do for the protection of freedom and the rights necessarily inhering in a state of freedom.

Did the freedom established by the Thirteenth Amendment involve nothing more than exemption from actual slavery?

Was it the purpose of the nation simply to destroy the institution, and then remit the race, theretofore held in bondage, to the several states for such protection, in their civil rights, necessarily growing out

of freedom, as those states, in their discretion, might choose to provide? Were the states against whose protest the institution was destroyed, to be left free, so far as national interference was concerned,
to make or allow discriminations against that race, as such, in the
enjoyment of those fundamental rights which by universal concession,
inhere in a state of freedom?

Congress, contended Harlan, has the power by direct and primary legislation to eradicate burdens and disabilities which are
the badges and incidents of slavery and servitude. He said:

I do not contend that the Thirteenth Amendment invests Congress
with authority, by legislation, to define and regulate the entire body
of civil rights which citizens enjoy, or may enjoy, in the several
states. But I hold that since slavery, as the court has repeatedly declared, was the moving or principal cause of the adoption of that
amendment, and since that institution rested wholly upon the inferiority, as a race, of those held in bondage, their freedom necessarily involved immunity from, and protection against, all discrimination
against them, because of their race, in respect of such civil rights as
belong to freemen of other races.

Congress could pass laws to protect Negroes against deprivation,
because of their race, of any civil rights granted to other freemen in the same state; and such legislation may operate against
officers and agents of the state, *"and also, upon, at least, such
individuals and corporations as exercise public functions and
wield power and authority under the state."* [7]

According to Harlan, then, the power of Congress under the
Thirteenth Amendment was not restricted to legislation against
slavery as an institution. It may be extended to the protection of
Negroes *against discrimination in respect of civil rights belonging to freemen where such discrimination is based upon race.*

What, then, are the legal rights of Negroes in respect of public conveyances, inns, and places of public amusement?

Public Conveyances. Harlan pointed out that it had been held
by the court that a common carrier exercises a sort of public
office and has public duties to perform; railways are public high-

[7] Italics supplied.

ways, established by authority of the state for public use; they are intended for public use and benefit; a railway corporation is a government agency, subject to be controlled for the public benefit; the government may regulate the rates of fares, all matters relating to the convenience and safety of the public; it may prohibit discriminations and favoritism.

Such being the relations these corporations hold to the public, it would seem that the right of a colored person to use an improved public highway, upon the terms accorded to freemen of other races, is as fundamental . . . as are any of the rights which my brethren concede to be so far fundamental as to be deemed the essence of civil freedom.

Blackstone had said that the power of locomotion is an element of personal liberty.

But of what value is this right of locomotion, if it may be clogged by such burdens as Congress intended by the act of 1875 to remove? They are burdens which lay at the very foundation of the institution of slavery as it once existed. They are not to be sustained, except upon the assumption that there is, in this land of universal liberty, a class which may still be discriminated against, even in respect of rights of a character so necessary and supreme, that, deprived of their enjoyment in common with others, a freeman is not only branded as one inferior and infected, but, in the competitions of life, is robbed of some of the most essential means of existence; and all this solely because they belong to a particular race which the nation has liberated.

Inns. The same observations made as to railways, said Harlan, apply to inns. An innkeeper may not select his guests. Innkeepers are a sort of public servant, exercising a quasi-public employment. The law gives the innkeeper special privileges, and, in consideration of these, he is charged with certain duties to the general public. He may not discriminate against any person asking admission as a guest on account of the person's race or color.

Places of Public Amusement. Such places, Harlan pointed out, are established and maintained under direct license of the law. The authority to establish and maintain them comes from the public. "The colored race is part of that public. The local government granting the license represents them as well as all other races within its jurisdiction."

In brief, it was Harlan's contention that discrimination practiced by individuals in the exercise of public or quasi-public functions "is a badge of servitude" which Congress may prevent under the Thirteenth Amendment.

THE STATUTE UNDER THE FOURTEENTH AMENDMENT

Harlan reminded the majority that in an earlier case the court had said that the one pervading purpose found in all the Civil War amendments, lying at the foundation of each, and without which none of them would have been suggested, was "the freedom of the slave race, the security and firm establishment of that freedom, and the protection of the newly-made freeman and citizen from the oppression of those who had formerly exercised unlimited dominion over him." Positive rights and privileges, he said, were intended to be secured by the Fourteenth Amendment.

Section 5 of the amendment gives power to Congress to enforce by appropriate legislation provisions of the amendment. But the majority in this case held that this section gives to Congress the power to legislate only for the purpose carrying into effect the *prohibition on state action*. But for this purpose, Harlan argued, the judicial power is adequate: courts could nullify all hostile state proceedings. The section grants not judicial but legislative power—power to Congress.

Nor is the amendment merely a prohibition upon *state* action. For the first clause of the first section provides that "all persons born or naturalized in the United States, and subject to the jurisdiction thereof, are citizens of the United States, and of the state wherein they reside." This provision is of an affirmative character: it grants Negroes citizenship in the United States and in the states wherein they reside. This provision introduced the Negroes into the political community known as the "people of the United States." It extended to them Article IV, Section 2:

"the citizens of each state shall be entitled to all the privileges and immunities of citizens in the several states."

"No state," said Harlan,

can sustain her denial to colored citizens of other states, while within her limits, of privileges or immunities, fundamental in republican citizenship, upon the ground that she accords such privileges only to her white citizens and withholds them from her colored citizens. The colored citizens of other states, within the jurisdiction of that state, could claim . . . every privilege and immunity which that state secures to her white citizens. . . . A colored citizen of Ohio or Indiana, while in the jurisdiction of Tennessee, is entitled to enjoy any privilege or immunity, fundamental in citizenship, which is given to citizens of the white race in the latter state. It is not to be supposed that any one will controvert this proposition.

What was secured to Negro citizens by the grant to them of state citizenship by the nation? There was secured at least exemption from race discrimination in respect of any civil right belonging to citizens of the white race in the same state—"unless the recent amendments be splendid baubles, thrown out to delude those who deserved fair and generous treatment at the hands of the nation." As was stated in four previous opinions of the court, the purpose of the amendments was to raise Negroes from the condition of inferiority and servitude to perfect equality of civil rights with all other persons.

It is fundamental in American citizenship that, in respect of such rights, there shall be no discrimination by the state, or its officers, *or by individuals or corporations exercising public functions or authority,* against any citizen because of his race or previous condition of servitude.[8]

If exemption from discrimination in respect of civil rights is a new constitutional right, why may not Congress guard, protect, and enforce that right? Congress may protect and enforce any right derived from or created by the Constitution. The court said in an earlier case that "rights and immunities created by

[8] Italics supplied.

and dependent upon the Constitution of the United States can be protected by Congress." The means to be adopted to protect such rights and immunities are within the discretion of Congress:

it is for Congress, not the judiciary, to say that legislation is appropriate—that is—best adapted to the end to be attained. The judiciary may not, with safety to our institutions, enter the domain of legislative discretion, and dictate the means which Congress shall employ in the exercise of its granted powers. That would be sheer usurpation of the functions of a co-ordinate department, which, if often repeated, and permanently acquiesced in, would work a radical change in our system of government.

The principle of construction or interpretation when a constitutional provision is before the court should be different from the one applied to a private contract.

Are constitutional provisions, enacted to secure the dearest rights of freemen and citizens, to be subjected to that rule of construction, applicable to private instruments, which requires that words to be interpreted must be taken most strongly against those who employ them?

Prior to the amendments, Congress, with the sanction of the court, passed the most stringent laws, operating upon the states, their officers and agents, and also upon individuals, in vindication of slavery and the rights of the master; but now the court has decided that Congress may not, by legislation of like character, guard, protect, and secure the freedom established by the amendments. Congress may, said Harlan,

without transcending the limits of the Constitution, do for human liberty and the fundamental rights of American citizenship, what it did, with the sanction of this court, for the protection of slavery and the rights of masters of fugitive slaves. If fugitive slave laws, providing modes and prescribing penalties, whereby the master could seize and recover his fugitive slave, were legitimate exercises of an implied power to protect and enforce a right recognized by the Constitution, why shall the hands of Congress be tied, so that—under an express power, by appropriate legislation, to enforce a constitutional provision granting citizenship—it may not, by means of direct legislation, bring the whole power of this nation to bear upon states and their officers, *and upon such individuals and corporations exercising public functions* as assume to abridge, impair, or deny rights confessedly secured by the supreme law of the land? [9]

The fact that the Fourteenth Amendment prohibited *states* from making or enforcing laws abridging privileges and immunities of citizens of the United States furnishes no reason for maintaining that the Fourteenth Amendment was intended to deny to *Congress* the power, by legislation, to protect the citizens of the several states, being also United States citizens, against all discrimination, in respect of their rights as state citizens, founded on race, color, or previous condition of servitude. In other words, the fifth section of the amendment confers upon Congress the power, by legislation, to enforce not merely the prohibition upon the states but all previous provisions of the amendment.

It was perfectly well known that the great danger to the equal enjoyment by citizens of their rights, as citizens, was to be apprehended not altogether from unfriendly state legislation, but from the hostile action of corporations and individuals in the states. And it is to be presumed that it was intended, by that section, to clothe Congress with power and authority to meet that danger.

Harlan foresaw in the decision of the court the future development of Jim Crowism and other forms of race discrimination, and the passivity of the Federal government in the face thereof. If it be adjudged, he said,

that *individuals and corporations, exercising public functions, or wielding power under public authority,* may, without liability to direct primary legislation on the part of Congress, make the race of citizens the ground for denying them that equality of civil rights which the Constitution ordains as a principle of republican citizenship; then . . . we shall enter upon an era of constitutional law, when the rights of freedom and American citizenship cannot receive from the nation that efficient protection which heretofore was unhesitatingly accorded to slavery and the rights of the master.[10]

[9] Italics supplied.   [10] Italics supplied.

Assuming with the majority that the amendment was intended to be directed only against action by the states and their officers, agents and instrumentalities, "keepers of inns, and managers of places of public amusement are agents or instrumentalities of the state, because they are charged with duties to the public, and are amenable, in respect of their duties and functions, to government regulation." *A denial by them of equality of civil rights is a denial by the state.* "If it be not, then the race is left, in respect of the civil rights in question, practically at the mercy of corporations and individuals wielding power under the states." The 1875 act endeavored to protect legal, not social, rights. It endeavored to provide that no state, nor officers of a state, nor any corporation or individual wielding power under state authority for the public benefit or public convenience, shall discriminate against citizens in their civil rights because of race.

It will be recalled that the court reserved the question whether Congress, in the exercise of its power to regulate interstate commerce, might or might not pass a law regulating rights in public conveyances moving in interstate commerce. But this question, said Harlan, should not have been reserved, for it was directly presented in one of the cases, in which a citizen of Mississippi bought a ticket from Tennessee to Virginia. Might not the 1875 act apply at least to this situation?

The underlying purpose of the legislation was to enable the Negro to take the rank of citizen accorded to him by the Fourteenth Amendment.

At every step, in this direction, the nation has been confronted with class tyranny. . . . If the constitutional amendments be enforced, according to the intent with which, as I conceive, they were adopted, there cannot be, in this republic, any class of human beings in practical subjection to another class, with power in the latter to dole out to the former just such privileges as they may choose to grant.

SUMMARY OF BRADLEY'S DECISION

The purpose of the 1875 act was to declare that in the enjoyment of accommodations and privileges of inns, public conveyances, theaters, and other places of public accommodation or amusement, no distinction shall be made between citizens differing in race or color. It is directed against action by individuals not acting as officers, agents, or instrumentalities of states or their political subdivisions. But the Fourteenth Amendment is directed only against action by states, their political subdivisions, and their officers, agents, and instrumentalities acting on their behalf. The subject matter of the act is confined to the states.

The Thirteenth Amendment, however, is not a limitation on state action only. Congress may pass legislation under this amendment directed against individuals who impose slavery or involuntary servitude upon another person. But a denial to a person of admission to the accommodations and privileges of an inn, a public conveyance, or a theater is not a subjection of that person to slavery or involuntary servitude. The inseparable incidents of slavery are compulsory work; restraint of movements; disability to hold property, make contracts, have standing in courts, act as a witness against a white person; and to be subject to severer punishments than those imposed upon white persons. These, and similar burdens and incapacities, differentiate the slave from the freeman, and only these were outlawed by the Thirteenth Amendment. The amendment has not outlawed all race or color distinctions.

SUMMARY OF HARLAN'S DISSENT

Constitutional rights should not be construed narrowly. The Thirteenth Amendment involves more than exemption from actual slavery; under its provisions, Congress may undertake to eradicate burdens and disabilities which are the badges and incidents of slavery and involuntary servitude. Such civil rights as belong to freemen of other races now belong to the Negro, too; and Congress may pass laws to protect Negroes against deprivation of civil rights granted to other freemen in the state; and such laws may operate against the officers and agents of the state, and upon such individuals as exercise public functions and wield power and authority under state law, license, or grant.

Operators of public conveyances, inns, and places of public amusement exercise a sort of public office and have public duties to perform; such accommodations are intended for public use and benefit, and are subject to public control or regulation in all matters affecting the public safety and convenience.

The Fourteenth Amendment prohibits states from abridging the privileges or immunities of citizens of the United States; but the amendment also provides, in positive rather than in prohibitive terms, that all persons born or naturalized in the United States are citizens of the United States and of the state wherein they reside. The amendment also provides that Congress shall have the power to enforce, by legislation, the provisions of the amendment. Congress, therefore, has the power, by direct and positive legislation, to protect state citizenship, not merely against *state* interference or abridgment, but against *all* interference or abridgment.

Negroes, by becoming citizens, are entitled to all the privileges and immunities of citizens in the several states. This means that a Negro citizen of Ohio is entitled, while in Tennessee, to enjoy all the privileges and immunities granted by Tennessee to its white citizens.

The grant of state citizenship implies, at least, freedom from race discrimination in respect of the civil rights enjoyed by white citizens; at any rate, from such discrimination practiced by the state, its officers, or by individuals exercising public functions or authority (such as innkeepers, carriers, theater owners).

Assuming with the majority that the Fourteenth Amendment was intended to be directed only against action by states, their officers, agents and instrumentalities, then keepers of inns, carriers, and theater owners come within its terms; for a denial by them of equality of civil rights is a denial by the state; the denial, in contemplation of the amendment, is *state action.*

SIGNIFICANCE OF THE DECISION

The decision in the Civil Rights Cases is one of the most farreaching in the social history of the people of the United States. Specifically it has meant these things:

1. Race distinctions with respect to enjoyment of facilities in carriers, inns (hotels, restaurants), theaters, and places of public accommodation and amusement generally, violate no constitutional guarantee.

2. Individuals are free to make such distinctions without interference from the Federal government.

3. States are free to make (or even compel) such distinctions without violating any constitutional guarantee.

CIVIL RIGHTS IN THE DISTRICT OF COLUMBIA

Mr. Justice Bradley said that as to territories and the District of Columbia, Congress has plenary power, implying that if the Civil Rights Act of 1875 were not of national scope, but limited to the District of Columbia, it might be constitutional. The cases presented, however, came from the states and not from the district, and so the question of the constitutionality of congressional civil rights legislation for the District of Columbia was not passed upon.

At the present time there is no such legislation for the district, and Negroes in the nation's capital city do not enjoy freedom from discrimination in places of public resort. Only under rare circumstances are they permitted to stay at a hotel or eat in a restaurant; nor are they permitted to sit with white persons in public theaters.[11]

In 1943 a bill[12] was introduced in Congress, known as the "Equal Rights Law of the District of Columbia." The bill provided that within the district any person who shall make any distinction, discrimination, or restriction on account of race, color, or creed, or for any reason not sanctioned by law and not applicable alike to persons generally, in the admission of any person to, or the accommodation or service of any person in any place of public accommodation, resort, entertainment, or amusement, or any public conveyance, or any public meeting, or assemblage,

[11] Separate schools are required by law; also separate school superintendents, a white person for white schools and a Negro for Negro schools. There is a separate school for Negro deaf-mute children; and the law requires segregation of girls in reform schools. 31 Stats. 109, 602, 1011, 1110–1113; 32 Stats. 906.
[12] H.R. 1995, 78th Cong., 1st Sess. (1943).

shall be guilty of a misdemeanor and liable to a penalty to be recovered by the aggrieved person.

The bill has not been passed; and it is very likely that if such a bill were to reach the floor of the Senate, it would be killed by a filibuster or the threat of one.

There is no legislation enacted by Congress, then, effective in the states or in the District of Columbia, outlawing discrimination by individuals against Negroes, because of their race or color, in hotels, restaurants, theaters, or other places of public accommodation. This statement needs to be qualified when applied to public carriers engaged in interstate commerce.[13]

[13] See Mitchell v. U.S., 313 U.S. 80 (1941). See 49 U.S.C. 3. In 1945 a bill was introduced in Congress to amend the above act so that segregation of passengers in interstate traffic would be a violation of the Interstate Commerce Act. See H.R. 1925, 79th Cong., 1st Sess. (1945). See Charles S. Mangum, Jr., *The Legal Status of the Negro* (1940), pp. 181 ff. Cf. Morgan v. Virginia, 90 L. Ed. (U.S.) 982 (Adv. Op.), 1946.

CHAPTER 3

General Federal Civil Rights
Statutes: Criminal

W E HAVE ALREADY called attention to the 1870 Civil Rights Act, and to the statement by Mr. Justice Bradley that that act is constitutional. One of its sections has become Section 51 of Title 18 of the United States Code—one of the important federal laws relevant to our present discussion.

18 U.S.C. 51

The section provides:

If two or more persons conspire to injure, oppress, threaten, or intimidate any citizen in the free exercise or enjoyment of any right or privilege secured to him by the Constitution or laws of the United States, or because of his having so exercised the same, or if two or more persons go in disguise on the highway, or on the premises of another, with intent to prevent or hinder his free exercise or enjoyment of any right or privilege so secured, they shall be fined not more than $5,000 and imprisoned not more than ten years, and shall, moreover, be thereafter ineligible to any office, or place of honor, profit or trust, created by the Constitution or laws of the United States.[1]

This provision was originally Section 6 of the 1870 act; it appeared in the 1875 Revised Statutes with some alteration; it became Section 19 of the Criminal Code; and now is generally known as 18 U.S.C. 51. For its adoption the Ku Klux Klan must be thanked.[2]

A reading of the act shows a number of limitations: (1) it is a conspiracy statute; it cannot be violated by a single person

[1] Constitutionality upheld in Ex parte Yarbrough, 110 U.S. 651 (1884); U.S. v. Waddell, 112 U.S. 76 (1884); Baldwin v. Franks, 120 U.S. 678 (1887); Logan v. U.S., 144 U.S. 263 (1892); Motes v. U.S., 178 U.S. 458 (1900).
[2] U.S. v. Mosley, 238 U.S. 383 (1915), at p. 387.

acting alone; (2) the victim or intended victim must be a citizen; aliens are not covered; (3) the purpose of the conspiracy must be the invasion of rights or privileges secured by the Constitution or laws of the United States.[3]

The Bill of Rights and some of the later amendments secure the rights and privileges; but they are not, as we have seen in the *Civil Rights Cases,* secured against invasion by private individuals (except in rare instances, to be noted hereinafter). The rights guaranteed by the Bill of Rights are secured against invasion by the Federal government; and in so far as they have been incorporated by construction into the Fourteenth Amendment,[4] the rights are secured also against state invasion. The Fourteenth Amendment guarantees no right against private invasion, but only against state action. The Fifteenth Amendment is enforceable against both the Federal and state governments, but not against private persons.[5] Only the Thirteenth Amendment is enforceable against the Federal government, states, and private persons.[6] In so far, then, as *express* provisions of the Constitution or federal laws are concerned, Section 51 may not be used against conspirators who are not public officers or agents but are private persons, unless the latter are charged with a crime under the Thirteenth Amendment.

This brings us to the point where it becomes necessary to consider the *privileges and immunities* clause of the Fourteenth Amendment.

The original Constitution (Article IV, Section 2, Clause 1) provides that the citizens of each state shall be entitled to all privileges and immunities of citizens in the several states. The purpose of the clause was to prevent a state from discriminating against the citizens of another state. The point of departure was *state citizenship*. The Civil War, however, emphasized the need of the concept of *national citizenship*. The Fourteenth Amend-

[3] Baldwin v. Franks, 120 U.S. 678 (1887). Annot. in 107 A.L.R. 1363 (1937).
[4] Cases will be cited *post,* but see, e.g., Lovell v. Griffin, 303 U.S. 444 (1938); Schneider v. State, 308 U.S. 147 (1939); Hague v. C.I.O., 307 U.S. 497 (1939).
[5] James v. Bowman, 190 U.S. 127 (1903).
[6] Smith v. U.S., 157 F. 721 (1907); cert. den. 208 U.S. 618 (1908).

ment embodies this concept: it deals with rights, privileges, and immunities of national, as distinguished from state, citizenship. Section 1 of the amendment provides that "No state shall make or enforce any law which shall abridge the privileges or immunities of citizens of the United States." The clause in the original Constitution protects a citizen against discrimination by another state; it does not protect the citizen against discrimination by his own state. The clause in the amendment protects the citizen against state action invading his rights derived from national citizenship. It protects him against his own state.

But what are the rights, privileges, and immunities of national citizenship?

The Fourteenth Amendment was adopted in 1868. The Supreme Court was called upon to interpret the amendment for the first time in 1873 in the important *Slaughterhouse Cases*,[7] which we must now consider.

A Louisiana statute chartered a private corporation, giving to it the exclusive right to establish and maintain stockyards, landing places, and slaughterhouses in New Orleans, and providing that all animals intended for food should be slaughtered there. It was the duty of the new corporation to permit any person to slaughter in its houses at charges restricted by statute. The statute purported to be a public health measure and provided for the inspection of animals. Butchers of New Orleans attacked the statute as unconstitutional. The Supreme Court upheld the statute. The argument that the act violated the due process clause of the Fourteenth Amendment was brushed aside by Mr. Justice Miller in his opinion for the majority. The principal argument was over the meaning and application of the privileges and immunities clause of the amendment. The plaintiffs' argument was that before the adoption of the Constitution an individual as the citizen of a state had certain fundamental rights to which he was entitled by reason of his state citizenship. By the Fourteenth Amendment, they argued, the citizen became primarily a citizen of the United States and only secondarily of the state;

[7] 16 Wall. (U.S.) 36 (1873).

therefore, the fundamental rights which formerly attached to him as a citizen of the state now belonged to him as a citizen of the United States and cannot be abridged by the state.

The majority of the court refused to accept this position. Only the privileges and immunities of citizens of the United States, and not of states, are safeguarded by the amendment. There was no intention to transfer from the states to the Federal government the security and protection of civil rights. To hold otherwise, said Miller, would make of the court "a perpetual censor upon all legislation of the states, on the civil rights of their own citizens." It would mean the fettering and degradation of the states.

For the protection of the privileges and immunities of citizens of states the citizen must look to his state. The fundamental civil rights, said the court, are granted by the states, not by the United States; they are rights which belong to the individual as a citizen of the state; they are "the class of rights which the state governments were created to establish and secure." The clause created no privileges or immunities; nor did it grant to the citizen of a state a claim against his own state.

Before the adoption of the amendment, said Miller, practically the only restraints on state action were the constitutional prohibitions against *ex post facto* laws, bills of attainder, and laws impairing the obligation of contracts.

Was it the purpose of the 14th Amendment, by the simple declaration that no state shall make or enforce any law which shall abridge the privileges and immunities of citizens of the United States, to transfer the security and protection of all the civil rights . . . from the states to the federal government?

There is no need, said the court, to define the privileges and immunities of citizens of the United States (as distinguished from citizens of the several states), which no state may abridge; but the court none the less ventured to suggest some which owe their existence to the Federal government, its national character, its Constitution, or its laws. Those enumerated by Miller were the following:

the right of a citizen to come to the seat of government, to assert
any claim he may have upon that government, to transact any
business he may have with it, to seek its protection, to share its
offices, to engage in administering its functions;

free access to seaports where foreign commerce is carried on;

free access to the subtreasuries;

free access to the land offices;

free access to the courts of the several states;

federal protection on the high seas;

federal protection within the jurisdiction of a foreign government;

the right to peaceably assemble and petition for redress of grievances;

the privilege of the writ of *habeas corpus;*

right to use navigable waters within the territory of the states;

rights secured to citizens by treaties;

right of a citizen of the United States to become a citizen of any
state by *bona fide* residence therein;

rights secured by the Thirteenth Amendment;

rights secured by the Fifteenth Amendment.

Under the Civil War amendments the states still have the power,
said the court, to regulate civil rights, the rights of person and
of property.

Mr. Justice Bradley, in his dissenting opinion, indicated a
willingness to go further than his colleagues in recognizing the
existence of a substantial body of rights, privileges, and immunities that go with national citizenship. These may be enumerated
under the following heads:

protection by the government;

enjoyment of life and liberty;

right to acquire and possess property;

right to pursue and obtain happiness and safety;

right of a citizen of one state to pass through or reside in any other
state for purposes of trade, agriculture, professional pursuit, or
otherwise;

benefit of writ of *habeas corpus;*

to institute and maintain actions in state courts;

to take, hold, and dispose of property, real and personal;

exemption from higher taxes than are paid by other citizens of the
    same state;
to be free from bills of attainder;
to be free from *ex post facto* statutes;
to be free from laws impairing obligation of contracts;
right of trial by jury;
right of free exercise of religious worship;
right of free speech and a free press;
right peaceably to assemble for discussion of public measures;
right to be secure against unreasonable searches and seizures;
"and above all, and including almost all the rest, the right of not
    being deprived of life, liberty or property, without due process of
    law."

These are among the rights not merely of citizens of the United
States, but "of all persons whether citizens or not." The Fourteenth Amendment is more than "a guaranty of mere equality of
privileges with other citizens." The rights set forth above would
exist even if not named in the Constitution. There is no need for
the Constitution to provide that citizens of the United States
should have and exercise all the privileges of citizens: "Their
very citizenship conferred these privileges," said Bradley.

And these privileges they would enjoy whether they were citizens of
any state or not. Inhabitants of federal territories and new citizens,
made such by annexation of territory or naturalization, though without any status as citizens of a state, could nevertheless, as citizens of
the United States, lay claim to every one of the privileges and immunities which have been enumerated.

Bradley took a broad view of the purposes of the Fourteenth
Amendment, comparable to the view expressed by Harlan in his
dissenting opinion in the *Civil Rights Cases*. Said Bradley:

The mischief to be remedied was not merely slavery and its incidents
and consequences; but the spirit of insubordination and disloyalty
to the national government which had troubled the country for so
many years in some of the states, and that intolerance of free speech
and free discussion which often rendered life and property insecure,
and led to much unequal legislation. The amendment was an attempt

to give voice to the strong national yearning for that time and that condition of things, in which American citizenship should be a sure guaranty of safety, and in which every citizen of the United States might stand erect in every portion of its soil, in the full enjoyment of every right and privilege belonging to a freeman, without fear of violence or molestation.

Mr. Justice Swayne, in a separate dissenting opinion, said that the protection of life, liberty, and property is a right and obligation vested in the Federal government, which must see to it that no one is deprived of life, liberty, or property without due process of law, and that every one enjoys equal protection of the laws. All are entitled to enjoy these rights; the government of the nation must secure them to all.

Without such authority any government claming to be national is glaringly defective. The construction adopted by the majority of my brethren is, in my judgment, much too narrow. It defeats, by a limitation not anticipated, the intent of those by whom the instrument was framed and of those by whom it was adopted. To the extent of that limitation it turns, as it were, what was meant for bread into a stone.

In his dissenting opinion Mr. Justice Field quoted from the opinion of Mr. Justice Washington of the Supreme Court, in the case of *Corfield v. Coryell.*[8] In this case, decided in 1823 in the federal circuit court of appeals, an attempt was made to enumerate the rights protected by the privileges and immunities clause in the original Constitution. Washington said that the only rights protected are those that are *"fundamental;* which belong, of right, to the citizens of all free governments; and which have, at all times, been enjoyed by the citizens of the several states which compose this union."[9] These fundamental rights, he said, may be comprehended under the following general heads:

protection by the government;
the enjoyment of life and liberty, with the right to acquire and possess property, and to pursue and obtain happiness and safety;

[8] Federal Cas. 3230 (1823); 6 Fed. Cas. 546. Cf. Carl Brent Swisher, *American Constitutional Development* (1943), p. 340.
[9] Italics in original.

the right of a citizen of one state to pass through or reside in any
    other state;

the benefit of the writ of *habeas corpus;*

the right to institute and maintain actions in state courts;

exemption from higher taxes than are paid by others;

the elective franchise.

The majority of the court, as we have seen, refused to accept
this position. Its decision, as Field said, rendered the clause "a
vain and idle enactment."

Despite the vigorous dissents [10] the principle of the decision
still stands; namely, that the right of an individual to life, liberty, and property is the right of *a citizen of the state* of which
the individual is an inhabitant. These are not rights enjoyed by
reason of one's *national citizenship.* The number of rights inherent in national citizenship is extremely limited. The only significant advance that has been made since the period when the
question of the constitutionality and scope of the Civil Rights
Acts was decided by the Supreme Court has been the reading
into the Fourteenth Amendment, against state infraction, of some
of the rights named in the Bill of Rights. The decision of the
court in the *Slaughterhouse Cases* rendered the privileges and immunities clause nugatory: the Fourteenth Amendment, in defining
a citizen of the United States, did not add any additional privileges and immunities to those which were enjoyed by citizens
before its adoption. Only those rights which owe their existence
to the Federal government, its national character, its Constitution, or its laws, may be protected by the Federal government.
The scope and protection of civil rights are matters for the states,
exclusively.

Two years later the court decided the earliest and leading case
on Section 51; namely, the *Cruikshank* case.[11] In the case a group
of private individuals prevented Negroes from attending meetings. This was the basis for an indictment under the section
charging a conspiracy to hinder citizens in the free exercise and

[10] Chief Justice Chase also dissented. The decision was 5–4.
[11] 92 U.S. 542 (1875).

enjoyment of their "lawful right and privilege to peaceably assemble together with each other and with other citizens of the
United States for a peaceable and lawful purpose." The court held
the indictment insufficient, pointing out that had the meeting of
Negroes been an assembly "for the purpose of petitioning Congress for a redress of grievances, or for anything else connected
with the powers or the duties of the national government," the
section would have applied; not, however, because of the First
Amendment, but because "the very idea of a government, republican in form, implies a right on the part of its citizens to meet
peaceably for consultation in respect to public affairs and to petition for a redress of grievances."

Thus it is apparent that the basis for an indictment against
private individuals under the section need not be a right expressly
granted by the Constitution (as under the Thirteenth Amendment), but may be a right implied from a consideration of what
is essential to the effective functioning of the Federal government. It is like the right of a citizen to come to the seat of government, mentioned by Miller in the *Slaughterhouse Cases.*

Under the *dictum* in the *Cruikshank* case, the right of assembly
is not an attribute of national citizenship, but the right of assembly to petition Congress is.

In later cases it was urged that the privileges and immunities
clause be used to protect the rights set forth in the first eight
amendments (the Bill of Rights) against state action; [12] but to
no avail. In nearly fifty cases,[13] parties before the court tried
in vain to get the court to put some meaning or life into the
clause; in spite of these efforts, the clause has been consistently
construed as suggesting only those interests growing out of the
relation between the citizen and the national government.

In *Colgate v. Harvey,*[14] decided in 1935, the decision seemed
to indicate that the court had at last agreed to broaden the scope
of the clause. The court held invalid, as a violation of the privi-

[12] E.g., Twining v. New Jersey, 211 U.S. 78 (1908).
[13] See list in 296 U.S. 404 (1935), at p. 445, n. 2. See also Ferry v. Spokane &c.
Ry., 258 U.S. 314 (1922).
[14] 296 U.S. 404 (1935).

leges and immunities clause, a Vermont statute relating to the individual income tax; the statute imposed a tax on dividends earned outside the state while exempting dividends earned within the state. Justices Stone, Brandeis, and Cardozo dissented. Four years later the decision was expressly overruled.[15]

The *dictum* of the *Cruikshank* case almost came to life also in the *Hague* case.[16] In this case Mr. Justice Roberts (Mr. Justice Black agreeing with him) found the requirements of appropriate jurisdiction statutes to be met in that the acts and ordinances of Jersey City violated the privileges and immunities clause. The purpose of the respondents was to discuss the National Labor Relations Act and their rights under it, and it is a privilege of national citizenship, he said, to assemble for the discussion of national legislation and to communicate with respect to it by speech or writing.

Mr. Justice Stone (with Mr. Justice Reed concurring) did not agree that the facts as to the respondents' citizenship or as to the purpose of the meetings were sufficiently apparent in the record, or that the privileges and immunities clause was applicable to them even if these facts were present. He said that the case was covered by the due process, rather than the privileges and immunities, clause. Chief Justice Hughes agreed with Roberts "with respect to the merits." On the jurisdiction point he concurred with Roberts as to the scope of the privileges and immunities clause but with Stone as to the lack of factual support in the record.

The decree, however, forbade in the broadest terms any limits upon the respondents' rights peaceably to communicate their ideas *upon any subject* to other persons within Jersey City; the decree was not limited to discussion of national legislation. Had Roberts been followed, the rights would have been limited to a discussion of national legislation.

The decision in the *Hague* case was followed by the decision of the court overruling the decision in *Colgate v. Harvey*.[17] In

---

[15] James Stewart & Co. v. Sadrakula, 309 U.S. 94 (1940). Madden v. Kentucky, 309 U.S. 83 (1940).
[16] Hague v. C.I.O., U.S. 497 (1939).   [17] Note 15, *supra*.

so far as the usefulness of the privileges and immunities clause is concerned, therefore, the court was back where it was when the decision in the *Slaughterhouse Cases* was announced.

At the end of 1941, in *Edwards v. California*,[18] the Supreme Court had another opportunity to decide an important case on the basis of this same clause, but failed to do so. In that case Edwards, a resident of California and a citizen of the United States, left for Texas to take back to California his brother-in-law, who was an indigent person employed by the WPA. When they got to California the brother-in-law obtained financial assistance from the Farm Security Administration. Edwards was convicted of violation of a California statute which made it a misdemeanor to bring into the state an indigent person who was not a resident of the state. The Supreme Court reversed the conviction, holding that the statute was an unconstitutional barrier to interstate commerce.

Mr. Justice Douglas, in a concurring opinion, said that the right to move freely from state to state occupies a more protected position in our constitutional system than does the movement of coal and cattle across state lines: This right is an incident of *national* citizenship, protected by the privileges and immunities clause of the Fourteenth Amendment.

Similarly, Mr. Justice Jackson found the commerce clause insufficient, and criticized the majority opinion by Mr. Justice Byrnes for employing that clause as the basis for the court's decision. He said that, notwithstanding the fact that the court had failed in the past to find specific instances of privileges and immunities, it should now squarely hold that

[18] 314 U.S. 160 (1941). See S. P. Meyers, "Federal Privileges and Immunities: Application to Ingress and Egress," 29 *Cornell L.Q.* 489 (1944). Note in 39 *Columbia L. Rev.* 1237 (1939). D. O. McGovney, "Privileges and Immunities Clause," 4 *Iowa L. Bull.* 219 (1918). Pendleton Howard, "Privileges and Immunities of Federal Citizenship and Colgate v. Harvey," 87 *U. of Pennsylvania L. Rev.* 262 (1939). Note, "Depression Migrants and the States," 53 *Harvard L. Rev.* 1031 (1940). Note, 52 *Harvard L. Rev.* 1136 (1939). Cf. Charles W. Collins, *The Fourteenth Amendment and the States* (1912), ch. 1; Horace E. Flack, *The Adoption of the Fourteenth Amendment* (1908), pp. 55 ff.

it is a privilege of citizenship of the United States, protected from state abridgment, to enter any state of the Union, either for temporary sojourn or for establishment of permanent residence therein and for gaining resultant citizenship thereof. If national citizenship means less than this, it means nothing.

As we have seen, then, the argument for fundamental rights, as expressed by Mr. Justice Washington in 1823, has not been adopted by the court in construing and applying the privileges and immunities clause of the Fourteenth Amendment. It has, however, been followed by the court in the definition of due process of law. The beginning of this development was seen in *Allgeyer v. Louisiana*,[19] in 1879, when the court undertook to protect corporations against state control. Later the court agreed to read some of the rights named in the first eight amendments into the due process clause of the Fourteenth Amendment. Thus the court has upheld freedom of speech,[20] freedom of the press,[21] freedom of religion,[22] freedom of assembly,[23] and the right to benefit of counsel,[24] against invasion by state action.

In summary it may be pointed out that the privileges and immunities clause in the Fourteenth Amendment is practically useless. Reliance on it is hazardous and is not likely to lead to a desirable result.

There are, however, a number of federal rights implied in the Constitution, resulting from the relation between the citizen and the Federal government. These rights are protected against in-

[19] 165 U.S. 578 (1897).
[20] De Jonge v. Oregon, 299 U.S. 353 (1937); Herndon v. Lowry, 301 U.S. 242 (1937).
[21] Grosjean v. Amer. Press Co., 297 U.S. 233 (1936); Near v. Minn., 283 U.S. 697 (1931).
[22] Hamilton v. Regents, 293 U.S. 245 (1934); Pierce v. Society of Sisters, 268 U.S. 510 (1925); Lovell v. Griffin, 303 U.S. 444 (1938); Schneider v. State, 308 U.S. 147 (1939); Cantwell v. Conn., 310 U.S. 296 (1940); Chaplinsky v. New Hampshire, 315 U.S. 568 (1942); Jamison v. Texas, 318 U.S. 413 (1943); Largent v. Texas, 318 U.S. 418 (1943); Murdock v. Penna., 319 U.S. 105 (1943); Martin v. Struthers, 319 U.S. 141 (1943); Jones v. Opelika, 319 U.S. 103 (1943); Douglas v. Jeannette, 319 U.S. 157 (1943).
[23] Cases cited in note 20, *supra*.
[24] Powell v. Ala., 287 U.S. 45 (1932); Glasser v. U.S., 315 U.S. 60 (1942); Betts v. Brady, 316 U.S. 455 (1942).

vasion by private persons as well as by officials. What are these rights? In a recent case, *Powe v. United States*,[25] they were defined as including the following:

   (1) The right to assemble peaceably for the purpose of petitioning the Federal government for redress of grievances; [26]

   (2) The freedom of speaking and printing on subjects relating to the Federal government, federal elections, federal laws, federal operations and officers; [27]

   (3) The Federal government must protect persons from violence while in federal custody; [28]

   (4) Federal elections may be protected by Congress.[29]

In the *Powe* case the defendants were indicted under Section 51 for conspiring to injure, oppress, threaten, and intimidate a named citizen of the United States in the free exercise of his right and privilege as a citizen to speak and publish his views in certain newspapers; more particularly, they were charged with a conspiracy to injure and oppress the executive editor of newspapers in Mobile, Alabama, in the exercise of his right to write and print editorials exposing and condemning various forms of illegal gambling and lotteries, and calling upon city and county officials to take action to suppress the same and to punish the offenders. The plan charged in the indictment was to procure a photograph of the editor in a lewd or obscene act and to threaten him with the use of it as evidence in prosecuting him.

---

[25] 109 F. (2d) 147 (1940); cert. den. 309 U.S. 679 (1940).

[26] U.S. v. Cruikshank, 92 U.S. 542 (1876). Cf. Hague v. C.I.O., 307 U.S. 496 (1939).

[27] The ground is that the government is a republican one in which the will of the people ought to prevail, and the will ought to be expressive of an informed public opinion.

[28] Logan v. U.S., 144 U.S. 263 (1892).

[29] U.S. v. Classic, 313 U.S. 299 (1941). Ex parte Yarbrough, 110 U.S. 651 (1884).

   Other cases having a bearing on national privileges and immunities: In re Quarles v. Butler, 158 U.S. 532 (1895), right to inform federal officer of violation of federal criminal laws. Cf. Motes v. U.S., 178 U.S. 458 (1900). On right to enter United States by citizen, see Chin Yow v. U.S., 208 U.S. 8 (1908). On privilege of expatriation, see Talbot v. Jansen, 3 Dall. 133 (1795). On right to resort to federal courts, Terral v. Burke Construction Co., 257 U.S. 529 (1922).

The federal circuit court of appeals held that these facts did not make an offense against the United States; because the right to freely speak and print about matters in general is not (to use the language of Section 51) "secured by the Constitution and laws of the United States"; the speaking and printing related to matters with which the city and county were concerned, and with which the United States had no concern.

The Federal government filed a petition for *certiorari*, in which it was contended that disclosure of local crime was not necessarily a local matter, but might have national interest because of the possibility of revealing violations of federal laws. But the Supreme Court denied the petition.[30]

The point may be made that the principle involved in rights implied from a consideration of what is essential to the effective functioning of the Federal government is a dynamic one, subject to expansion or progressive refinement. The time may come when the Supreme Court will consider all the personal rights protected against federal or state invasion as essential attributes of national citizenship to be protected against invasion by private individuals conspiring together, and thus subject to protection under Section 51. Such a development would be as natural as has been the reading into the Fourteenth Amendment, against *state* infraction, of the Bill of Rights. Due process incorporates the rights enumerated in the first eight amendments, not because they are set forth in those amendments, but because they are of such a nature that they must be included in the conception of due process of law. The test whether a right is included in the due process clause was said by the Supreme Court to be:

Is it a fundamental principle of liberty and justice which inheres in the very idea of free government and is the inalienable right of a citizen of such a government? If it is, and if it is of a nature that pertains to process of law, this court has declared it to be essential to due process of law.[31]

Shortly after this decision, the court affirmed in principle what it had only intimated before; it laid down the rule that the

[30] 309 U.S. 679 (1940).   [31] Twining v. New Jersey, 211 U.S. 78 (1908).

due process clause requires that state action shall be consistent with the fundamental principles of liberty and justice which are at the base of all our civil and political institutions.[32]

The principle used in this development of constitutional law is one which opens large windows: what may not have been thought of as an essential right two generations ago may be asserted and maintained as one today. Our view of the fundamental principles of liberty and justice may be taken from a point of vantage other than the one used by our grandparents: we may see them, for one thing, as requiring protection from individual encroachment as well as from federal and state encroachment.

Several things said in the opinions in the *Schneiderman*[33] denaturalization case may be taken as pointing in this direction. In a denaturalization case the question of what are the essential attributes of American citizenship may be of central importance. In his opinion for the majority of the court in the *Schneiderman* case, Mr. Justice Murphy said that if any provisions can be singled out as requiring unqualified attachment, they are the guarantees of the Bill of Rights. It may well be argued that if these guarantees require unqualified attachment as evidence of proper awareness of possession of the attributes of national citizenship, then the Federal government has the correlative duty to protect the citizen in his enjoyment of those guarantees, even against invasion by private individuals.

In his dissenting opinion, Chief Justice Stone (Justices Roberts and Frankfurter agreeing with him) said that there are principles of the Constitution attachment to which Congress may make a condition precedent to the granting of citizenship; and among such principles one may name, said Stone, the following: protection of civil rights; protection of life, liberty and property; representative government.

It would seem that here, in the statements by Murphy and Stone, we see a promise of an expansion of the principle vaguely adumbrated in the *Cruikshank* case. When the expansion will have been effected, the citizen will receive much more protection

[32] Cases cited in note 20, *supra*. [33] Schneiderman v. U.S., 320 U.S. 118 (1943).

from federal authorities than he has been able to get up to the present. This development would only recall us to the original intent of Section 51; for, as has been pointed out by a federal judge in Missouri: "The statute [Section 51] behind these cases, it is true, had its origin in the determination of the sovereign to protect the humblest citizens, poor, helpless Negroes, to protect them in their constitutional rights from the oppression and abuse of the Ku Klux Klan." [34]

Up to now we have considered protection of rights and privileges secured by the Constitution (expressly or by implication). The section speaks, however, of rights and privileges secured by the Constitution and *laws* of the United States. What rights and privileges secured by federal statutes have been protected against invasion by private persons?

The reported cases dealing with the enforcement of federal statutory rights have all been homestead cases, involving prosecution under Section 51 of persons who intimidated homesteaders in order to cause them to leave their homesteads.

The homestead laws, although they provide a machinery for obtaining title to land in the public domain on compliance with statutory conditions, do not contain specific criminal provisions penalizing interference with homesteaders. The theory of those cases is that the homesteader has a federal statutory right to acquire title on compliance with conditions including the residence requirement, and that running him off the homestead deprives him of this right, and hence falls within section 51. [35]

It has been pointed out that this theory is susceptible of generalization to any case of coercion of a person who has acquired rights under a federal statute if the purpose of the coercion is to cause him to renounce his statutory rights or benefits. [36] Thus, if a person has secured rights under the federal Social Security Act, the Wage and Hour Act, or the National Labor Relations Act, under Section 51 he may seek to have criminal sanctions im-

[34] See U.S. v. Clark, 19 F. Supp. 981 (1937).
[35] Dept. of Justice, Circular 3356, Supp. 2, April 4, 1942, p. 4.   [36] *Ibid.*, p. 5.

posed to punish attacks by *private or public officials,* upon the exercise of his acquired rights.

An indictment drawn on this theory has been sustained in the federal district court against demurrer in cases in Kentucky and Georgia. Both cases involved the use of thugs hired to break up union activity; in one case they beat employees, in the other, an organizer who was the accredited bargaining representative of employees. In both cases it was established that the victims had been intimidated in exercising rights under the National Labor Relations Act.[37]

If Congress passes a Fair Employment Practice Act,[38] it may be that Negro workers will then be in a position to protect their rights to hold a job, and to upgrading and promotions within it, under Section 51, against conspiracies by two or more white workers to deprive them of their statutory rights.

The annual reports of the Attorney General show that Section 51 is being used to protect persons other than Negroes. Thus, in the report for 1938 it is stated that, as a result of an investigation into the outrages in Harlan County, Kentucky, more than twenty coal-mining companies and more than forty individuals were indicted for alleged violation of the section by conspiring to injure, oppress, threaten, and intimidate employees of the coal-mining companies with intent to hinder their free exercise and enjoyment of rights guaranteed by the National Labor Relations Act. The case involved the civil rights of some 20,000 coal miners.[39]

Although Sections 51 and 52 were adopted under the Fourteenth Amendment, the Attorney General reported for the year 1941 a case against two defendants charged with violation of Section 51 by conspiring to deprive citizens of rights secured to them by the Thirteenth Amendment; namely, the right to be free from slavery and involuntary servitude.[40] And in the *Classic* case [41] the indictment charged violations of Sections 51 and 52,

---

[37] *Ibid.* Cases unreported.
[38] See H.R. 2232, 79th Cong., 1st Sess. (1945), in Appendix.
[39] Annual Report of Attorney General (1938), p. 81.
[40] See *ibid.*, p. 99.   [41] 313 U.S. 299 (1941).

alleging a conspiracy to deprive citizens of the right of qualified voters to have their ballots counted in a Congressional primary election.

Summary. Section 51 is a criminal conspiracy act. It protects only the citizen. It protects the citizen in the enjoyment of rights and privileges secured by the Constitution or laws of the United States. Under it private individuals may be prosecuted. It does not protect the citizen in the exercise of constitutional privileges and immunities, or civil rights generally, for these are attributes of state, as distinguished from national, citizenship. It protects the citizen in the exercise of those rights or privileges which are essential to the maintenance of the Federal government; for example, against fraud and intimidation at federal elections, against intimidation of federal witnesses. It will also protect the citizen in the exercise of rights granted by federal statutes where protection under any other act may be difficult or impossible; for example, the homestead acts.

The *Slaughterhouse Cases* made the concept of civil rights a matter of state concern exclusively. The Federal government may not define and protect civil rights. When it protects federal witnesses or federal elections it protects itself: that is the theory and the fact. For the definition and protection of his civil rights the citizen must look to his state.

This case, taken together with the *Civil Rights Cases,* denied the doctrine that after the passage of the Fourteenth Amendment the fundamental rights, privileges, and immunities, which formerly attached to an individual as a citizen of the state in which he lived, now belonged to him as a citizen of the United States. All that the privileges and immunities clause protects is the interest growing out of the relationship between the citizen and the Federal government. But this relationship is narrowly viewed; it does not entail the fundamental rights of free men. For such rights the citizen must look to his state.

This narrow construction is certainly not in keeping with the object of the framers of the Fourteenth Amendment.[42] The de-

---

[42] See Collins, *The Fourteenth Amendment and the States* (1912), ch. 1; Flack, *The Adoption of the Fourteenth Amendment* (1908), pp. 55 ff.

cision to make this construction has been justified on the ground that a different interpretation would "enlarge judicial control of state action and multiply restrictions upon it to an extent difficult to define, but sufficient to cause serious apprehension for the rightful independence of local governments." [43] But in rendering protection to property rights the Supreme Court was not afraid that use of the due process clause for such a purpose would enlarge judicial control of state action and multiply restrictions upon states. The court was not slow in exercising control of state action in the protection of public utility and other corporations, whom the framers of the amendment did not contemplate.[44]

18 U.S.C. 52

Based on Section 2 of the 1866 Civil Rights Act, this is also Section 20 of the Federal Criminal Code. The legislative history indicates that the immediate occasion for its adoption was the more adequate protection of the Negro race and their civil rights; but the purpose of its first clause was to protect the constitutional rights of all inhabitants of the states.[45] The section reads as follows:

Whoever, under color of any law, statute, ordinance, regulation, or custom, willfully subjects, or causes to be subjected, any inhabitant of any state, territory, or district to the deprivation of any rights, privileges, or immunities secured or protected by the Constitution and laws of the United States, or to different punishments, pains, or penalties, on account of such inhabitant being an alien, or by reason of his color, or race, than are prescribed for the punishment of citizens, shall be fined not more than $1,000, or imprisoned not more than one year, or both.

In the *Classic* case [46] the Supreme Court pointed out that the section authorizes the punishment of two separate offenses:

[43] Colgate v. Harvey, 296 U.S. 404 (1935), dis. op.   [44] See note 42, *supra*.
[45] 313 U.S. 299 (1941), at p. 327. For fuller statement of history see Screws v. U.S., 325 U.S. 91 (1945). See also Francis Biddle, "Civil Rights and the Federal Law," in *Safeguarding Civil Liberty Today* (Edward L. Bernays Lectures, Cornell University, 1945), pp. 109–144. Robt. K. Carr, "Screws v. U.S.", *Cornell L. Quar.*, Sept. 1945.
[46] 313 U.S. 299 (1941).

(1) willfully subjecting any inhabitant to the deprivation of rights secured by the Constitution and federal laws;

(2) willfully subjecting any inhabitant to different punishments on account of his alienage, color or race, than are prescribed for the punishment of citizens.

At the outset a number of elements are to be noted: (1) The act may be violated by a single individual. Unlike Section 51, this is not a conspiracy statute. (2) While Section 51 is for the protection of citizens, this section is for the protection of "any inhabitant." (3) The act must be done under color of authority. While Section 51 is directed against both individual persons and officers, Section 52 is directed only against officers, or persons acting under color of authority.

The Screws Case. It is not possible to discuss this section critically without giving a full analysis of the decision of the Supreme Court in *Screws v. United States*,[47] decided in 1945. To a consideration of this case we now turn.

Screws was sheriff of Baker County, Georgia. With the assistance of Jones, a policeman, and Kelley, a deputy sheriff, he arrested Hall, a Negro of Georgia. The arrest was made late at night at Hall's home, on a warrant charging Hall with the theft of a tire. Hall, about thirty years of age, was handcuffed and taken by car to the court house. As he alighted from the car at the court-house square, the three officers began beating him with their fists and with a solid-bar blackjack about eight inches long and weighing two pounds. After Hall had been knocked to the ground, they continued to beat him for at least fifteen, or possibly thirty, minutes, until he was unconscious. Then he was dragged, feet first, through the court-house square into the jail and thrown upon the floor dying. An ambulance was called and Hall was removed to a hospital where he died within the hour and without regaining consciousness. Mr. Justice Douglas, in his opinion for the court, was not exaggerating when he said that

[47] 325 U.S. 91 (1945). J. Cohen, "The Screws Case. Federal Protection of Negro Rights," 46 *Columbia L. Rev.* 94 (1946).

the case "involves a shocking and revolting episode in law enforcement."

An indictment was returned against the officers, one count charging them with violation of Section 52, and another charging a conspiracy to violate Section 52 contrary to 18 U.S.C. 88.[48] The indictment charged that the officers, acting under color of the laws of Georgia, "willfully" caused Hall to be deprived of "rights, privileges, or immunities secured or protected" to him by the Fourteenth Amendment: the right not to be deprived of life without due process of law; the right to be tried by due process of law, and, if found guilty, to be punished in accordance with the laws of the state. The jury returned a verdict of guilty. The circuit court of appeals affirmed the judgment of conviction, with one judge dissenting.[49]

Before the Supreme Court it was argued on behalf of the officers that Section 52 is unconstitutional in so far as it makes criminal activities which are in violation of the due process clause of the Fourteenth Amendment. For no ascertainable standard of guilt is provided. The due process clause has been broadly defined by the court; but these broad definitions, it was contended, provide, by reason of their broadness, no ascertainable standard of guilt. Section 52 has content only if it is permitted to incorporate into it by reference a large body of changing and uncertain law, expressible in general terms, and not always reducible to specific rules. But under our system of government criminal statutes must be specific. In order to determine what Section 52 outlaws, the interested citizen must have access to a comprehensive law library.

In his opinion for the court, Mr. Justice Douglas called attention to the fact that the section had been before Congress for passage, amendment, revision, and further amendment in the years 1866, 1870, 1874, and 1909. He said:

We hesitate to say that when Congress sought to enforce the Four-

---

[48] This statute makes it a crime for two or more persons to conspire to commit any offense against the United States or to defraud the government.
[49] 140 F (2d) 662.

teenth Amendment in this fashion it did a vain thing. We hesitate to conclude that for 80 years this effort of Congress, renewed several times, to protect the important rights of the individual guaranteed by the Fourteenth Amendment has been an idle gesture.

The court, he said, can construe the act in such a way that it will be constitutional, and this means confining its scope within narrower limits than those used by the lower courts.

The court found a way out of the difficulty by pointing out that the statute requires the proscribed act to be done "willfully." While the constitutional vice in such a statute may be the essential injustice to the accused in placing him on trial for an offense the nature of which the statute does not define and of which, hence, it can give no warning, however,

where the punishment imposed is only for an act knowingly done with the purpose of doing that which the statute prohibits, the accused cannot be said to suffer from lack of warning or knowledge that the act which he does is a violation of law. The requirement that the act must be willful or purposeful may not render certain, for all purposes, a statutory definition of the crime which is in some respects uncertain. But it does relieve the statute of the objection that it punishes without warning an offense of which the accused was unaware.

In other words, the statute requires a specific intent; this requirement saves the section from the charge that it lacks an ascertainable standard of guilt.

Yet the question remains as to how an officer can determine with sufficient definiteness the range of rights that are protected by the Constitution. Douglas answered this question by saying:

The specific intent required by the act is an intent to deprive a person of a right which has been made specific either by the express terms of the Constitution or laws of the United States or by decisions interpreting them. . . . He who defies a decision interpreting the Constitution knows precisely what he is doing. If sane, he hardly may be heard to say that he knew not what he did. Of course, willful conduct cannot make definite that which is undefined. But willful violators of constitutional requirements, which have been defined, certainly are in no position to say that they had no adequate advance notice that they would be visited with punishment.

The defendants in this case apparently acted "in reckless disregard of constitutional prohibitions or guarantees"; for those "who decide to take the law into their own hands and act as prosecutor, jury, judge, and executioner plainly act to deprive a prisoner of the trial which due process of law guarantees him."

The case, said Douglas, follows the precedent of the *Classic* case.[50] In that case the court dealt with the validity of an indictment charging election officials with willful failure and refusal to count the votes cast, with altering the ballots cast and falsely certifying the number of votes for the respective candidates. Since the right to vote considered in that case is guaranteed by the Constitution, the indictment was adequate, "since he who alters ballots or without legal justification destroys them would be acting willfully in the sense in which section [52] uses the term."

But in the *Screws* case, said Douglas, the difficulty was that the trial judge did not charge the jury on the element of willfullness. To convict properly, it was necessary for the jury to find that the defendants "had the purpose to deprive the prisoner of a constitutional right, e.g., the right to be tried by a court rather than by ordeal." While no exception was taken to the court's charge, and while normally, under these circumstances, the Supreme Court would not take note of this error, since, however, the error was so fundamental as not to submit to the jury the essential ingredients of the offense, the court thought it necessary to take note of it on its own motion, and so reversed the judgment and sent the case back for a new trial.

The opinion of Douglas cannot, however, be left at this point, for it covered other points which are significant for our discussion.

It was contended on behalf of the defendants that they are not within the terms of Section 52 because they had not acted "un-

[50] 313 U.S. 299 (1941).

der color of any law." In fact, they argued, their actions were *contrary* to the laws of the state; they acted *against*, rather than *under*, color of any law. But the court thought otherwise:

They were officers of the law who made the arrest. By their own admissions they assaulted Hall in order to protect themselves and to keep their prisoner from escaping. It was their duty under Georgia law to make the arrest effective. Hence, their conduct comes within the statute.

The case is no different from the situation in the *Classic* case. In that case election officials misused power which they possessed by virtue of state law, and the misuse of power was made possible only because the wrongdoer was clothed with the authority of state law; the wrongdoing was performed in the course of duties under state law. In the present case,

the defendants were officers of the law who had made an arrest and who by their own admissions made the assault in order to protect themselves and to keep the prisoner from escaping, i.e., to make the arrest effective. That was a duty they had under Georgia law. . . . In each [case] officers of the state were performing official duties; in each the power which they were authorized to exercise was misused.

"Under color of law" means under pretense of law. It has no application to a situation where an officer not authorized to act nevertheless takes action. Under color of law applies to one who acts in the name of, and for, the state, and is clothed with the state's power; but acts of officers in the ambit of their personal pursuits are not covered by the term.

The court was asked to abandon the holding in the *Classic* case, which had been unanimously decided in 1941. But a majority of the court refused to do so.

Mr. Justice Rutledge, concurring in the result, wrote a separate opinion. The evidence, he said, has nullified any pretense that defendants acted as individuals; they used the power of official business in all that was done. The act and the amendment were aimed at just such a case as this: "Abuse of state power was the target," he said.

It is too late now . . . to question that in these matters abuse binds the state and its act, when done by one to whom it has given power to make the abuse effective to achieve the forbidden ends. . . . For it was abuse of basic civil and political rights, by states and their officials, that the amendment and the enforcing legislation were adopted to uproot.

The violation of the amendment and the statute here was clear. This should be the end of the matter. The defendants have not denied that they acted "willfully" within the meaning of Section 52. They claimed justification, but could not prove it, as the verdict against them shows. The question of willfullness was first raised in the dissenting opinion in the court of appeals, then by inquiry at the argument, and finally in the opinion of Mr. Justice Douglas for the majority.

Sections 51 and 52 show no differences in the basic rights guarded. If one is vague, so is the other; they fall or stand together. They have stood together for nearly eighty years. In the *Mosley* case [51] the Supreme Court upheld the constitutionality of Section 51, and in the *Classic* case the court upheld the constitutionality of both sections. "These more recent pronouncements but reaffirmed earlier and repeated ones. The history should not require retelling. But old and established freedoms vanish when history is forgotten. . . . If time and uniform decision can give stability to statutes, these have acquired it."

Rutledge admitted, however, that Section 52 had not been much used in direct application until recently, when it has been applied more frequently and in a variety of situations. If the sections are valid in general coverage of other constitutional rights, they are not void in the application to rights under the Fourteenth Amendment. In view of their history, the sections apply more clearly to rights under this amendment than to others. "To strike from the statute the rights secured by the Fourteenth Amendment, but at the same time to leave within its coverage the vast area bounded by other constitutional provisions, would contradict both reason and history." Among the rights heretofore

[51] 238 U.S. 383 (1915).

protected by the sections have been, said Rutledge, the following:

> the right to a fair trial;
> the right to be free from arrest and detention by methods constitutionally forbidden;
> the right to be free from extortion of property by such methods;
> the right to be free from extortion of confessions;
> the right to be free from mob action incited or shared by state officers;
> the right to police protection on proper occasion and demand;
> the right to be free from interference with the free exercise of religion;
> the right to be free from interference with the freedom of the press and speech;
> the right to be free from interference with the freedom of assembly.

And now the decision in the instant case adds:

> the right to be free from deprivation of life itself without due process of law.

Statutory specificity, said Rutledge, has two purposes: (1) to give due notice that an act has been made criminal before it is committed; (2) to inform the accused of the nature of the offense charged, so that he may adequately prepare his defense. As to (2), the indictment is usually specific enough; if it is not, the defendant may make a motion to quash or a motion for a bill of particulars. In this case the defense provided showed clearly that the defendants knew well enough what was the charge against them and why they were brought to trial. As to (1): in the first place, Sections 51 and 52 are no more general and vague, Fourteenth Amendment rights included, than other criminal statutes. Secondly, Section 52 strikes only at abuse of official functions by state officers; and generally

state officials know something of the individual's basic legal rights. If they do not, they should, for they assume that duty when they assume their office. Ignorance of the law is no excuse for men in general. It is less an excuse for men whose special duty is to apply it, and therefore to know and observe it. If their knowledge is not comprehensive, state officials know or should know when they pass the limits of their authority, so far at any rate that their action exceeds honest error of judgment and amounts to abuse of their office and its function. When they enter such a domain in dealing with the citizen's rights, they should do so at their peril, whether that be created by state or federal law. . . . Since the statute, as I think, condemns only something more than error of judgment, made in honest effort at once to apply and follow the law, officials who violate it must act in intentional or reckless disregard of individual rights and cannot be ignorant that they do great wrong.

Certainly the act clearly applies to well-established, clear-cut fundamental rights, including many secured by the Fourteenth Amendment. When an attempt is made to apply the act to a case where it is doubtful if a right exists which is alleged to have been violated, then that particular charge might be invalidated; but the statute as a whole would not need to be outlawed.

In this case there was no mere error of judgment, made in good faith, on the part of defendants. The trial judge's charges were wholly adequate. Accordingly, Rutledge would affirm the judgment of conviction. But since four Justices have voted for reversal and a new trial, and since his views concerning appropriate disposition are more nearly in accord with those stated by Douglas than they are with the views of those who favor outright reversal, in order that disposition may be made of the case, he cast his vote for a reversal and a new trial.

Mr. Justice Murphy dissented, holding that the judgment of conviction should be affirmed. The statute, he said, may be vague as to certain criminal acts but definite as to others; but this does not mean that, therefore, the statute must fall. The court is not deciding any case but the one presented on the facts herein; and on those facts it is clear enough that the statute is constitutional. The reference in Section 52 is to rights protected by the Constitution; at the same time, the right not to be deprived of life without due process of law is lucidly protected by the Fourteenth Amendment.

There is nothing vague or indefinite in these references to this most basic of all human rights. Knowledge of a comprehensive law library is unnecessary for officers of the law to know that the right to murder individuals in the course of their duties is unrecognized in this nation. No appreciable amount of intelligence or conjecture on the part of the lowliest state official is needed for him to realize that fact; nor should it surprise him to find out that the Constitution protects persons from his reckless disregard of human life and that statutes punish him therefor.

The evidence, said Murphy, is more than convincing that the defendants willfully, or at least with wanton disregard of the consequences, deprived Hall of his life without due process of law. "A new trial could hardly make that fact more evident; the failure to charge the jury on willfulness was at most an inconsequential error."

From the opinion of Murphy it appears that the State of Georgia had refused to prosecute the officers for murder or manslaughter. He said:

Too often unpopular minorities, such as Negroes, are unable to find effective refuge from the cruelties of bigoted and ruthless authority. States are undoubtedly capable of punishing their officers who commit such outrages. But where, as here, the states are unwilling for some reason to prosecute such crimes the federal government must step in unless constitutional guarantees are to become atrophied.

Mr. Justice Roberts wrote a dissenting opinion, in which Justices Frankfurter and Jackson concurred.

Section 52, said Roberts, although it goes back to 1866, has, for all practical purposes, remained a dead letter for nearly eighty years. Under the Georgia law defendants committed a criminal homicide. The only issue is whether Georgia alone has the power and duty to punish them, or whether "this patently local crime" can be made the basis of a federal prosecution under Section 52.

The practical question is whether the states should be relieved from responsibility to bring their law officers to book for homicide, by allowing prosecutions in the federal courts for a relatively minor offense carrying a short sentence. The legal question is whether, for the purpose of accomplishing this relaxation of state responsibility, hitherto settled principles for the protection of civil liberties shall be bent and tortured.

Roberts, at the outset of his opinion, attempted to discredit the civil rights legislation adopted after the Civil War under the various amendments: "It is familiar history that much of this legislation was born of that vengeful spirit which to no small degree envenomed the Reconstruction era." Furthermore, when the laws were enacted, there was little legislative respect for constitutional limitations, "and Congress passed laws clearly unconstitutional." As proof of this assertion, Roberts cited the *Civil Rights Cases*.[52] Section 52, he said, is before the court now for the first time on full consideration as to its meaning and constitutionality, "unembarrassed by preoccupation both on the part of counsel and court with the more compelling issue of the power of Congress to control state procedure for the election of federal officers."

The statute, said Roberts, was not intended to apply to situations where the state officer acted contrary to state law. The Fourteenth Amendment (and the statute adopted under it) was intended to prohibit a state from authorizing any one of its officers to do acts which the Constitution prohibited. Here the state duly obeyed the Constitution, but its officers flouted the law; they are subject to punishment by the state, but not by the Federal government. The Federal government may prosecute persons who violate federal rights under claim of state authority; it may not prosecute persons who offend state authority: "such a distortion of federal power devised against recalcitrant state authority never entered the minds of the proponents of the legislation." In support of this assertion, Roberts quoted from the statements by Senators Trumbull and Sherman, leading Reconstruction statesmen. To attribute any other purpose to the legislators responsible for the act would be to assume that they intended to revolutionize the balance of the political relations between the national government and the states "without reason."

[52] 109 U.S. 3 (1883).

State courts, like federal courts, are guardians of the constitutional rights of individuals; the Supreme Court and Congress should not do anything to disturb the balance that exists between the federal and the state judiciary. This is a fundamental policy of our federal system. There is nothing in the act, nor in its history, nor in the practice of government for seventy-five years, nor in the body of judicial opinion "which bids us find in the unbridled excess of a state officer, constituting a crime under his state law, action taken 'under color of law' which federal law forbids."

Before the decision in the *Classic* case, only two reported cases [53] considered Section 52, and neither of these is in point, because in those cases the defendants attempted to justify their conduct under existing state law. Only the *Classic* case, said Roberts, "looks the other way." But in that case the court did not focus attention on the problem herein presented. "The views in the *Classic* case thus reached ought not to stand in the way of a decision on the merits of a question which has now for the first time been fully explored and its implication for the workings of our federal system have been adequately revealed."

It may be that Congress could, under the Fourteenth Amendment, treat action by a state official, even though done in defiance of state law, as the action of a state; but it has not done so by Section 52; for this section is narrower than the power of Congress.

The presuppositions of our federal system, the pronouncements of the statesmen who shaped this legislation, and the normal meaning of language powerfully counsel against attributing to Congress intrusion into the sphere of criminal law traditionally and naturally reserved for the states alone. When due account is taken of the considerations that have heretofore controlled the political and legal relations between the states and the national government, there is not the slightest warrant in the reason of things for torturing language plainly designed for nullifying a claim of acting under a state law

[53] U.S. v. Buntin, 10 F. 730 (1882); U.S. v. Stone, 188 F. 836 (1911).

that conflicts with the Constitution so as to apply to situations where state law is in conformity with the Constitution and local misconduct is in undisputed violation of that state law. In the absence of clear direction by Congress we should leave to the states the enforcement of their criminal law, and not relieve states of the responsibility for vindicating wrongdoing that is essentially local or weaken the habits of local law enforcement by tempting reliance on federal authority for an occasional unpleasant task of local enforcement.

Then Roberts turned to a consideration of the constitutionality of Section 52. Basic to civil liberties is the requirement that criminal statutes be definite.

But four members of the court are of the opinion that this plain constitutional principle of definiteness in criminal statutes may be replaced by an elaborate scheme of constitutional exegesis whereby that which Congress has not defined the courts can define from time to time, with varying and conflicting definiteness in the decisions, and that, in any event, an undefined range of conduct may become sufficiently definite if only such undefined conduct is committed "willfully." . . . To base federal prosecutions on the shifting and indeterminate decisions of courts is to sanction prosecutions for crimes based on definitions made by courts. This is tantamount to creating a new body of federal criminal law . . . crimes must be defined by the legislature. . . . What the Constitution requires is a definiteness defined by the legislature, not one argumentatively spelled out through the judicial process which, precisely because it is a process, cannot avoid incompleteness.

The section, said Roberts, does not become more definite by the requirement that a person "willfully" commit what Congress has not defined. How can vagueness be made to evaporate by the suggestion that "what is otherwise too vaguely defined must be 'willfully' committed"?

Since the word "willfully" was added only in 1909, argued Roberts, then the act must have been unconstitutional before that time. But the term was not put into the statute with eyes on the constitutional question now under consideration.

In conclusion, Roberts said: "There can be no doubt that this shapeless and all-embracing statute can serve as a dangerous instrument of political intimidation and coercion in the hands of those so inclined."

Summary of Decision and Opinions. Douglas, Stone, Black, Reed, Rutledge, and Murphy agreed that Section 52 is constitutional.

1. The act is constitutional in face of the argument that it is indefinite and vague.
2. The act is constitutional when applied to a state officer who violates a right guaranteed by the Constitution even though the officer acted in contravention of state law.

Douglas, Stone, Black, and Reed said the act is constitutional in face of the argument that it is indefinite and vague, because the act of the officer, to be within the terms of the statute, must have been done "willfully."

Douglas, Stone, Black, and Reed reversed the judgment of conviction and sent the case back to the trial court for a new trial because the trial judge had failed to charge the jury adequately on the element of willfullness.

Rutledge said that the act is constitutional in face of the argument that it is indefinite and vague; and that the officers had acted willfully, within the meaning of the statute. He said the judgment of conviction should be affirmed; but he voted to reverse and remand, only to avoid a stalemate in the court and make a decision possible.

Murphy said that the act is constitutional in face of the argument that it is indefinite and vague; that the officers had acted willfully, within the meaning of the statute; and that the judge's charge was entirely adequate. He said the judgment should be affirmed.

Roberts, Frankfurter, and Jackson, dissenting, said:

1. The act is unconstitutional because of its indefiniteness and vagueness.
2. If constitutional, the act was intended by Congress to apply only

to that unconstitutional conduct of state officers which has been authorized by state law, but not to such conduct which is opposed to state law.

Significance of the Decision. Following the Supreme Court decision in the *Civil Rights Cases* that the 1875 Civil Rights Act is unconstitutional, the chief important statutes whereby the Negro could look to the Federal government for protection in his constitutional rights were Sections 51 and 52. If these were taken from him, the Negro would be at the mercy of the state governments, with but few exceptions (under the Thirteenth and Fifteenth Amendments). By a 6–3 vote the constitutionality of Section 52 (and, by clear implication, Section 51 also) has been saved. There continues to exist, then, a link between the Federal government and the protection of the Negro against deprivation of his life, liberty, and property without due process of law by state officials acting under state law or acting contrary to state law, and against deprivation of his rights or privileges under the Constitution or federal law by two or more private persons acting together in a conspiracy. Just as the decision in the *Civil Rights Cases* is of the utmost significance for what it took away from the Negro (or failed to give him), so the decision in the *Screws* case is of the utmost significance, for what it left remaining to the Negro.

The Future of Section 52. As Roberts points out in his dissenting opinion, up to the present only two reported cases have been brought under the section, apart from the *Classic* case. The reason why the volume of prosecutions and convictions has been small or negligible (an amazing fact in view of the importance of the subject matter and the length of time the section has been in force) was set forth by Rutledge in his concurring opinion. First place must be given to the "self-restraint of federal prosecuting officials." Another reason is that a strong case must be made to show abuse of official function in order to secure indictment or conviction. The trial must generally be within the state of which the accused is an officer. The jury must consist of citizens of that state, and such citizens have not and will not be ready to indict or convict their local officers in doubtful cases.

A federal official therefore faces both a delicate and a difficult task when he undertakes to charge and try a state officer under the terms of sections 19 and 20 [51 and 52]. The restraint which has been shown is as much enforced by these limitations as it has been voluntary.

While the reasons stated by Rutledge are undoubtedly important, nevertheless, as Roberts has said, the chief reason why, for all practical purposes, the statute has remained a dead letter all these years must be looked for elsewhere. It is to be found in the ingrained tradition of Negro suppression in the South.

The fact that minor public officials, judges, prosecuting attorneys, sheriffs, court attendants, and in some communities even the police force, are elected by the people, means that the administration of justice is dependent upon local voters, and this, Myrdal points out, means discrimination against an unpopular minority group, "particularly when this group is disfranchised as Negroes are in the South."

The elected judge knows that sooner or later he must come back to the polls, and that a decision running counter to local opinion may cost him his position. He may be conscious of it or not, but this control of his future career must tend to increase his difficulties, in keeping aloof from local prejudices and emotions. Of course, the judge's attitudes are also formed by conditions prevalent in his local community, but he has a degree of acquaintance with the law, and with public and legal opinion outside his community. This would tend to emancipate him from local opinion were it not for his direct dependence on it.[54]

While it is true that federal judges are appointed by the President and that their term is for life (or during good behavior), in the administration of federal criminal justice it is not the federal judge but the United States attorney for the district that plays the central role; and this official is a local lawyer appointed by the President chiefly for political reasons; the attorney's term is for four years, "unless sooner removed by the President."[55]

[54] Myrdal, *An American Dilemma* (Harper, 1944), I, 523.   [55] 28 U.S.C. 482.

The attorney is the one who is supposed to initiate criminal proceedings; there is no review of his discretion unless the Department of Justice goes out of its way to look into the conduct of his office. What Myrdal says of elected judicial officers applies to the United States attorneys in almost every detail.

Even if the district attorney were willing to go against the current of strong prejudice in his community, he is generally practical enough to anticipate the reactions of the grand jury and the trial jury. While the jury system works well enough "in a reasonably homogeneous, highly educated and public spirited community," says Myrdal,

it causes, however, the gravest peril of injustice in all cases where the rights of persons belonging to a disfranchised group are involved, particularly if this group is discriminated against all around and by tradition held as a lower caste upon whose rights it has become customary to infringe. *The extreme democracy in the American system of justice turns out, thus, to be the greatest menace to legal democracy when it is based on restricted political participation and an ingrained tradition of caste suppression.* Such conditions occur in the South with respect to Negroes.[56]

As a result of his experiences, the Negro in the South has come to look upon law and justice "not as protecting safeguards, but as sources of humiliation and oppression."[57] In the South, Myrdal states,

the Negro's person and property are practically subject to the whim of any white person who wishes to take advantage of him or to punish him for any real or fancied wrongdoing or "insult." A white man can steal from or maltreat a Negro in almost any way without fear of reprisal, because the Negro cannot claim the protection of the police or courts, and personal vengeance on the part of the offended Negro results in organized retaliation in the form of bodily injury (including lynching), home burning or banishment.[58]

Court officials are white; the jury, too, is usually all-white, "except for cases in the federal courts and in some of the larger

[56] Myrdal, *An American Dilemma,* I, 524. Italics in original.
[57] *Ibid.,* p. 525.   [58] *Ibid.,* p. 530.

cities"; [59] Negro lawyers are scarce in the South; the Negro's testimony is generally disregarded; for offenses which involve any actual or potential danger to whites, Negroes are punished more severely than whites, though the higher state courts and the federal courts are less likely to discriminate against Negroes; the jury is more guilty of obvious partiality than are the judge and public prosecutor. "When the offender is a white man and the victim a Negro, a grand jury will often refuse to indict. Even the federal courts find difficulty in getting indictments in peonage cases." [60] It is notorious, says Myrdal,

that practically never have white lynching mobs been brought to court in the South, even when the killers are known to all in the community and are mentioned by name in the local press. When the offender is a Negro, indictment is easily obtained and no such difficulty at the start will meet the prosecution of the case. The petit jury is even less impartial than the grand jury.[61]

It is in the light of these facts that one must understand Rutledge's reference to the "self-restraint of federal prosecuting officials"—a self-restraint which is both voluntary and a recognition of objective limitations.

Because of his profound concern for civil liberties, Mr. Justice Murphy, when he was Attorney General of the United States, set up, in 1939, a Civil Rights Unit (or Section) in the Criminal Division of the Department of Justice. In his annual report for 1939, Murphy referred to this activity in the following statement:

The maintenance of civil liberties of the individual is one of the mainstays and bulwarks of democracy. It is fundamental that in the United States certain civil rights are guaranteed by the state governments, while others are assured by the federal government. In respect to the latter group the Department of Justice has an important function to perform. With that end in view, I caused to be organized a Civil Liberties Unit in the Criminal Division of the Department. One of the

[59] Myrdal, *An American Dilemma*, I, 549.   [60] *Ibid.*, p. 552.
[61] *Ibid.*, p. 553. These quotations are reprinted by permission of the publisher.

functions of this unit is to study complaints of violations of the Civil Rights Acts and to supervise prosecutions under those statutes.[62]

As far as we know, Murphy was the first Attorney General who recognized an obligation on the part of the Department of Justice with respect to civil rights guaranteed by federal law.

It is important to note that the Civil Rights Unit was charged with the duty to investigate complaints and to supervise prosecutions. These activities, it was expected, would tend to counteract the self-restraint of federal district attorneys. It was also expected that whenever a community would know that the Department of Justice in Washington is interested in a case, the impact of prejudice will be considerably weakened by a desire to show the rest of the country that the community has respect for law and order, and a civilized sense of justice.

But the Department of Justice soon imposed on itself a policy of self-limitation. Roberts quoted as follows from a statement prepared by the Attorney General:

The Department of Justice has established a policy of strict self-limitation with regard to prosecutions under the civil rights acts. When violations of such statutes are reported, the Department requires that efforts be made to encourage state officials to take appropriate action under state law. To insure consistent observance of this policy in the enforcement of the civil rights statutes, all United States Attorneys have been instructed to submit cases to the Department for approval before prosecutions or investigations are instituted. The number of prosecutions which have been brought under the civil rights statutes is small.

The statement pointed out that since 1939 the number of complaints received annually by the Civil Rights Unit has ranged from 8,000 to 14,000; but in no year have prosecutions under both Sections 51 and 52 exceeded 76. In the fiscal year 1943 there were only 31 full investigations of alleged violations under Section 52, and only three cases were brought to trial. In the fiscal

[62] Annual Report of the Attorney General (1939), p. 2. See also Frank Coleman, "Freedom from Fear on the Home Front," 29 *Iowa L. Rev.* 415 (1944).

year 1944 there were only 55 such investigations, and prosecution in only twelve cases was instituted (though in neither year were there less than 8,000 complaints).

It is to be hoped that the decision in the *Screws* case will strengthen the Civil Rights Unit and prompt the Department of Justice to assume a policy of more vigorous investigation and prosecution of violations; though it should be noted the Department was not restrained by fear that the Supreme Court might hold Sections 51 and 52 unconstitutional, or narrowly limited. It is much more likely that the restraint was self-imposed lest the Southern Representatives and Senators in Congress decide to supervise the Department's policies and "curb excesses by withdrawal of funds,"—as was suggested or implied by the Department itself in the statement from which Roberts quoted in his dissenting opinion. It is, unfortunately, possible that the dissent of three Justices may tend to restrict the Civil Rights Unit still further, lest it risk converting a minority of three into a majority of five.

When it comes to the vindication of his civil rights, it is thus by only a slender thread that the Negro maintains a connection with the national government. The Negro does not fear unconstitutional state legislation directed against him; that specter has been reduced to a minimum. What he does fear is the lawless administration of justice by state officials and conspiracies by private individuals to deprive him of his constitutional and legal rights. That fear may be strengthened by the dissenting votes of the three Justices, rather than weakened by the decision of the six Justices.

The dissenting opinion, despite the fact that much of it is written in conventional legal terminology, is based fundamentally on a policy judgment, namely, "states' rights"; and such a policy judgment may readily serve as a rallying cry for the Southern forces in a campaign to abolish or paralyze the work of the Civil Rights Unit, or at least as much of the work as may involve the protection of the rights of Negroes under Sections 51 and 52.

Despite the fact that it was stated that the authorities in Georgia took no steps to bring Screws and his henchmen to account (the Solicitor General of the Albany Circuit in the State of Georgia, which includes Baker County, testified that he took no measures against Sheriff Screws and the other two defendants because no complaint had been filed in connection with the death of Hall), Roberts none the less said:

We are told that local authorities cannot be relied upon for courageous and prompt action, that often they have personal or political reasons for refusing to prosecute. If it be significantly true that crimes against local law cannot be locally prosecuted, it is an ominous sign indeed.

What is the cure? Here we see the fundamental policy judgment (though questions of policy or wisdom are not for the courts): "In any event, the cure is a re-invigoration of state responsibility. It is not an undue incursion of remote federal authority into local duties with consequent debilitation of local responsibility."

Earlier in his opinion Roberts touched on the same theme:

In the absence of clear direction by Congress we should leave to the states the enforcement of their criminal law, and not relieve states of the responsibility for vindicating wrongdoing that is essentially local or weaken the habits of local law enforcement by tempting reliance on federal authority for an occasional unpleasant task of local enforcement.

Roberts himself pointed out that Sections 51 and 52 have remained a dead letter, for all practical purposes, for about seventy-five years. If the statutes are a dead letter, then they cannot be charged with having relieved the states of the responsibility for vindicating local wrongdoing or weakening the habits of local law enforcement. No one with any acquaintance with the facts ventured to intimate that the people of Georgia did not undertake to prosecute the Sheriff of Baker County and his deputy and the policemen because of the "tempting reliance on federal authority." If Roberts, Frankfurter, and Jackson were thinking of the administration of justice in the State of Georgia in terms of the future rather than of the past, the authoritative studies by Myrdal and others should have disclosed to them the fact that the situation could hardly be made worse by a vigorous policy of investigation and prosecution on the part of federal authorities.

If Justices of the Supreme Court start their reasoning in a case with (1) the assumption or conviction that the civil rights legislation adopted after the Civil War "was born of that vengeful spirit which to no small degree envenomed the Reconstruction era" and was largely unconstitutional; and (2) the slogan of states' rights, and the consequent prejudice that federal authority, law, and officials are "remote," while state authority, law, and officials are "local," then it should not be difficult for them to resurrect Congressional debates in order to learn from them that the envenomed Reconstructionists intended, when they proposed and urged adoption of Sections 51 and 52, to have put on the statute books perfectly innocuous and largely meaningless acts of Congress. The spuriousness of the argument and the historiography may be underscored if the argument is put this way:

1. The Reconstructionists in Congress were motivated by venom and hatred against the South.
2. They enacted civil rights statutes which were clearly unconstitutional.
3. Senators Trumbull and Sherman were leading Reconstruction statesmen. They were against states' rights and against the South.
4. Sections 51 and 52 were part of the Reconstruction legislative civil rights program.
5. Senators Trumbull and Sherman, in their speeches in Congress, indicated clearly that Sections 51 and 52 were intended to be interpreted or construed with full respect for the states' rights doctrine.
6. Therefore, in order to carry out the intention of the Reconstruction Congress, the statutes must be construed or interpreted narrowly so as not to invade states' rights—the doctrine opposed and negated by Reconstructionists.

It is interesting to note that the dissenting Justices stated that they were dissenting on the ground that the decision by the majority was a threat to civil liberties. "As misuse of the criminal machinery," said Roberts, "is one of the most potent and familiar instruments of arbitrary government, proper regard for the rational requirement of definiteness in criminal statutes is basic to civil liberties." Because Section 52 is indefinite and vague, it is a threat to civil liberties and should be declared unconstitutional.

While the constitutional requirement that criminal statutes be definite is an important bulwark of civil liberties, no less important is the constitutional guarantee that no person shall be deprived of his life without due process of law. At the best, then, one might say that the court faced the problem of vindicating posthumously Hall's constitutional right to life or the constitutional right of his murderers not to be tried except under a statute whose terms are definite, in a legal sense.

Six of the Justices thought that the terms of Section 52 are definite enough to meet the constitutional test. In the light of precedents, there is no doubt but that the majority were right. Let us look at a number of the precedents.

In a case before the Supreme Court in 1936 it was argued that the phrase "fair and open competition" in the Illinois Fair Trade Act was fatally vague and indefinite, and therefore, if the Act were enforced, there would be a denial of due process of law. The court unanimously held that the point lacked substance; that the phrase was as definite as the phrase "unfair methods of competition" in the Federal Trade Commission Act, which the court had never regarded as fatally defective. Mr. Justice Roberts did not dissent in that case.[63]

In 1913 the court [64] considered the contention that the criminal provisions of the Sherman Anti-Trust Act were unconstitutional on the ground of uncertainty. As construed in the cases

---

[63] Old Dearborn Co. v. Seagram Corp., 299 U.S. 183 (1936).
[64] Nash v. U.S., 229 U.S. 373 (1913). Sherman anti-trust act is 26 Stat. 209 (1890).

brought before the court, the act applied only to such contracts and combinations that, either by reason of intent or by the nature of the contemplated action, prejudice the public interests by unduly restricting competition or unduly obstructing the course of trade. It was argued that the crime thus defined contains an element of degree as to which estimates may differ, with the result that a person might find himself in prison because his honest judgment did not anticipate the judgment of a jury. It was argued that the act was indefinite and uncertain; it made the criminality of conduct depend upon whether a jury may think it reasonable or unreasonable.

In his opinion for the court, Mr. Justice Holmes said:

But apart from the common law as to restraint of trade . . . the law is full of instances where a man's fate depends on his estimating rightly, that is, as the jury subsequently estimates it, some matter of degree. If his judgment is wrong, not only may he incur a fine or a short imprisonment, as here; he may incur the penalty of death. "An act causing death may be murder, manslaughter, or misadventure according to the degree of danger attending it." . . . "The very meaning of the fiction of implied malice in such cases at common law was, that a man might have to answer with his life for consequences which he neither intended nor foresaw." . . . "The criterion in such cases is to examine whether common social duty would, under the circumstances, have suggested a more circumspect conduct."

In 1942 the court [65] considered a New Hampshire statute which provided that no person shall address "any offensive, derisive or annoying word to any other person" on any street, "nor call him by any offensive or derisive name, nor make any noise or exclamation in his presence and hearing with intent to deride, offend or annoy him." The Supreme Court unanimously held that

It is a statute narrowly drawn and limited to define and punish specific conduct lying within the domain of state power, the use in a public place of words likely to cause a breach of the peace. . . . A statute punishing verbal acts, carefully drawn so as not unduly to impair liberty of expression, is not too vague for a criminal law.

[65] Chaplinsky v. New Hampshire, 315 U.S. 568 (1942).

Justices Roberts, Frankfurter, and Jackson did not dissent in that case.

In the *Screws* case, the dissenting Justices did not indicate that they thought an injustice was done by the majority decision. Rather, they had their eyes upon the future development of the law. "This court," said Roberts, "now creates new delicate and complicated problems for the enforcement of the criminal law." He feared that the decision was "bound to produce a confusion detrimental to the administration of criminal justice." Although the officials of the Department of Justice may be following a "policy of strict self-limitation," there is no assurance that these officials will enjoy permanent tenure and immortality. "Evil men are rarely given power; they take it over from better men to whom it had been entrusted. There can be no doubt that this shapeless and all-embracing statute can serve as a dangerous instrument of political intimidation and coercion in the hands of those so inclined."

This type of reasoning has been condemned by the court time and again. In *Fox v. Washington,* a case involving freedom of speech, Mr. Justice Holmes said for a unanimous court:

We understand the state court by implication at least to have read the statute as confined to encouraging an actual breach of law. Therefore the argument that this act is both an unjustifiable restriction of liberty and too vague for a criminal law must fail. It does not appear and is not likely that the statute will be construed to prevent publications merely because they tend to produce unfavorable opinions of a particular statute or of law in general. In this present case the disrespect for law that was encouraged was disregard of it—an overt breach and technically criminal act. . . . *That is all that has happened as yet, and we see no reason to believe that the statute will be stretched beyond that point.* If the statute should be construed as going no farther than it is necessary to go in order to bring the defendant within it, there is no trouble with it for want of definiteness.[66]

Similarly, in *United States v. Keitel,* Mr. Justice White said for a unanimous court:

[66] 236 U.S. 273 (1915). Italics supplied.

Nor do we deem it necessary to do more than briefly refer to . . . the fear . . . that if the words to defraud in any manner or for any purpose receive a broad significance charges of crime may be hereafter predicated upon acts not prohibited and innocuous in and of themselves, and which, when they were committed, might have been deemed by no one to afford the basis of a criminal prosecution. *It will be time enough to consider such forebodings when a case arises indicating that the dread is real and not imaginary.*[67]

As we have seen, in the *Classic* case the Supreme Court pointed out that Section 52 authorizes the punishment of two separate offenses:

(1) willfully subjecting any inhabitant to the deprivation of rights secured by the Constitution or federal laws;

(2) willfully subjecting any inhabitant to different punishments on account of his alienage, color, or race, than are prescribed for the punishment of citizens.

The question of color or race, then, is pertinent only when a different punishment is imposed. In all other cases under the section, the consideration of color or race is irrelevant.

Thus, in the *Screws* case, the fact that Hall was a Negro was not a strictly relevant fact, from the standpoint of the language of the act. It was, however, a relevant fact from another point of view: the life, liberty, and property of Negroes in Georgia do not receive equal protection with the life, liberty, and property of whites. Hall was deprived of his life without due process of law because he was a Negro; the Sheriff of Baker County and the other two officers were not prosecuted under state law because their victim was a Negro. These facts were important because they were not exceptional or singular; they were part of an established social pattern. If a Negro of Georgia is not to be deprived of his life without due process of law by a person acting under color of law, his constitutional right must be protected by federal law. If the choice was between the abstraction of states' rights and the concrete need of a helpless group to have

---

[67] 211 U.S. 370 (1908). Italics supplied.

their constitutional rights protected, six of the Supreme Court Justices chose the latter.

The annual reports of the Attorney General show that Section 52 is being used to protect persons other than Negroes and aliens. Thus for the year 1941 a case is reported in which defendants were charged under Section 52 with having, under color of law, willfully deprived a person of the free exercise of rights secured to him by the Constitution; namely, the right and privilege of pursuing his means of livelihood in the business of photography.[68]

In view of the fact that Section 52 was adopted under the Fourteenth Amendment, it is doubtful if the courts would apply it to federal officials (although its language is broad enough to cover officials of any jurisdiction). Thus far no case has been brought under the section against any one who was not a state or municipal officer.

[68] Annual Report of the Attorney General (1941), p. 99.

CHAPTER 4

Lynching as a Federal Crime

THE OPINION may be ventured that the decision in the *Screws* case [1] provides an effective answer to the opponents of federal antilynching legislation. Before we consider this point, however, it may be well to place the movement for antilynching legislation in its broad historical and legal setting.

PROPOSED FEDERAL ANTILYNCHING LEGISLATION

The movement for a federal antilynching bill first received official support in 1891, in the recommendation of President Harrison that Congress pass a law to protect aliens from mob violence.[2] The recommendation came as the result of difficulties arising from an outbreak that year in New Orleans, when eleven Italians awaiting trial were taken from jail and lynched. The state made no effort to apprehend the mob leaders. The Italian government protested under the terms of a treaty; the Federal government answered that it had no power under our federal system; strained relations ensued, until the Secretary of State offered compensation to the families of the victims.

A bill was submitted to Congress in 1892, providing that when acts which were crimes under the laws of the states were committed against aliens in violation of treaty rights, the offenders should be prosecuted in the federal courts, but the state statutes should define the crime, prescribe the punishment, regulate the rules of evidence and procedure; in other words, the act made criminal by state law shall be tried and punished in a federal court if the act committed was a violation of treaty rights.

[1] Screws v. U.S., 325 U.S. 91 (1945).
[2] History of proposed antilynching legislation in David O. Walter, "Proposals for a Federal Anti-Lynching Law," 28 *Amer. Pol. Sc. Rev.* 436 (1934).

Although bills of similar purport were introduced in the Senate in 1893, 1899, and 1908, and in the House in 1900, 1902, 1903, 1905, and 1907, no action was taken until 1908. In that year the House passed a bill recommended by the Department of State. Differing from the earlier bills, it provided that

if two or more persons conspire to injure, oppress, threaten, or intimidate any alien in his free exercise of any right secured to him under any treaty of the United States, or because of his having so exercised the same, they shall be fined not more than $5,000 or imprisoned not more than ten years or both.

The bill, however, died in a Senate committee. Similar measures were introduced in 1909, 1915, 1917, 1919, and 1920, but no action was taken on any bill. In 1922 the Dyer antilynching bill included a clause for the protection of aliens, following, however, the 1892 rather than the 1907 model; and since then the protection of aliens has been treated as part of the general problem of antilynching legislation.

In 1892 President Harrison urged Congress, on behalf of the Negro race, to adopt the strongest antilynching measures. But Congress failed to respond. In 1894 a resolution for an investigation of lynching was introduced in the House. In 1900 a Negro Congressman introduced the first general antilynching bill. In 1901 a bill was introduced in the House and one in the Senate; the Senate Committee on the Judiciary reported the bill adversely. In 1902 another resolution for an investigation (this time a Senate resolution) was introduced, only to suffer the fate of its predecessor. The next measure was introduced in 1918, in the form of a House bill offered by Representative Dyer of Missouri. Similar bills were introduced in succeeding Congresses until 1921, when Dyer reported favorably for the House Committee on the Judiciary on H.R. 13, a bill similar in form to that introduced in the Senate in 1901.

The Southern Democrats opposed the bill vehemently. It was argued that the Fourteenth Amendment applied only as a prohibition on state action, not on the action of individuals. Further, when police officers fail to afford reasonable protection to prisoners, they are violating duties imposed by state law, and so cannot be considered agents of the state.

In 1922 the Dyer bill passed the House after five weeks of consideration. The bill was killed in the Senate by a filibuster. There was no action on bills introduced in 1923, 1925, 1927, 1929, 1933, 1935. In 1937 a bill again passed the House; it was favorably reported by the Senate Committee on the Judiciary, but was killed by a filibuster.[3]

For the purpose of our discussion we may examine the anti-lynching bill considered by Congress in 1940.[4] The preamble stated that the bill is adopted, under the Fourteenth Amendment, for the purpose of better assuring by the several states equal protection and due process of law to all persons charged with, or suspected or convicted of, any offense within the states' jurisdiction. The bill provided that:

1. Any assemblage of three or more persons which attempts to exercise by violence any power of correction or punishment over any person in the custody of any peace officer, or suspected of, charged with, or convicted of the commission of any offense, with the purpose or consequence of preventing the apprehension, or trial, or punishment by law of such person, shall constitute a "mob."

2. Any such violence by a mob which results in the death or maiming of the victim shall constitute a "lynching."

3. Whenever a lynching occurs, any officer of a state or subdivision thereof who is charged with the duty or possesses the authority to protect such person from lynching, and neglects or refuses to make diligent efforts to protect the person from lynching, or who has custody of the person and neglects or refuses to make diligent efforts to protect him from lynching, or who is charged with the duty or possesses the authority to apprehend, keep in custody, or prosecute the members of the lynching mob, and neglects or refuses to make diligent efforts so to do, shall be guilty of a felony.

[3] Note, 38 *Columbia Law Rev.* 199 (1938).
[4] H.R. 801, 76th Cong., 3d Sess. (1940). See Hearings on bill before subcommittee of Senate Committee on Judiciary (1940). See also H.R. 51, 78th Cong., 1st Sess. (1943), in Appendix.

4. Whenever a lynching occurs, and information on oath is submitted to the Attorney General that an officer of a state or subdivision thereof has violated the provisions of paragraph 3, the Attorney General shall cause an investigation to be made, to determine if there has been a violation of the act.

5. Every subdivision of a state having police functions shall be civilly liable for any lynching within its jurisdiction, to each person injured or his next of kin, for a sum of $2,000 to $10,000.

6. Civil action may be brought in the federal court, prosecuted by the Attorney General, for the benefit of the real party in interest, or by claimant's counsel.

It is apparent that the bill is directed against state officers or officers of a governmental subdivision of the state, in so far as criminal liability is concerned. It is not directed against members of the mob. As for civil liability, the bill is directed only against the subdivision of the state in which the lynching takes place.

Would this bill, if enacted, be constitutional? In the light of the decision in the *Screws* case, it is submitted that the question can no longer even be raised in good faith.

First in importance has been the contention that action by state officers is not state action, and the Fourteenth Amendment is aimed only against state action. But the court in the *Screws* case has answered that argument: Hall was deprived of his life without due process of law, within the meaning of the Fourteenth Amendment, by the State of Georgia, when he was beaten to death by the sheriff of Baker County, the deputy sheriff, and a policeman. The antilynching bill is aimed only against persons such as the defendants in the *Screws* case: officers of a state or its subdivisions.

The only other important question is whether a *failure* to act in accordance with official duty may also be defined as state action. On this point the decision in the *Screws* case is instructive. The court in that case said that Hall had been deprived of his life without due process of law, by state action. But the court put the matter in another way, too: for the jury to convict the defendants, it was necessary for the jury to find that the defendants "had the purpose to deprive the prisoner [Hall] of a constitutional right, e.g., the right to be tried by a court rather than by ordeal." And the dissenting Justices agreed with this statement; for Roberts said: "There is no question that Congress could provide for a penalty against deprivation by state officials 'acting under color of any law' of 'the right to be tried by a court rather than by ordeal.'" The dissenting Justices only questioned the proposition that Congress by Section 52 had so provided.

What does the antilynching bill propose except to punish state officers who deprive a person of his right to be tried by a court rather than by ordeal?

"It is plain," said Mr. Justice Douglas in the *Screws* case, "that basic to the concept of due process of law in a criminal case is a trial—a trial in a court of law, not a 'trial by ordeal.'"

In principle there is no difference between dereliction in the performance of official duty by active conduct or such dereliction by neglect, failure, or refusal to act. Would it have made any difference in the *Screws* case, if, after the defendants had brought Hall to the courthouse square, they had permitted third parties to murder him instead of accomplishing the result with their own hands? Would the deprivation of his life, or his right to a trial in a court of law rather than by ordeal, have been any the less state action, within the meaning of the Fourteenth Amendment?

According to Willoughby such dereliction in the performance of official duties is state action or state violation of the due process and equal protection clauses. It seems reasonably clear, he says,

that, where the officials of the states have been derelict in the performance of their official duties with regard to the protection of persons against lynching, or, it may be said, against any other form of violence, whether to persons or to their property, or have conspired with others to that end, there is ground for saying that there has been a deprivation of life, liberty or property by the state and therefore, that the prohibition of the Fourteenth Amendment has been violated, and therefore, that an act of Congress directed to the punishment of such dereliction would be constitutional. Equal protection of the laws would also be denied in cases in which it would appear that such derelictions had been motivated by animosities against persons because of their race, nationality, or because of their inclusion within a certain social or religious or other class, group or association. It is also probably correct to say that private individuals conspiring with state officials to deny to persons in the custody of state officials due process of law or the equal protection of the laws could be held responsible in the federal courts, for, in such cases, under the general law of conspiracies according to which all the parties are principals, such private persons would, as to their status, be grouped with the state officials.[5]

Congress cannot, under the Fourteenth Amendment, make lynching itself a federal crime; but it may reach lynching by reaching state officials who, acting under color of law, may be responsible for the lynching by failure to perform their duty. Since the decision in the *Screws* case clearly interprets as state action any unlawful action on the part of a state officer, the heart of the constitutional question is, then, whether *failure to act* can be considered *state action*. While, as we have noted, the opinions of Douglas and Roberts in the *Screws* case shed some light on this question, it may be said that the Supreme Court has never squarely decided this point. In at least two cases,[6] however, the notion that inaction may be state action, and may constitute a denial of due process, was present. At any rate, while the court has not yet held that inaction may constitute a denial of due process or equal protection of the laws, it has never held the contrary to be true.

There is no logical difficulty in the notion that failure to afford protection to the threatened victim constitutes a denial of due process or of equal protection.

[5] *Constitutional Law of the United States* (2d ed., 1929), III, 1934–35.
[6] Truax v. Corrigan, 257 U.S. 312 (1921); Powell v. Alabama, 287 U.S. 45 (1932). Cf. statement by William H. Hastie, in Senate committee Hearings referred to in note 4, *supra*, at p. 87, where cases are cited to show that the Supreme Court has held that failure to act may be a denial of due process of law.

An impressive array of statistics can be brought forward to show the frequent complete breakdown of state law enforcement agencies in the face of a lynching. It can be safely asserted that few lynchings occur without warning; sometimes the prospect of a lynching is known sufficiently in advance for newspapers and radio to announce the coming event long before it takes place. In this situation the failure of the proper officers to act amounts to little less than coöperation with the mob.[7]

The *Screws* decision for the first time applies the concept of due process to police matters *preceding* a trial (apart from cases in which confessions were held to have been extorted by force and violence—but in such cases it is the use of the confession at the trial, its admission as evidence, rather than the extortion itself, that constituted a denial of due process). The principle of that decision is that a right to trial by law, rather than by ordeal, is embraced by the concept of due process of law. The principle also includes the requirement that if a person is to lose his life as the consequence of a sentence of death, he is to lose it by legal execution and not by a mob lynching. A lynching is a deprivation of life without due process of law. The Fourteenth Amendment, which is the basis for the antilynching bill,

merely prohibits a denial or a deprivation, not a denial or deprivation by affirmative action. If a record of state inaction with respect to lynching, chiefly of Negroes, covering the entire period since the Civil War, does not justify corrective legislation by Congress, then the Fourteenth Amendment, intended primarily at least for the protection of Negroes, has completely missed its mark.[8]

As we have said, we see no logical basis for a constitutional difference between these two situations: (1) where Screws and the other defendants, all state officers, beat the prisoner to death in the courthouse square; and (2) where the officers stand by and permit a mob to beat the prisoner to death. In each case the officers have prevented the disposition of the accused or prisoner

[7] Note in 38 *Columbia Law Rev.* 199 (1938), at p. 204. Cf. McNabb v. U.S., 318 U.S. 332 (1943); Anderson v. U.S., 318 U.S. 350 (1943).
[8] Note, 38 *Columbia Law Rev.* 199 (1938), at p. 207.

by due process of law; they have made it impossible for the state to afford him the enjoyment of proceedings which make up the state's established course of judicial procedure; and, in the strict constitutional sense, they have prevented and destroyed the person's right, privilege and immunity to have the state afford him due process of law.[9]

The antilynching bill would have been passed years ago if Southern members of the United States Senate had not abused the democratic process by a filibuster, and if other Southern spokesmen had not carried on a campaign to misrepresent the facts concerning the proposed measure and the facts relating to lynchings in the South. Typical of the strategy used is the following statement from the publication of the University of South Carolina School of Law:

A storekeeper in New York who is brutally shot and killed by a mob for not contributing to a protection association is not protected. But the family of a Negro who has raped innocent white girls and has been lynched is allowed to recover much from the county or the officer. In the single city of Chicago during 1926 and 1927 there were 130 slayings by gangsters. There were not as many lynchings in that period in the whole United States. The title of the bill belies its substance. The bill does not guarantee equal protection under the law. We reiterate, the Anti-Lynching Bill, if enacted, is unconstitutional.[10]

The persons responsible for the above statement could not have been so ignorant of the law that they failed to distinguish between slayings by gangsters, and the mob lynchings within contemplation of the bill; for any one who has had an elementary course in constitutional law must know that the Federal government cannot make either a slaying by gangsters or a mob lynching a federal crime; all it can do is attempt to punish state officers responsible for state action (affirmative action or neglect of duty). There is no body of facts showing that the failure of officers to prevent gangster killings amounts to cooperation with the gangsters; but the facts do show that the failure of officers

[9] Cf. note in 2 *Geo. Washington Law Rev.* 498 (1934'
[10] 2 *Selden Soc. Year Book* 12 (1938'

to act to prevent lynchings (particularly where Negroes are the victims) "amounts to little less than cooperation with the mob."[11]

And the reference to the lynched Negro having raped innocent white girls is a typical attempt to appeal to race prejudice, the fiction of white superiority and the subhumanity of the Negro race. At the 1940 hearings on the antilynching bill, before a sub-committee of the Senate Committee on the Judiciary, it was shown that, in the period 1889 to 1930, 3,714 persons were lynched. Of these only 622 had been *accused* of rape, and 249 of attempted rape—a total of 871 victims who were *accused* of rape or attempted rape (about 25 per cent of the total).[12] The other victims had been accused of other "crimes," including 66 who were charged with having merely insulted white women. In the five years 1931–1935, 84 persons were lynched. Of these only nine had been *accused* of rape, and thirteen of attempted rape— a total of 22 (less than 25 percent). In this period four Negroes were lynched for "insulting" white women. Raper, in *The Tragedy of Lynching*, reporting on statistics for the years 1889–1929, says:

The accusations of rape and attempted rape combined accounted for less than one-fourth of the lynchings, and investigations after the lynchings often proved these accusations to have been unfounded. Many Negroes accused of rape or attempted rape, and saved from mobs by courageous peace officers or other means, have been acquitted by the courts. In some cases, girls and women who had posed as victims acknowledged that they made these charges to cover their own derelictions, to divert suspicion from some white man, to reconcile their parents, to attract attention, or "just to have a little excitement." Also numerous cases are on record of white criminals who have blackened their faces to disguise themselves.[13]

The Tuskegee Institute [14] reported three lynchings in 1943: (1) Robert Hall, in Georgia (the victim in the *Screws* case). (2) Cel

[11] Note in 38 *Columbia Law Rev.* 199 (1938), at p. 204.
[12] See Hearings cited in note 4, *supra*, at p. 7.   [13] P. 37.
[14] Florence Murray, ed., *The Negro Handbook* (1944), p. 169.

los Harrison, in Florida. He had been accused of murdering a
white man in a robbery attempt in 1940; he was taken from
jail by four white masked men and clubbed to death. Harrison
had been convicted of the crime in a lower court, and the conviction was affirmed by the Florida Supreme Court; but on rehearing the latter court reversed itself on the ground that the
"confession" was not properly admissible as evidence. The circuit
court later *nolle prossed* the indictment and Harrison was released (there was no evidence against him but the "confession").
But a new indictment was returned in 1943 and Harrison was
scheduled to be tried on the Monday following his death. (3)
Holley Willis, a soldier, in Illinois; accused of insulting a white
woman over the telephone.

These, and not cases of Negroes raping innocent white girls,
are typical lynching situations, as the writings of James H. Chadbourn, Arthur Raper, and Walter White, and the reports of the
Tuskegee Institute and the National Association for the Advancement of Colored People clearly show.[15]

Are the lynchers ever apprehended and punished? Professor
Chadbourn, of the University of North Carolina, has said:

Although 1,741 persons were lynched for the period 1900–1930,
there is record of only twelve instances in which convictions have been
secured in prosecutions for these lynchings . . . this means that only
about eight-tenths of one per cent of the lynchings in the United
States since 1900 have been followed by convictions of any of the
lynchers.[16]

In the light of these facts, the argument of states' rights means
the right of states to remain inactive where lynchings are concerned; it means that, from the standpoint of the law-in-action,
as distinguished from the law-on-the-law-books, mob lynchings
are not against the law of the United States. This situation is, of
course, an intolerable one; and the Department of Justice, recog-

---

[15] James H. Chadbourn, *Lynching and the Law* (1933); Arthur Raper, *The
Tragedy of Lynching* (1933); Walter White, *Rope and Faggot* (1929). See
also James E. Cutler, *Lynch Law* (1905).
[16] "Lynching and the Law," 20 *Amer. Bar Ass'n Jour.* 71 (1934).

nizing the national shame involved, especially while the nation was fighting a war for basic freedoms, sought a way of meeting it in the absence of a specific federal antilynching law.

LYNCHING AND 18 U.S.C. 51

Victor W. Rotnem, Chief of the Civil Rights Unit of the Department of Justice, and Frank Coleman, Special Assistant to the Attorney General, have related how the Department came to employ federal law for the first time in a lynching case. The story is not without tragic elements.[17]

In January of 1942 Cleo Wright, a Negro of Sikeston, Missouri, was arrested and placed in the local jail, facing charges of assault and attempted rape. On January 25, 1942, in broad daylight, a mob broke into the jail, seized and removed Wright, tied his feet to the rear of an automobile, dragged him through the Negro section of the town, poured gasoline on his body, and burned him to death.

Within forty-eight hours the German and Japanese short-wave radio broadcasters featured discussions of the Sikeston lynching. The broadcasts were relayed to the peoples of the Dutch East Indies and India.

On February 13, 1942, Wendell Berge, Assistant Attorney General, requested the F.B.I. to make a full inquiry into the lynching. In a press release, Francis Biddle, Attorney General, said:

With our country at war to defend our democratic way of life throughout the world, a lynching has significance far beyond the community, or even the state, in which it occurs. It becomes a matter of national importance and thus properly the concern of the federal government.

Biddle directed that the evidence be presented to a federal grand jury in St. Louis. The grand jury returned no indictments but made an advisory report recommending a federal statute to make lynching of a person in legal custody of the state a federal crime. The grand jury described the lynching as a "shameful outrage" and censured the police for having "failed completely

[17] V. W. Rotnem, "The Federal Civil Right 'Not to be Lynched,'" 28 *Washington Univ. Law Q.* 57 (1943).

to cope with the situation." But the facts, said the jury, did not constitute a federal crime under existing law. In this opinion the grand jury differed with the Department of Justice.

The Department has taken the position that once a person has been accused of a crime under state law, especially once he is in the legal custody of the state, he has the right, under the federal Constitution, to a fair and impartial trial; that a mob by lynching him deprives him of this right; that this deprivation is an obstruction of federal justice; that, besides Sections 231–251 of title 18 of the United States Code, which are general statutes prohibiting under penalty the obstruction of justice, Sections 51 and 52 make the lynching a federal crime.

Are the private members of a lynch mob within 18 U.S.C. 51? The Department of Justice proceeded in the Sikeston case on the theory that the mobsters were within this statute. This was the rationale:

When a prisoner in custody of the state is taken from such custody by a mob and lynched, the victim does not exercise or enjoy the right secured to him by the Constitution to have a fair trial. But does not the Fourteenth Amendment operate only against state action? How can the private members of the mob be reached? Is not the decision of the Supreme Court in the *Civil Rights Cases* in the way of federal prosecution of private persons?

But, it is argued, this decision of the court is not in point, for the following reasons: (1) the 1883 case involved a federal statute granting equal accommodations in hotels, restaurants, and similar places, and the court held that equality in such places is not a privilege or immunity of national citizenship under the Constitution, and Congress by legislation cannot make it such a privilege or immunity. What the court said beyond deciding this point was mere *obiter dicta*. (2) That decision was under the narrower privileges or immunities clause and not under the broader due process clause. (3) The act before the court in the 1883 case sought to create new social and business rights in private intercourse—an end which Congress may not seek to accomplish. In any case, the court did not need to decide the case on the broad ground asserted; namely, that legislation under the Fourteenth Amendment may not *in any case* be against individual action or conduct.

When the functioning of due process of law in a state criminal action is prevented by private persons, is there no congressional power to make such interference with due process of law a federal crime? . . . Even to ask that question should startle American ears! [18]

Yet the question, Rotnem points out, has been asked and has been answered previously with diverse results. In a case before a federal court in Alabama in 1904,[19] the indictment of mobsters under Section 51 was sustained. The *Classic* [20] case is also cited as a favorable precedent. Three Supreme Court decisions are cited as adverse.[21] But it is significant to note, says Rotnem,

that all three of these cases were decided long before the development of the idea that an appeal lies to the federal courts by virtue of the Fourteenth Amendment from a state court if it fails to provide due process of law. . . . Many of the rights we now regard as secured by the Constitution were at that time unrecognized; but, since they are now recognized, decisions denying that they are within the purview of a statute that makes prevention of their exercise a federal offense should no longer be controlling. As the concept of constitutional rights and privileges expands, so must— and should—the statute that provides a sanction against interference with them enlarge. And in this direction the court pointed in *United States v. Classic* in 1941.[22]

The grand jury in the *Sikeston* case, says Rotnem, should have returned indictments against members of the mob.

Reference at this point should be made to our previous discussion of the law on prosecution of private persons under Section 51, in so far as rights and privileges secured by the Constitution are concerned. We there pointed out that (1) decisions applying the statute are in situations involving peonage, fraud

---

[18] *Ibid.*   [19] Ex parte Riggins, 134 F. 404 (1904).   [20] 313 U.S. 299 (1941).
[21] U.S. v. Harris, 106 U.S. 629 (1882); Hodges v. U.S., 203 U.S. 1 (1906); Powell v. U.S., 212 U.S 563 (1909).
[22] 28 *Washington Univ. Law Q.* 57 (1943).

and intimidation at federal elections, and intimidation of federal informers and witnesses; (2) *dicta* point to the permissible use of the act in cases involving the right to assemble peaceably to petition the Federal government for the redress of grievances; the freedom to speak and print on subjects relating to the federal government, federal elections, laws, operations, and officers. The *dicta* point to a right implied from a consideration of what is essential to the effective functioning of the Federal government. We said that the time may come when the Supreme Court will consider all the personal rights protected against federal or state invasion as essential attributes of national citizenship and protected against invasion by private individuals conspiring together, and thus subject to protection under Section 51. Recognition of the applicability of Section 51 to private persons who are members of a lynching mob may point the way to the formulation of a general principle which may either overrule the *Civil Rights Cases* or narrowly limit its scope.

Willoughby has argued that it would be unconstitutional to provide by act of Congress for the prosecution by federal authorities of private members of a lynching mob, relying, in part, on the proposition

that the right to life, liberty and property and to equality of protection of the laws are not, in themselves, affirmatively considered, federal rights; they are, and remain, rights created or recognized by the laws of the states, though the persons enjoying them are federally guaranteed against their impairment by the states.[23]

But if Negroes cannot look to certain states for the creation or recognition of the right to life, liberty, and property, and the right to equal protection of the laws, are they then to be without these rights? Under such circumstances may not the test of the asserted right be: "Is it a fundamental principle of liberty and justice which inheres in the very idea of free government and is the inalienable right of a citizen of such a government?"[24] Is not the asserted right not to be deprived of one's

[23] *Constitutional Law of the U.S.* (2d ed., 1929), III, 1936.
[24] Twining v. New Jersey, 211 U.S. 78 (1908).

life without due process of law such a fundamental principle of liberty and justice, inherent in the very idea of free government, and the "fundamental" right of a citizen of such a government? [25] May it not be, then, a federal right, regardless of whether or not it is also a state right?

LYNCHING AND 18 U.S.C. 52

While there is still uncertainty as to the application of Section 51 to private individuals who are members of a lynching mob, there should be no uncertainty, since the decision in the *Screws* case, as to the applicability of Section 52 to state officers who willfully withhold police protection from the victims of such mobs. If one grants that, from the standpoint of the Fourteenth Amendment, willful failure to perform official duty (state inaction) may be the same as state action, then nothing should stand in the way of full use of Section 52 against guilty state officers.

Even before the decision in the *Screws* case, the Department of Justice attempted to break new ground on the basis of this theory, and succeeded. Failure in the *Sikeston* case, where Section 51 was relied on, did not end the Department's efforts in lynching cases.

On October 12, 1942, at Quitman, Mississippi, the bodies of two Negro boys, aged sixteen and fourteen, were found hanging on a bridge after a group of hooded men had taken them from an unguarded town jail, where they had been confined for molesting a young white girl. On October 18, 1942, at Laurel, in the same state, a Negro farmer, convicted by a white jury in a state court the day before for killing his white employer during an altercation, and awaiting sentence to life imprisonment, was seized from jail in full public view and lynched.[26]

---

[25] Cf. H. Lauterpacht, *An International Bill of the Rights of Man* (1945), p. 70. Cf. indictment of major war criminals before the international military tribunal, with charges of crimes against humanity, based on charter of the tribunal. *New York Times,* October 19, 1945, pp. 11 and 12; Robert H. Jackson, *Case against Nazi War Criminals* (1946); M. R. Konvitz, "Will Nuremberg Serve Justice?" 1 *Commentary* January, 1946. See note 15 in ch. 6, *post* (p. 105).
[26] Frank Coleman, "Freedom from Fear on the Home Front," 29 *Iowa Law Rev.* 415 (1944).

A federal grand jury was convened to consider these two cases. For lack of identifying evidence the first case was no-billed; but in the Laurel case the grand jury returned the first federal lynching indictment in forty years (the first since the indictment in the Alabama case in 1904, referred to above).[27] The jailer and four individual members of the Laurel mob were indicted under Sections 51 and 52 (as well as supporting Sections 88 and 550 of title 18 of the United States Code).[28]

In April, 1943, the defendants were brought to trial. After a week-long trial they were acquitted. But the judge of the federal district court sustained the several counts of the two indictments.

Another case reported by Coleman is of a lynching near Paris, Illinois, on October 12, 1942. Person, a Negro resident of Tennessee, was hunted down and shot to death by a mob of white farmers, organized under the leadership of an Indiana sheriff and his deputies. Baseless rumors had circulated about Person and had aroused the farm community.

In June, 1943, a federal grand jury in Illinois indicted the sheriff and his three deputies, and nine private individuals, alleging a conspiracy in violation of Section 52 to deprive Person of his right not to be deprived of his life or liberty without due process of law, or to be denied the equal protection of the law. Defendants demurred to the indictment; the demurrer was overruled. The case is of special interest for the reason that the court held that the indictment is not defective as to the defendants who were not state officials.

It is immaterial that they themselves may not have had the capacity to violate the statute for they became liable criminally if they conspired to violate that statute and if one or more of their fellow conspirators had the capacity to commit the substantive offense.[29]

Summarizing the circumstances under which lynchings lie within the prosecutive power of the Federal government, Coleman points out the following categories:

[27] Ex parte Riggins, 134 F. 404 (1904).
[28] Section 88 is a conspiracy statute; Section 550 defines "principals."
[29] U.S. v. Trierweiler, 52 F. Supp. 4 (1943). Cf. U.S. v. Chaplin, 54 F. Supp. 926 (1944).

(1) *A mob lynches a person not in state custody.* No basis for federal jurisdiction.

(2) *Mob seizes prisoner from state custody; state officers without fault.* Procedure under Section 51, conspiracy of private persons.

(3) *State officers conspire with mob, or actively assist mob, to lynch prisoner.* Section 52 may apply to both the officers and the private persons, as in the *Trierweiler* case,[30] discussed *supra*.

(4) *State officers willfully fail to protect prisoner.* Section 52 applies.

A survey of all the lynchings occurring since 1931 indicates that over 60% involved victims seized from the custody of the law. If federal power is ultimately established to prosecute in 60% of the lynchings, federal prosecutors and federal juries should play an important part in banishing lynchings from our land forever.[31]

This recent legal development, a product of the war, should not stand in the way of the enactment of the federal antilynching bill. If Sections 51 and 52 can act as deterrents, all the more will a specific law do so—a law providing compensation to the victims or their families, as well as criminal sanctions against the perpetrators of the most bestial of all crimes in a civilized community.

[30] Cited in note 29, *supra*.   [31] 29 *Iowa Law Rev.* 415 (1944).

CHAPTER 5

Federal Legislation against Discrimination in Employment

URING THE PAST SEVERAL YEARS a number of bills [1] have been introduced in Congress to prohibit discrimination in employment because of race, creed, color, national origin, or ancestry. The bills are substantially identical. We shall here take as the basis of our discussion H.R. 2232 (79th Cong., 1st Sess.) offered by Mrs. Norton.[2]

The bill declares that, according to the findings of the Congress, discrimination in employment because of race, creed, color, national origin, or ancestry (1) leads to interracial tension and conflict; (2) forces large segments of the population permanently into substandard conditions of living; (3) creates a drain upon the resources of the nation; (4) causes a diminution of employment and wages which disrupts the market for goods in commerce; all of which (5) burden, hinder, and obstruct commerce. The bill is directed against discrimination practiced by (1) em-

[1] At the beginning of the 1st Session of the 79th Congress thirteen bills having this purpose were introduced in the House of Representatives. The provisions of ten of these bills were identical. The best features of the bills, in the judgment of the House Committee on Labor, were directed to be embodied in a new bill, H.R. 2232, here considered. In the Senate, in the same Session, S. 101 and S. 459 were introduced. S. 101 is substantially like H.R. 2232.

S. 459, introduced by Senator Taft, has received no support. It does not mention national origin or ancestry. It provides for the appointment of a commission, but fails to provide for the prohibition of unfair employment practices. The commission is charged with the duty to bring about unfair practices by making comprehensive studies of discrimination, formulating plans for the elimination of such discrimination, by publishing reports, by making investigations when complaints have been filed and making recommendations to the parties as to ways and means of elimination of discriminatory practices. In short, the Taft bill provides no criminal sanctions.

In February, 1946, the bill was killed in the Senate by a filibuster; an attempt to impose closure failed.

[2] The bill appears in the Appendix.

ployers who have in their employ six or more workers and are engaged in interstate commerce; (2) labor unions having six or more members; (3) agencies of the Federal government. The right to work without discrimination is declared to be an immunity of all citizens of the United States.

The bill calls for the creation of a Fair Employment Practice Commission, composed of five members appointed by the President, by and with the consent of the Senate. The members of the Commission are to serve full time and receive an annual salary of $10,000. Whenever it is alleged that any person has engaged in an unfair employment practice, the Commission shall serve on him a complaint. If the case is decided against the person, the Commission is to issue a cease and desist order. The order may include a direction to hire or rehire. The orders of the Commission are to be subject to judicial review. The Commission is to have authority to issue regulations.

Every contract to which the Federal government is a party is to contain a provision that the contractor will not engage in any unfair employment practice; and no contract shall be made by the government with any person found to have engaged in any unfair employment practice.

The orders of the Commission are to be subject to judicial enforcement in the same manner as in the case of orders of the National Labor Relations Board.

The House Committee on Labor, to whom the bill was referred, reported favorably without amendment and recommended that the bill be passed.[3] Only two members of the committee dissented: Clark Fisher of Texas, and Clare E. Hoffman of Michigan. Among the reasons offered by Mr. Fisher is that the bill "is manifestly unfair to the American Negro because it would retard his progress and would be calculated to foment racial feeling and bitterness against him."[4] Representative Hoffman said that

---

[3] "The Fair Employment Practice Act," 79th Cong., 1st Sess., Report 187 (1945). See Hearings before House Committee on Labor, H.R. 3986, H.R. 4004, and H.R. 4005 (2 vols., 1944). See Hearings on S. 101 and S. 459, before Senate Subcommittee of the Committee on Education and Labor (1945).

[4] 79th Cong., 1st Sess., Report 187 (1945), p. 9

the fate of the bill should be decided "upon a consideration of how the Negro can best be given equality of opportunity, not only for employment but for education and the exercise of his religious freedom." [5] There was no objection on constitutional grounds.

THE CONSTITUTIONAL QUESTION

The right to work free from discrimination is declared by the bill to be an immunity of the citizens of the United States, which shall not be abridged by any federal or state agency.

We have seen how narrow is the scope of the privileges and immunities clause of the Fourteenth Amendment. It is doubtful if this clause in the bill will be given great weight by the Supreme Court; for, apart from this declaration that the right to work free from discrimination is an immunity of citizens, the bill is founded on the theory that the law is within the power of Congress under the commerce clause of the Constitution. The bill, in so far as it affects private employment, apart from any contractual relation with the Federal government, is limited to employment involved in interstate commerce. It is under the guise, then, of regulating interstate commerce that Congress proposes to outlaw discrimination in employment.

The bill is founded on the same constitutional base as are the National Labor Relations Act,[6] the Fair Labor Standards Act,[7] and similar legislation upheld by the Supreme Court. The theory of the National Labor Relations Act is that Congress is entitled to provide reasonable measures to prevent disruption of interstate commerce by enacting the law. The act declares that it shall be an unfair labor practice for employers to interfere with, restrain, or coerce employees in the exercise of rights of self-organization and to bargain collectively. The employer is forbidden to discriminate in regard to the hiring or tenure of employees or in regard to any term or condition of employment by encouraging or discouraging membership in any labor organization. The employer may not discharge or otherwise discriminate

[5] *Ibid.*, p. 11.   [6] 29 U.S.C. 151 (1935).   [7] 29 U.S.C. 201 (1938).

against an employee because he has filed charges or given testimony against the employer. This act has been held by the Supreme Court as not an arbitrary or capricious restraint on the employer's right to conduct his business in his own way.[8]

It was argued before the court that the National Labor Relations statute supervises and restrains employers only, and so is one-sided; but the court held that this was not a constitutional objection.[9] The Fair Employment Practice Act does not suggest this objection, because it is directed against both employers and unions.

So, too, the court has upheld the wage and hour provisions of the Fair Labor Standards Act, saying that Congress has the constitutional power to legislate against labor conditions detrimental to the minimum standard of living required for the general well-being of workers engaged in interstate commerce or the production of goods for such commerce.[10]

Similarly, the court has upheld the labor provisions of the Bituminous Coal Act of 1937,[11] the Motor Carriers Act,[12] the Walsh-Healy Public Contracts Act,[13] and analogous legislation.[14] It is doubtful if the court will be able to distinguish successfully, on constitutional grounds, between those acts and the Fair Employment Practice Act.[15]

[8] Consolidated Edison Co. v. N.L.R.B., 305 U.S. 197 (1938); Associated Press v. N.L.R.B., 301 U.S. 103 (1936); N.L.R.B. v. Jones & Laughlin Steel Corp., 301 U.S. 1 (1936).
[9] N.L.R.B. v. Jones & Laughlin Steel Corp., 301 U.S. 1 (1936).
[10] U.S. v. Darby Lumber Co., 312 U.S. 100 (1940); Opp Cotton Mills v. Dept. of Labor, 312 U.S. 126 (1940); Overnight Motor Transportation Co. v. Missel, 316 U.S. 572 (1941), rehearing denied, 317 U.S. 706 (1942); Kirschbaum v. Walling, 316 U.S. 517 (1942).
[11] 15 U.S.C. 828 (1937). Gray v. Powell, 314 U.S. 402 (1941); Sunshine Anthracite Coal Co. v. Adkins, 310 U.S. 381 (1940).
[12] 49 U.S.C. 301 (1935). U.S. v. Carolina Freight Carriers Corp., 315 U.S. 475 (1942).
[13] 41 U.S.C. 35 (1936). The minimum wage provision does not represent exercise by Congress of regulatory power over private business. Perkins v. Lukens Steel Co., 310 U.S. 113 (1940).
[14] Cf. Steward Machinery Co. v. Davis, 301 U.S. 548 (1937).
[15] Cf. statement by Mr. Justice Roberts in New Negro Alliance v. Sanitary Grocery Co., 303 U.S. 552 (1938): "The desire for fair and equitable conditions on the part of persons of any race, color, or persuasion, and the removal of discrimination against them by reason of their race or religious beliefs is quite

As to the provisions in the bill directed against discrimination by labor unions, two recent decisions of the court indicate that these provisions will in all probability successfully withstand a constitutional attack. In the *Steele* [16] and *Tunstall* [17] cases the court upheld the claims of Negro workers who charged the Brotherhood of Locomotive Firemen and Enginemen with the policy to exclude Negro firemen from jobs within the union's jurisdiction. The court held that the union could not claim to be the exclusive bargaining representative of the craft unless it assumed the duty to represent all persons in the craft without discrimination because of race.[18]

Although the Railway Labor Act, under which the union claimed the rights of representation, contains no specific provision against race discrimination by unions, the court decided the case on the basis of an interpretation of the act. But Mr. Justice Murphy, in a concurring opinion, said that he would put the decision against the union on constitutional grounds. The Constitution, he said,

voices its disapproval whenever economic discrimination is applied under authority of law against any race, creed or color. A sound democracy cannot allow such discrimination to go unchallenged. Racism is far too virulent today to permit the slightest refusal, in the light of a Constitution that abhors it, to expose and condemn it wherever it appears in the course of a statutory interpretation.[19]

---

as important to those concerned as fairness and equity in terms and conditions of employment can be to trade or craft unions or any form of labor organization or association. Race discrimination by an employer may reasonably be deemed more unfair and less excusable than discrimination against workers on the ground of union affiliation."

[16] Steele v. Louisville & Nashville Railroad Co., 323 U.S. 192 (1944). Unanimous decision.

[17] Tunstall v. Brotherhood of Locomotive Firemen and Enginemen, 323 U.S. 210 (1944). Unanimous decision. This is a companion case to the Steele case.

[18] As to racial discrimination by labor organizations, see Senate Hearings on S. 101 and S. 459 (1945), pp. 126, 127, and House Hearings, on H.R. 3986, H.R. 4004, and H.R. 4005 (2 vols., 1944), I, 221. See Herbert R. Northrup, *Organized Labor and the Negro* (1944); Sterling Spero and A. L. Harris, *The Black Worker* (1931); Robt. C. Weaver, *Negro Labor: a National Problem* (1946).

[19] Cf. Milton R. Konvitz, *The Alien and the Asiatic in American Law* (Cornell University Press, 1946), ch. VI, "The Right of Aliens to Work," a discussion of

As to outlawing discrimination by federal agencies, it has been pointed out [20] that Congress on at least twenty-three different occasions in the years 1933–1944 has outlawed racial and religious discrimination in legislation for public works projects, the Civilian Conservation Corps, unemployment relief, civil service classification, National Youth Administration, and other acts. No serious question as to the constitutionality of such provisions can be raised.[21]

It seems ironical that under our Constitution, as construed by the Supreme Court, the evil of discrimination in employment can be reached only under the guise of regulation of interstate commerce. It is through a back door that the new concept, the new "immunity" of the right to work at gainful employment, will be received into the Constitution.[22]

---

constitutional bases of a number of Supreme Court decisions: Truax v. Raich, 239 U.S. 33 (1915); Clarke v. Deckebach, 274 U.S. 392 (1927); Heim v. McCall, 239 U.S. 175 (1915).

It might be noted in passing that while the bill speaks of the immunity of *citizens* to be free from discrimination in employment, the rest of the bill speaks of *individuals*. The bill would seem to protect aliens as well as citizens, though it does not expressly so provide. The phrase "national origin, or ancestry" might apply to citizens alone, but when taken together with the term "individuals" a more proper interpretation, it would seem, especially in the light of the liberal and broad purposes of the measure, is that it should be construed as applying to aliens as well as citizens.

[20] 90 Cong. Rec., Part 10, p. A3325 (1944).

[21] Perkins v. Lukens Steel Co., 310 U.S. 113 (1940); Heims v. McCall, 239 U.S. 175 (1915).

[22] For this type of legislation generally see Harold Dublirer, "Legislation Outlawing Racial Discrimination in Employment," 5 *Lawyers Guild Rev.* 101 (1945); Report of Fair Employment Practice Committee (1945). See also *Jobs without Creed or Color,* pamphlet by the Workers Defense League and Winifred Raushenbush (1945); A. Wilson, "The Proposed Legislative Death Knell of Private Discriminatory Employment Practices," 31 *Va. L. Rev.* 798 (1945); Felix S. Cohen, "The People vs. Discrimination," *Commentary,* March, 1946.

CHAPTER 6

General Federal Civil Rights
Statutes: Civil

THE IMPORTANT general federal civil rights acts, giving the right to bring a civil suit for damages when civil rights are violated, are 8 U.S.C. 41, 43, and 47(3).[1] In a general sense they might be said to be correlative with the criminal civil rights acts already considered.

Section 41 is derived from the civil rights statutes of 1866 and 1870; Section 43 is derived from an act of 1871, while Section 47 is derived from 1861 and 1871 acts. All the provisions, therefore, stem from the Reconstruction program.[2]

8 U.S.C. 41

All persons within the jurisdiction of the United States shall have the same right in every state and territory to make and enforce contracts, to sue, be parties, give evidence, and to the full and equal benefit of all laws and proceedings for the security of persons and property as is enjoyed by white citizens, and shall be subject to like punishment, pains, penalties, taxes, licenses, and exactions of every kind, and to no other.

The substance of Section 41 was adopted in 1866, under the Thirteenth Amendment (which was adopted in 1865). In 1868 the Fourteenth Amendment was adopted, and two years later the statute was reenacted. The question at once suggests itself, Is Section 41 to be read in the light of the Thirteenth or the Fourteenth Amendment? The answer may be important. For, as we have said, the Thirteenth Amendment is directed against individual as well as against official action; while the Fourteenth Amendment is directed against only official action. Are the rights

[1] Cf. 8 U.S.C. 48. [2] Cf. 28 U.S.C. 13, 14, 41.

mentioned in Section 41 to be asserted against private individuals as well as against officers?

In the *Civil Rights Cases,* Mr. Justice Bradley said that the 1866 and 1870 acts were to be distinguished from the 1875 act, which alone was before the court for consideration. The former acts, he said, were limitations on the states only; they were corrective in their character, intended to counteract and furnish redress against state laws and proceedings, and against customs having the force of law. At a later point in his opinion Bradley said that the 1866 act was passed under the Thirteenth Amendment and before the adoption of the Fourteenth, and that it undertook to wipe out the incidents of slavery which constituted "its substance and visible form." This act, he said, certainly since its reenactment under the Fourteenth Amendment, is constitutional, for it enumerates the fundamental rights which are the essence of civil freedom, rights which constitute the essential distinction between freedom and slavery. Among the rights named by Bradley in this connection were the following which are enumerated in the section under consideration: the right to make and enforce contracts, to sue, be parties, and give evidence. Since the court in the *Civil Rights Cases* said that the statute is constitutional, especially since its reenactment under the Fourteenth Amendment, and since the court held that the amendment is a limitation only on state, but not on private, action, it would follow that the view of the court was that Section 41 asserts rights against states only. It is to be noted, however, that the court's statements concerning this statute were only *obiter dicta.*

Our conclusion that the court in the *Civil Rights Cases* meant that Section 41 asserts rights against state action only is strengthened by a consideration of the *Harris* case,[3] decided the year before. In that case the constitutionality of another civil rights statute was before the court, but Mr. Justice Woods, in his opinion for the court, discussed the substance of Section 41 (referring to it as the 1866 civil rights act). This act, he said, was adopted under the Thirteenth Amendment. "Even if the amendment is held to be directed against the action of private individ-

[3] 106 U.S. 629 (1882).

uals, as well as against the action of the states and United States," it cannot be said that Congress has the power to punish every crime by which the right of any person to life, property, or reputation is involved; it cannot declare criminal the deprivation by a private person of the right to make a contract, bring suit, or give evidence, nor a conspiracy to bring about deprivation of such rights. Such provisions "clearly cannot be authorized by the amendment which simply prohibits slavery and involuntary servitude."

In the following year, in the *Civil Rights Cases*, the court, probably wishing to mitigate the sharpness of these strictures on the 1866 act, asserted the constitutionality of the act, under the Fourteenth Amendment, thereby clearly implying that its provisions are aimed only at state action.

In a recent case decided by the circuit court of appeals [4] it was said generally of the civil rights act considered in this section that "they did not have the effect of taking into federal control the protection of private rights against invasion by individuals." The protection of such rights and the redress for such wrongs "was left with the states." It might, however, be argued, that the rights enumerated in Section 41, since they are of the essence of freedom and constitute the essential distinction between freedom and slavery, are subject to protection by the Federal government against invasion by private persons.

The section carries with it no civil or criminal sanctions: it is a general statement of constitutional policy. As was said by Mr. Justice Strong in *Strauder v. Virginia*,[5] it merely puts in the form of statute what had been substantially ordained by the Fourteenth Amendment; it merely provides a partial enumeration of rights and immunities intended to be guaranteed by the Constitution.

8 U.S.C. 43

Every person who, under color of any statute, ordinance, regulation, custom, or usage, of any state or territory, subjects, or causes to be subjected, any citizen of the United States or other person within the

[4] Love v. Chandler, 124 F. (2d) 785 (1942).   [5] 100 U.S. 303 (1879).

jurisdiction to the deprivation of any rights, privileges, or immunities secured by the Constitution and laws, shall be liable to the party injured in an action at law, suit in equity, or other proper proceeding for redress.

By its own terms, Section 43 is directed only against state action. The only question raised is as to the rights, privileges, and immunities secured by the United States Constitution and laws embraced by its terms. This takes us back to the question of rights inherent in national citizenship, which we discussed in connection with the criminal statutes (18 U.S.C. 51 and 52). There we pointed out that the *Cruikshank* and *Slaughterhouse* decisions extremely limited the number of rights inherent in *national citizenship, as such,* under the Constitution. Here we would only add that the decisions have rendered the privileges and immunities clause of the Fourteenth Amendment practically a dead letter. The Civil War Amendments have not nationalized civil rights. The *Slaughterhouse Cases* stand in importance with the *Dred Scott* case and the *Civil Rights Cases* in the social history of the people of the United States.

Summarizing the situation as to 8 U.S.C. 43, we would say: the rights, privileges, and immunities protected by it and by the Fourteenth Amendment, under which it was adopted, are those arising under the Constitution and laws of the United States, which accrue from *national* citizenship only, and not those which accrue from state citizenship. The section offers protection against state action only. Neither the amendment nor the act created new rights or privileges. The number of rights inherent in national citizenship are extremely limited. Later decisions of the court have not broadened the class of federal privileges and immunities. As recently as 1944, Chief Justice Stone, in an opinion for the court, in a case in which Sections 41 and 43 were relied on, said that

The protection extended to citizens of the United States by the privileges and immunities clause includes those rights and privileges which, under the laws and Constitution of the United States, are incident to citizenship of the United States, but does not include rights pertaining to state citizenship and derived solely from the relationship of the citizen and his state established by state law. . . . It was not intended by the Fourteenth Amendment and the Civil Rights Acts that all matters formerly within the exclusive cognizance of the states should become matters of national concern.[6]

The court cited with approval the *Slaughterhouse Cases* and held that the right to become a candidate for state office, like the right to vote for the election of state officers, is a right or privilege of state citizenship and not one of national citizenship, "which alone is protected by the privileges and immunities clause."

8 U.S.C. 47(3)

If two or more persons in any state or territory conspire or go in disguise on the highway or on the premises of another, for the purpose of depriving directly or indirectly, any person or class of persons of the equal protection of the laws, or of equal privileges and immunities under the laws; or for the purpose of preventing or hindering the constituted authorities of any state or territory from giving or securing to all persons within such state or territory the equal protection of the laws; . . . in any case of conspiracy set forth in this section, if one or more persons engaged therein do, or cause to be done, any act in furtherance of the object of such conspiracy, whereby another is injured in his person or property, or deprived of having and exercising any right or privilege of a citizen of the United States, the party so injured or deprived may have an action for the recovery of damages, occasioned by such injury or deprivation, against any one or more of the conspirators.[7]

The constitutionality or usefulness of this section is in great doubt. In 1882, in *United States v. Harris*,[8] the court considered an indictment under a statute which was substantially identical with the statute set forth above, except that it provided a criminal, instead of a civil, sanction. The indictment in substance charged that some twenty defendants conspired with other per-

---

[6] Snowden v. Hughes, 321 U.S. 1 (1944).
[7] We have omitted from the statute a provision relating to interference with the suffrage, which falls outside the scope of this book.
[8] 106 U.S. 629 (1882).

sons to deprive four citizens of the United States of the equal protection of the laws; that when the four citizens were under arrest and in the custody of the deputy sheriff, the conspirators beat, bruised, and wounded the arrested persons, and prevented the deputy sheriff from giving them due and equal protection of the laws of the state of Tennessee.

In his opinion for the court, Mr. Justice Woods declared the statute unconstitutional. It appears from the terms of the statute that it was framed "to protect from invasion by private persons, the equal privileges and immunities under the laws, of all persons and classes of persons." There is no warrant for the act in the Fourteenth Amendment, for the amendment is "not a guaranty against the commission of individual offenses"; the amendment adds nothing to the rights of one citizen against another. Said the court: "the legislation under consideration finds no warrant for its enactment in the Fourteenth Amendment."

The statute, said the court, was not framed to be limited to state abridgment of the privileges or immunities, or state deprivation of life, liberty, or property without due process of law, or state denial of equal protection of the laws; under its terms private persons are liable to punishment; it is, therefore, not warranted by the Fourteenth Amendment.

Nor is the act warranted by the Thirteenth Amendment, for its terms are broader than those of the amendment. It

covers any conspiracy between two free white men against another free white man to deprive him of any right accorded him by the laws of the state or of the United States. A law under which two or more free white persons could be punished for conspiring or going in disguise for the purpose of depriving another free white citizen of a right accorded by the law of the state to all classes of persons—as, for instance, the right to make a contract, bring a suit, or give evidence—clearly cannot be authorized by the amendment which simply prohibits slavery and involuntary servitude. Those provisions of the law, which are broader than is warranted by the article of the Constitution by which they are supposed to be authorized, cannot be sustained . . . it is clear that the legislation now under consideration cannot be sustained by reference to the Thirteenth Amendment to the Constitution.[9]

If Congress can punish under the amendment a conspiracy to do an unlawful act, argued the court, it can punish the act itself, whether done by one or more persons. If this act were constitutional, it would follow that Congress has the power to punish every crime by which the right of any person to life, property, or reputation is invaded. Such a construction would invest Congress with power over the whole domain of crimes. "A construction of the amendment which leads to such a result is clearly unsound."

The section, including the provision relating to suffrage, has been relied on in recent cases involving the right to vote.[10] Apart from them, in the light of the decision in the *Harris* case, it is difficult to see how the section can be useful; yet it has been mentioned in a recent case in the circuit court of appeals, in a case which did not involve the right to vote, and the constitutionality of the section was not questioned in the opinion, though the suit under the section was not sustained.[11]

CONCLUDING STATEMENT

The people of the United States adopted the Thirteenth, Fourteenth, and Fifteenth Amendments, in the years 1865–1870. Congress adopted the Civil Rights Act of 1866, the Civil Rights Enforcement Act of 1870 and 1871, the Ku Klux Klan Act of 1871, and the Civil Rights Act of 1875. All this constitutional and statutory legislation was adopted chiefly to help the freed Negro. The Negro, however, has profited very little from their provisions. Only a small part of the statutes remain in force, and their force is largely nominal. The Civil Rights Act of 1875 was declared unconstitutional; of the many sections of the other acts, only a few remain on the books—the rest have been repealed or declared unconstitutional; and those that remain are a slender reed for the proclamation of liberty. Filibustering Southern Sena-

[9] *Ibid.*   [10] E.g., O'Sullivan v. Felix, 233 U.S. 318 (1914).
[11] Viles v. Symes, 129 F (2d) 828; cert. den. 317 U.S. 633 (1943).

tors will stand, as they have stood, in the way of more and better legislation. Liberal courts must make the best use of what is available: the laws are few and the adverse precedents are many. As far as the Negro is concerned, the Civil War amendments still lack, after nearly three generations, sufficient teeth with which to free him from the incidents and badges of servitude.

Students of the record may, however, take another view of the matter; they may approve all that has taken place. Charles Warren, in *The Supreme Court in United States History,* reflecting on the decisions in the *Civil Rights Cases,* the *Harris* case, and others of a similar character, says:

Viewed in historical perspective now, however, there can be no question that the decisions in these cases were most fortunate. They largely eliminated from national politics the Negro question which had so long embittered Congressional debates; they relegated the burden and the duty of protecting the Negro to the states, to whom they properly belonged; and they served to restore confidence in the national court in the Southern states.[12]

Warren quotes (with approval) the following statement by a Southern lawyer with respect to the decision in the *Cruikshank* case:[13]

When the decision was reached and the prisoners were released, the utmost joy succeeded in Louisiana, and with it a return of confidence which gave best hopes for the future. . . . What gave satisfaction to the South and strength to bear the affliction in which they found themselves was the determination of the court to maintain the true character of the government, and to hold, notwithstanding the excited feeling growing out of the war, that the existence of the states, with powers for domestic and local government including regulation of civil rights, the rights of persons and property, was essential to the perfect working of our complex form of government.[14]

One would agree, on a basis of policy, that where states respect and enforce civil rights, without distinction as to race, it is better that states retain control over this aspect of public affairs;

---

[12] *The Supreme Court in U.S. History,* III, 330 (1922); rev. ed. (1926).
[13] 92 U.S. 542 (1876).   [14] *The Supreme Court in History,* III, 330.

there is no problem when there is such respect and enforcement. The problem arises when states distinguish in the matter of civil rights between classes of citizens, making one group first-class citizens and the others second-class citizens. When that happens the issue of states' rights is used only as a screen, as a basis for the perpetuation of the discriminations; and, in that event, persons outside of the discriminating states have a valid interest to attempt to change conditions. What other explanation is there for the widespread interest in an international Bill of Rights? [15]

When Poland or Germany or Spain denies basic freedoms to a group of its own citizens, the citizens of other nations cannot stand by, out of respect for the principle of national self-determination; for a man is a citizen of the world as well as of the nation or state. If the San Francisco Conference in 1945 assumed that all the nations of the world are interested in the status of civil rights within any one nation, all the more have the people of the United States an interest in the status of civil rights within any one state in the union. Some of the cases considered in this chapter "have relegated the burden and duty of protecting the Negro to the states, to whom they properly belonged," said Mr. Warren. But the word "properly" expresses only his opinion, and the opinion of the majority of the Justices of the Supreme Court who decided those cases. But the *Dred Scott* case was also decided by a majority of Justices. On the other hand, a representative minority of Justices in the *Slaughterhouse Cases* and the *Civil Rights Cases* vigorously dissented, because some of them anticipated the further degradation of the

[15] Cf. H. Lauterpacht, *An International Bill of the Rights of Man* (1944); *Statement of Essential Human Rights,* drafted under auspices of American Law Institute and sponsored by Americans United for World Organization, reprinted in *Twice-a-Year,* XII–XIII (1945), 138–153; G. Gurvitch, *A Bill of Social Rights* (1946). But on August 2, 1946, the Senate accepted compulsory jurisdiction by the World Court, insisting, however, on the veto to protect United States sovereignty. Questions relating to this country's treatment of a minority group will rest solely within the domestic jurisdiction. Despite the claim that the Nuremberg trial of Nazi war criminals sets a precedent for international intervention when a country denies civil rights to a minority, the United States successfully opposed sanctions against Franco Spain; and no sanctions have been imposed against the Peron government of Argentina.

position of the Negro in the South, in the absence of national policy implemented by legislation and executive protection. Nor have the cases eliminated from national politics "the Negro question which had so long embittered Congressional debates." Senators and Representatives from Southern states can hardly be said *not* to embitter Congressional debates. The point is that the decisions of the court have left the question of the Negro almost precisely where it was in 1883. A solution within "the perfect working of our complex form of government" is still to be found.

PART TWO

State Civil Rights

CHAPTER 7

Statutes Prohibiting Discrimination

A FTER THE SUPREME COURT declared the 1875 federal civil rights act unconstitutional in the *Civil Rights Cases,* Northern states began to enact state civil rights acts to outlaw discrimination in places of public accommodation. The Supreme Court held that the matter of civil rights is one for the states exclusively, so the states north of the Mason and Dixon line undertook to define such rights and to prohibit violation of them on account of race or color. In time the concept of civil rights was extended to cover places and activities not originally contemplated, and the prohibition was extended to protect persons on account of religious differences as well as racial differences. In some instances the statutes protect aliens as well as citizens. We shall not here consider elaborately all the statutes directed against discrimination; our discussion at this point will be of a general, introductory character, summarizing state legislation and providing a general commentary on the statutes.

CONSTITUTIONALITY

Are state statutes which prohibit discrimination between persons on account of race or color in the enjoyment of civil rights constitutional? By indirection the court in the *Civil Rights Cases* answered the question in the affirmative; but strictly the Supreme Court in that case held only that federal legislation on the subject, when directed against individual conduct as distinguished from state action, is unconstitutional. It was not until June 18, 1945, when the court decided the *Railway Mail Association* case,[1] that one could point to a closer Supreme Court precedent on this point.

[1] Railway Mail Association v. Corsi, 326 U.S. 88 (1945).

One of the civil rights acts [2] adopted by the New York legislature provided that no labor organization shall deny a person membership by reason of race, color, or creed, or deny to any of its members, by reason of race, color, or creed, equal treatment in the designation of its members for employment, promotion, or dismissal by an employer. The New York Court of Appeals [3] unanimously sustained the constitutionality of the act, as did the Supreme Court, on appeal.

It was argued by the Association that the act offended the due process clause of the Fourteenth Amendment as an interference with its right of selection to membership, and that it was an abridgment of its property rights and liberty of contract. In his opinion for the court, Mr. Justice Reed said:

A judicial determination that such legislation violated the Fourteenth Amendment would be a distortion of the policy manifested in that amendment which was adopted to prevent state legislation designed to perpetuate discrimination on the basis of race or color. We see no constitutional basis for the contention that a state cannot protect workers from exclusion solely on the basis of race, color or creed by an organization, functioning under the protection of the state, which holds itself out to represent the general business needs of employees.

Mr. Justice Frankfurter, in a concurring opinion, said:

Of course a state may leave abstention from such discriminations to the conscience of individuals. On the other hand, a state may choose to put its authority behind one of the cherished aims of American feeling by forbidding indulgence in racial or religious prejudice to another's hurt. To use the Fourteenth Amendment as a sword against such state power would stultify that amendment. Certainly the insistance by individuals on their private prejudices as to race, color or creed, in relations like those now before us, ought not to have a higher constitutional sanction than the determination of a state to extend the area of non-discrimination beyond that which the Constitution itself exacts.

Reed spoke of an organization "functioning under the protection of the state," and Frankfurter spoke of private prejudices "in relations like those now before us"; but one need not con-

[2] New York Civil Rights Law, sec. 43   [3] 293 N.Y. 315 (1944).

sider these statements as words of limitation; for in the Supreme Court cases which passed on the constitutionality of the federal civil rights acts it was said time and again that the matter of the protection of civil rights pertains entirely to the states. If the matter belongs to the states, what constitutional limitation is there on the states defining for themselves the concept and scope of civil rights? The characterization of the Association as an organization "functioning under the protection of the state" was not relevant to the decision. It might have been relevant if the question before the court was one relating to the power of the Federal government to pass an act similar to the one enacted in New York; for then it might be a question of state action in violation of a federal act, and the action of an organization functioning under state protection might be said (as was said by Mr. Justice Harlan in his dissenting opinion in the *Civil Rights Cases*) to be state action. But here the statute was state legislation; it was directed against individual action; whether or not the Association functioned under state protection was, therefore, totally irrelevant.

If, however, the characterization of the Association was strictly relevant, then the question may arise (as it has arisen in state courts) whether or not state civil rights acts may be directed only against persons and corporations performing quasi-public functions (like carriers, innkeepers and theaters—only those mentioned in the 1875 federal act, which the court said would be constitutional if enacted by a state legislature), or whether such acts may be directed also against others—clothing merchants, department stores, golf courses. We submit, however, that it would be no proper function for the Supreme Court to review and invalidate a state's definition cf civil rights. Since the Federal government may not define and protect a state citizen's civil rights, certainly the definition and protection must rest with the state.

In 1907 the Supreme Court had an opportunity to pass upon this question but failed to do so. In that case [4] the defendant conducted a race course, for which tickets of admission were issued.

[4] Western Turf Association v. Greenberg, 204 U.S. 359 (1907).

After the plaintiff had been admitted, he was ejected by the defendant. The plaintiff then sued the defendant under a California act and recovered $1,000. The state court held the act constitutional as a valid exercise of the state's police power.

In the Supreme Court it was argued that the act deprived the defendant of liberty without due process of law; but the court said that, the defendant being a corporation, it had no liberty at all; for the constitutional prohibition against deprivation of liberty without due process applied only to natural, not artificial, persons. Nor did the statute deprive defendant of property with-. out due process. Said Mr. Justice Harlan for a unanimous court:

Decisions of this court . . . recognize the possession, by each state, of powers never surrendered to the General Government; which powers the state, except as restrained by its own constitution or the Constitution of the United States, may exert not only for the public health, the public morals and the public safety, but for the general or common good, for the well-being, comfort and good order of the people. . . . The statute is only a regulation of places of public entertainment and amusement upon terms of equal and exact justice to every one holding a ticket of admission . . . it is only a regulation compelling it to perform its own contract as evidenced by tickets of admission issued and sold to parties wishing to attend its race course. . . . The race-course in question being held out as a place of public entertainment and amusement is, by the act of the defendant, so far affected with a public interest that the state may, in the interest of good order and fair dealing, require defendant to perform its engagement to the public, and recognize its own tickets of admission in the hands of persons entitled to claim the benefits of the statute.

The opinion of the court limits the scope of the decision in two respects: (1) the case involved admission to a place of public entertainment and amusement, which the court considered an undertaking "affected with a public interest"—the quasi-public callings enumerated in the 1875 federal act, the regulation of which are clearly beyond question; (2) the California statute before the court called for admission to places of public amusement of persons who presented tickets of admission; the act did not require proprietors of such places to sell tickets of admission to all persons without discrimination; it only provided that if a ticket were bought, the holder had an irrevocable right of admission. As construed, this could hardly be called a civil rights act.

The question of the constitutionality of civil rights acts has been passed on by a number of state courts; in all cases general civil rights acts have been sustained as constitutional; but the scope of the decisions has frequently been rather narrow. Thus, in a Minnesota case,[5] the court spoke of a civil rights act "as to all kinds of business, of a public or quasi-public character."

In the same way, in an Illinois case,[6] the court, in upholding the civil rights act of that state, spoke of the regulation of certain businesses "in which the public have an interest." So, too, in an Iowa case [7] the court upheld the state act as constitutional as applicable to institutions "either public or quasi-public in character."

The courts placed the decisions on the ground that the state has the right to regulate places of public entertainment or amusement, or places of public resort, and not at all on the ground that the state has the right to define and protect civil rights. On the ground that a barber shop is a place of public resort, a civil rights act which applied to such shops has been sustained; [8] on the ground that the operation of a bootblack stand is a place of public accommodation, a civil rights act which applies to such an activity has been sustained.[9] While legislatures have recognized the existence of civil rights, as such, and have undertaken the regulation of businesses in the interests of such rights, courts have not, apparently, been eager to give clear and definite recognition of the right of a state to define and protect such rights. They have shown greater concern for the types of businesses affected than for the needs of citizens.

[5] Rhone v. Loomis, 77 N.W. 31 (1898).
[6] Picket v. Kuchan, 153 N.E. 667 (1926).
[7] Brown v. Bell, 123 N.W. 231 (1909).
[8] Messenger v. State, 41 N.W. 638 (Neb. 1889).
[9] Darius v. Apostolos, 190 P. 510; 10 A.L.R. 986 (1919).

An interesting case in this connection is *Harvey v. Sissle*,[10] decided by the Ohio Court of Appeals in 1936. The defendant, the proprietor of a retail shop, was sued under the civil rights act of Ohio for refusing to sell apparel to the plaintiff. The act did not specifically mention stores; but the plaintiff argued that the defendant's business came within the catch-all phrase in the statute, "or other place of public accommodation." The court reversed the judgment for the plaintiff given by the lower court, and said:

In olden times we were taught that the right of private contract was a constitutional guaranty. If a farmer had grain or cattle to sell or a manufacturer had machinery to sell or a merchant had merchandise to sell, we were told that he could sell it whenever, to whomsoever, and upon whatever terms he chose. He could refuse to sell to a German, Irishman, Negro, Jew, or any other person for any or no reason. It is now said that this former concept must be modified to the extent that any one who offers the market price for his wares may enforce the sale. Before this modification of the right of private contract becomes . . . law, it should at least receive express legislative declaration. . . . Retail stores are private businesses. . . .

The next year, 1937, the Ohio legislature amended the act to include stores or other places for the sale of merchandise. New York and Michigan have a similar provision, and Illinois has one directed against department stores. A court faced with such a provision needs to consider directly and squarely the question of the scope of the state's power to define and protect civil rights. It will not then be able to avoid the question by references to the power of the state to regulate public or quasi-public businesses. For the purpose of the state civil rights acts, like that of the 1875 federal act, is not to regulate public and quasi-public businesses: it is to protect persons in their civil rights, to entitle all persons, regardless of race or color, to the full and equal enjoyment of all accommodations, advantages, facilities, and privileges of the various places, institutions, or agencies enumerated in the acts, which invite the patronage of the public more or less

[10] 5 N.E. (2d) 410 (1936); one judge dissented.

generally. The purpose of such legislation is to compel recognition of the equality of persons in the right to the services offered by the agencies for the accommodation of the public.

In the absence of such legislation in a state, places of public accommodation have the right to select their patrons and customers; they may exclude whomsoever they please, for any reason whatsoever. In the absence of such legislation, the Negro has no civil rights, in the sense of a legal claim to the full and equal enjoyment of all accommodations, facilities, and advantages offered to white persons. For instance, in Baltimore, where the Negroes constitute 18 percent of the population, only one large department store accepts Negro trade and allows Negro customers to try on apparel. In the other stores two patterns are found: (1) as soon as a Negro enters the store, a floorwalker approaches and says that the store does not cater to Negro trade; and (2) Negroes are permitted to enter and buy articles across the counter, but are not allowed to try on hats, dresses, or gloves.[11] Similar discrimination is practiced in Washington, D.C.[12]

In the absence of protective legislation, the Negro is entirely at the mercy of the proprietors. While there is some authority for the view that civil rights statutes ___ merely declaratory of the common law,[13] no case within recent years has proceeded on this basis, and it is doubtful if such a case would succeed today. At one time, apparently, common law proceedings constituted a real "threat"; for in 1875 the Tennessee legislature adopted an act expressly abolishing the common law rule requiring the rendition of the full and equal accommodations to all who apply, without discrimination because of race or color.[14]

CIVIL RIGHTS ACTS IN THE STATES

Eighteen states have civil rights acts: California, Colorado, Connecticut, Illinois, Indiana, Iowa, Kansas, Massachusetts, Michigan, Minnesota, Nebraska, New Jersey, New York, Ohio, Pennsylvania, Rhode Island, Washington, Wisconsin.

[11] Charles S. Johnson, *Patterns of Negro Segregation* (1943), p. 167.
[12] *Ibid.*, p. 69.   [13] Ferguson v. Gies, 46 N.W. 718 (1890).
[14] Code of Tenn. 5262.

In addition,[15] three states have statutes that appear to be civil rights acts but are not. Maine [16] and New Hampshire [17] have acts which prohibit places of public accommodation from issuing advertising matter that suggests discrimination against persons of "any religious sect, creed, class, denomination, or nationality" (as phrased in the Maine act) or against "any religious sect, class or nationality" (as phrased in the New Hampshire act). There is no mention of discrimination on account of color or race in either statute, nor is the actual discrimination prohibited—the only thing prohibited is publicity that one is practicing discrimination. The third state which calls for a comment is Louisiana. In 1869 and 1870, when the Reconstruction program was being widely adopted, Louisiana adopted a civil rights act [18] which has never been repealed—except by implication. Since those days Louisiana has adopted many statutes which make segregation mandatory.

Thirty states and the District of Columbia have no civil rights acts; in some of these states segregation of the races is mandatory, in others the matter is determined by custom and the will of the proprietors.

The more significant provisions of the acts [19] may be summarized as follows:

Persons Covered. In California the act is for the protection of citizens only; in the other states it applies to all persons.

Basis of Discrimination. In some states the basis of the discrimination is immaterial; but in California, Kansas, Massachusetts, and Minnesota discrimination on account of race or color is prohibited; in Connecticut discrimination on account of race, color, or alienage is prohibited; in New York the act was amended in 1945 to ban discrimination on account of race, color, religion, or national origin.

Sanctions. California provides only for right of civil action; Colorado, Illinois, Indiana, Kansas, Massachusetts, Michigan, Minnesota, New York, and Wisconsin provide for both

[15] The civil rights acts of these eighteen states are set forth in the Appendix.
[16] Rev. Stats. (1930), ch. 134.   [17] Rev. Laws (1942), I, ch. 208.
[18] Gen. Stats., I, Title 13, secs. 1070 ff.
[19] See Appendix for full text of statutes; citations also appear in the Appendix.

civil and criminal actions; in Connecticut, Iowa, Nebraska, Ohio, Pennsylvania, Rhode Island, and Washington provision is made for only a criminal penalty; in New Jersey the party aggrieved sues for a money judgment, but the amount recovered goes to the state. In Illinois the place in which a violation takes place may be enjoined as a nuisance.

Enforcement. In New Jersey when the legislature in 1944 reorganized the office of the attorney general, it provided that one of his duties shall be the enforcement of the civil rights laws. A 1945 act in New York imposes similar duties on the attorney general.

In Illinois statutes passed in 1935 provide that it shall be the duty of all municipal, county, and state officials to cooperate in the enforcement of the act. If a sheriff, deputy sheriff, chief of police, marshal, policeman, or other peace officer obtains knowledge as to a violation, the act charges him with the duty to investigate, secure evidence, and sign a complaint. The act also charges the state's attorney in every county with the duty to prosecute diligently violators of the act, and the attorney general is charged with the duty to obtain evidence of violations and to make or cause to be made complaints against violators. If the state's attorney in the county or the attorney general fails to act within a reasonable time after an affidavit alleging a violation has been filed, the county circuit court may appoint a special assistant attorney general or state's attorney to prosecute the cause, the expenses to be paid by the county.

Types of Acts. The state of Washington has an act of a general nature, providing as follows:

Every person who shall deny to any other person because of race, creed or color, the full enjoyment of any of the accommodations, advantages, facilities, or privileges of any place of public resort, accommodation, assemblage or amusement, shall be guilty of a misdemeanor.

The act does not define or enumerate places of public resort, accommodation, assemblage, or amusement. All other statutes attempt to define and enumerate places of public accommodation;

though generally, after the enumeration of specific places, the acts add the phrase "and all other places of public accommodation and amusement."

Various types of places are named in the legislation of different states.

Public conveyances: named in all of the statutes except those of Washington.

Stations or terminals: New Jersey, New York, Pennsylvania.

Garages: New Jersey and Pennsylvania.

Rest rooms: Illinois.

Golf courses: New York.

Public library: New Jersey, New York, Pennsylvania.

Drug store: Pennsylvania.

Dispensary, clinic, hospital: New Jersey, New York.

Gymnasium: New Jersey, New York, Pennsylvania.

Cemeteries: New Jersey and New York. The Illinois act prohibits only discrimination in the price of cemetery lots because of race or color; it also prohibits discrimination in provision of funeral hearses.

Escalators: Michigan.

Elevators: Illinois, Michigan, New York.

Stores: Michigan.

Retail stores and establishments: New York and Ohio.

Department stores: Illinois.

Clothing stores: Illinois.

Hat stores: Illinois.

Shoe stores: Illinois.

Bathrooms: Illinois.

Boardwalk and public seashore accommodation: New Jersey.

Parks: Connecticut.

Bathhouses: California, Iowa, New York, Pennsylvania, Rhode Island.

Barber shops: California, Colorado, Illinois, Indiana, Iowa, Massachusetts, Michigan, Minnesota, Nebraska, New York, Ohio.

Beauty parlors: New York.

Theaters: California, Colorado, Connecticut, Illinois, Indiana, Iowa, Massachusetts, Michigan, Minnesota, Nebraska, New Jersey, New York, Ohio, Pennsylvania, Rhode Island.

Amusement parks: New York.

Skating rinks: California, Illinois, Massachusetts, New York, Rhode Island.

Race course: California.

Billiard and pool parlor, shooting gallery: New Jersey, New York, Pennsylvania.

Fairs, circus: California, New Jersey, New York, Pennsylvania.

Bowling alleys: New Jersey and Pennsylvania.

Boardinghouses: Kansas.

Licensed places of entertainment: Kansas and Rhode Island.

Hotels: California, Connecticut, Illinois, Indiana, Iowa, Kansas, Michigan, Minnesota, New Jersey, New York, Pennsylvania.

Eating places (restaurants and similar places): named in all the state civil rights acts except that of Washington (Massachusetts mentions only inns).

Soft drink and ice cream places: California, Illinois, Iowa, Michigan, Minnesota, New Jersey, New York, Pennsylvania.

This outline is not represented as being precise in all instances. It takes no account of shades of differences among the statutory provisions; for example, in some instances statutes mention theaters and movie houses, while the outline mentions only the former. The purpose of the enumeration is merely to convey to the reader general information as to the contents of civil rights acts.

Besides Maine and New Hampshire (see p. 116), other states that prohibit the advertising of discrimination include Colorado, Illinois, Massachusetts, Michigan, New Jersey, New York, and Pennsylvania. Some states also prohibit discrimination in the writing of different forms of insurance or in the rates charged. Such statutes are found in Connecticut, Minnesota, New Jersey, New York, and Wisconsin.

PRIVATE RIGHT OF ACTION

In states where provision is made only for criminal action, may the aggrieved party none the less sue for damages? This question has come up in a number of cases. Thus, in Michigan [20] a Negro dentist sought to procure a ticket for a seat on the first floor of a theater. Denied the privilege because of his race or color, he brought an action to recover damages. The theater owner contended that the act is a criminal statute only and does not give rise to an action for damages. He argued that at common law a theater was a private business; that no cause of action existed unless expressly created by statute. The court said that the civil rights act was not merely for the benefit of the public; if it were, then it would be strictly penal and no private action would be recognized. The statute is also for the benefit of particular individuals or groups; therefore, a private action may be maintained by the injured party, especially since the injured party is not entitled to the penalty expressly imposed by the act.

Another case that may be cited in this connection is one decided in 1938 by the Supreme Court of the State of Washington.[21] In that case a Negro was ejected from a movie theater because he insisted on occupying a seat on the lower floor and refused to go to the balcony. The Washington act is penal only; but the court held that an action for damages may be brought.

What happens in a state with no civil rights act is typified by a case decided by the Utah Supreme Court in 1933.[22] A Filipino bought four theater tickets for $1.40. He and his three friends, also Filipinos, tried to take seats on the lower floor but were told that Filipinos must sit in the balcony. He sued for damages. The court held that he could not recover on the theory of tort, but that he could recover $1.40 for breach of the contract. (Utah has a statute which provides only that an innkeeper who

[20] Bolden v. Grand Rapids Operating Corp., 214 N.W. 241; 53 A.L.R. 183 (1927). Cf. Grannan v. Western Racing Ass'n, 44 N.Y. Supp. 790 (1897); rev'd 153 N.Y. 449 (1897); Woolcott v. Shubert, 217 N.Y. 212 (1916); Brawner v. Irvin, 169 F. 964 (1909).
[21] Randall v. Cowlitz Amusements, Inc., 76 P. (2d) 1017 (1938).
[22] De La Ysla v. Publix Theatres Corp., 26 P. (2d) 818 (1933).

refuses, "without just cause or excuse," to receive and entertain any guest is guilty of a misdemeanor.) The reasoning of the court is interesting. A common carrier is a business affected with a public interest and must accommodate everyone. Not so a theater; it is a private business; in the absence of statute, the owner may admit or exclude anyone at his pleasure; a ticket of admission is a revocable license; the holder thereof may be refused admission or ordered to leave after being admitted. Where the license is revoked through no fault of the holder of the ticket (in the absence of misbehavior), the only remedy is for breach of contract: he may recover only the amount of damages sustained as a direct and proximate result of the breach, but not for the humiliation and mental suffering.

Despite the existence of a civil rights act, a common-law right of action may exist for breach of the common-law duty of an innkeeper toward a patron.[23] As will be seen later, it is doubtful if a common-law duty not to discriminate or exclude existed as to theaters and restaurants; it probably existed as to innkeepers and common carriers.

CONSTRUCTION OF CIVIL RIGHTS ACTS

With rare exception,[24] the courts have not given recognition to existence of civil rights under the common law and apart statute; they therefore have applied the rule of construction that statutes in derogation of the common law must be strictly construed. Such statutes have also been strictly construed because they are penal [25] and because they impose restrictions on the control or management of private property.[26]

A case decided by the New York Supreme Court [27] will serve as a good illustration. The plaintiffs alleged that the defendant denied them the privilege of using its golf course on the ground of their race or color. They sued for damages under the civil

[23] Odom v. East Ave. Copr., 34 N.Y. Supp. (2d) 312 (1942); aff'd 37 N.Y. Supp. (2d) 491 (1942).
[24] Brown v. Bell Co., 123 N.W. 231 (1912).
[25] Gibbs v. Arras Bros., 222 N.Y. 332   [26] Ibid.
[27] Delaney v. Central Valley Golf Club, 28 N.Y. Supp. (2d) 932 (1941); aff'd 31 N.Y. Supp. (2d) 834 (1941); app. denied, 32 N.Y. Supp. (2d) 1016 (1942).

rights act which did not include golf courses in its enumeration of places of public accommodation or amusement.

Plaintiffs offered proof that on a previous occasion one of them had been permitted to play on the course upon the payment of a fee; and, further, that two signs on the highway and two on the grounds indicated that the course was a public one. Defendant contended that it was not a public but a private club, and so not within the terms of the statute. It argued that when one of the plaintiffs played on the course on a previous occasion, the rules of the club had been relaxed; but the relaxation of the rules was only temporary. As to the signs, it argued that the club had not put them up, but that they had been put up by a group of businessmen in the neighboring town; besides, the signs said that the course was "public" but "under club rules."

The court held that plaintiffs had failed to sustain the burden of proving that the golf course was a place of public accommodation, resort, or amusement. Furthermore, the court pointed to the fact that the statute did not (then) specifically name golf courses among such public places. In view of the fact that the act enumerates public places, then one may say, the court stated that the legislature intended to limit the application of the statute to the places enumerated, and that if there is to be an extension the list, the legislature, rather than the courts, should exten

Finally, said the court, the act being penal, and restricti property rights, it is not to be extended through implication by analogy. Judgment was for the defendant.

Although, then, most civil rights acts contain words to the effect that the act shall not be limited to the places enumerated but shall apply also to "all other places of public accommodation," the courts have held this general language is limited and qualified by the specific designations which precede it. Thus it has been held [28] that the words "eating house" do not include an ice-cream parlor; that the words "inn, hotel or boarding house" do not include a restaurant or lunchroom; [29] that the

[28] Chochos v. Burden, 128 N.E. 696 (1921).
[29] State v. Brown, 212 P. 663 (1923).

a local legal-aid society or the branch of the National Association for the Advancement of Colored People to take the case; but in such instances it can be expected that only a few highly selected cases will be handled; now and then the owner of a place of public accommodation pays a penalty, but the vast majority of violators are left undisturbed. The existence of a civil rights act on the statute books does not, therefore, necessarily mean that discrimination has been eliminated. The passage of a statute guaranteeing equal rights is only the beginning.

As we have mentioned, in New Jersey, New York, and Illinois public officials are charged with the duty of enforcing the civil rights laws. This is a step in the right direction; but it does not provide the ultimate solution, for public officials will not ordinarily go out of their way to have such laws vindicated in the courts unless strong groups of representative citizens undertake to act as watchdogs.

Since a civil rights act is a *sine qua non* in the struggle to achieve equal civil rights, much thought has been given by the American Civil Liberties Union and the National Association for the Advancement of Colored People to the framing of a "model" bill. The latter organization aided in the drafting of the bill in Congress providing for civil rights in the District of Columbia, and the model state bill promulgated by the American Civil Liberties Union is fashioned, in some respects, after the Congressional bill. We would call attention to the following provisions in the model bill:

1. It provides against not only discrimination, but against, also, any distinction or restriction. This will make it impossible for a court to hold that segregation is not a violation of the act.

2. No distinction, discrimination, or restriction is to be made on account of race, color, creed, ancestry, or national origin.

3. It is directed against any place of public accommodation, resort, entertainment, or amusement, whether licensed or not, public conveyances, public meetings, or assemblages.

4. Places of public accommodation shall include hotels, restaurants, stores, or shops where foodstuffs, drinks, goods, or wares are sold, or offered, advertised, or displayed for sale to the public.

5. Such places shall also include hospitals, clinics, theaters, motion-picture houses, concert halls, amusement parks, public parks and public buildings under the jurisdiction of the national or municipal governments; buildings, residential or otherwise, receiving any tax exemption from any source, or the construction of which was directly financed in whole or in part by any public funds or grants.

6. Also public libraries, kindergartens, primary and secondary schools, high schools, academies, colleges and universities, extension courses, and all educational institutions under the supervision of the state authorities; and any such institution mentioned in this paragraph which is supported in whole or in part by public funds or by contributions solicited from the general public or obtaining any tax exemption, except those institutions admission to which is based on religious belief or affiliation.

7. It is provided, however, that the foregoing enumeration shall not be construed as limiting in any way the meaning of the general phrase "places of public accommodation, resort, entertainment, or amusement."

8. It shall be a violation to advertise that the place makes any distinction or discrimination; and a publication may be *prima facie* evidence that the publication was authorized by the owner or operator.

9. It shall be unlawful to revoke a ticket of admission to any public performance unless the holder is causing a breach of the peace.

10. Special provision is made against discrimination by a public school system, a public utility company, or by anyone engaged in the production or distribution of equipment or supplies for any public agency.

11. Special provision against discrimination by labor organizations.

12. Person aggrieved may recover from $100 to $500 for each violation.

13. Violation shall also constitute a misdemeanor, carrying a penalty of a fine from $100 to $500, or imprisonment from thirty to ninety days, or both fine and imprisonment.

14. Violation by a licensee two or more times within a twelve-month period shall lead to suspension of license for sixty days.

15. A cover-all provision that all persons shall be entitled to equal protection of the laws, and that no person shall, because of his race, color, creed, ancestry, or national origin, be subjected to any dis-

crimination in his civil rights by any other person, or firm, or the state, or any subdivision thereof. Violation is a misdemeanor, punishable by a fine of $100 to $500.

The bill has been drawn on the theory that it should not enumerate all places, for a bill enumerating a multitude of places where equality is required would be construed to exclude other places not mentioned. Nor is the bill drawn after the model of the State of Washington act, which mentions no places at all. The "model" bill tries to steer a course between the Scylla of specificity and the Charybdis of generality. It is difficult to foretell what the courts would do with such a law, except that one may say in a general way that liberal courts would construe the act broadly, with an eye on the civil rights of individuals, while unsympathetic courts would construe the act narrowly, with an eye on the fact that the law proposes to restrict the rights of owners of property. The bill is, no doubt, the best measure thus far devised. One specially interesting feature is the section which proposes to modify the common-law rule that theater tickets are licenses revocable at the will of the owner. This rule has been changed by statute in New York and the act has recently been held constitutional.[40]

The full scope of legislation directed to the elimination of discrimination has not yet been explored. Nearly every existing statute has a major fault or a group of minor ones which together render the act one of relatively small value. For example, the New Jersey act provides that the person aggrieved shall have a cause of action, but the amount he recovers as damages goes to the state. Such a provision makes it impossible for a lawyer to take the plaintiff's case on a contingent-fee basis. After two generations' experience with state civil rights acts it should not be a surprise that we now know more about this type of legislation than our forefathers knew, but this knowledge is of no value unless it is utilized through an improvement of the legislative method of vindication of rights.

[40] Christie v. 46th Street Theatre Corp., 292 N.Y. 520 (1944) ; cert. den. 323 U.S. 710 (1944).

A FAIR RACIAL PRACTICES ACT

Carey McWilliams has proposed the adoption of a new federal civil rights statute, in the form of a fair racial practices act, to be enforced by modern administrative methods as a matter of public policy, rather than by individual actions as a matter of personal privilege.[41]

It is extremely doubtful if the proposal is today feasible; but it might become feasible if it were first successfully tried out on a state level. One of the chief objections to the typical state civil rights act, in the minds of some persons, is its coercive feature: an owner of a place of public accommodation may be coerced into opening his place to all persons regardless of race, color, or creed, though neither he nor his employees may be ready, psychologically, to receive the patronage of Negroes or other persons not previously permitted to enter his place of business. As in the case of discrimination in employment, the thought is that the owner should first be exposed to persuasion through conferences; only if he obstinately persists in denying equal treatment should the civil and penal sanctions be brought to bear on him. Perhaps there is much to be said for this position; it would be eminently desirable to see a fair racial practices act adopted by a state and enforced in good faith for a number of years.

Under such a state act, a commission against discrimination might be established, which would receive, investigate, and pass upon complaints against owners, operators, or employees of places of public accommodation, resort, or amusement. Unlike a court, such a commission could send its investigators to a place of business and get firsthand reports. The commission could create advisory agencies throughout the state to study specific instances of discrimination, and to seek cooperation from the persons charged with violation of the act. If the local advisory agency is unsuccessful, the state commission could itself attempt to eliminate the discrimination by conference, conciliation, and persuasion. If these methods do not lead to success, then a formal hearing could be held; the hearing might result in an order

[41] "Race Discrimination and the Law," 9 *Science and Society* 1 (1945).

which would direct respondent to cease and desist and which would be subject to enforcement by court order.

If state fair employment practice acts were established to follow the procedure outlined above, and should prove successful, the example would in all likelihood spread to the treatment of discrimination in fields other than employment, and state fair racial and religious practice acts would be adopted to replace existing state civil rights acts.

STATE LEGISLATION AGAINST DISCRIMINATION IN EMPLOYMENT

In the twelve years preceding 1945 thirteen states enacted legislation forbidding discriminatory practices in employment on account of race, color, or creed.[42] The laws were directed against such practices by state civil service, in home or work relief, by public works contractors, war contractors, and trade unions.[43] In New York a law of 1933 prohibited discrimination by utility companies; [44] a law of 1940 prohibited discrimination by labor organizations; [45] a law of 1935 prohibited discrimination by public contractors.[46] But no state had a fair employment practice act. In 1945 the New York Legislature took the lead by passing the Ives-Quinn bill.[47] New Jersey followed with passage of the Hill law,[48] and Indiana passed a measure,[49] narrower in scope, but none the less covering discrimination in employment generally. In 1946 Massachusetts enacted a fair employment practice law. (The New York, New Jersey, and Massachusetts acts are set forth in the Appendix.) We shall here summarize the New York law.

[42] See First Report of F.E.P.C. (1945), 148–149.
[43] Legislation in New York, Pennsylvania, Nebraska, Kansas, and Indiana. See *Digest and Analysis of Existing and Proposed Laws Dealing with Discrimination* (N.Y. State Commission against Discrimination, Albany, 1944), p. 37.
[44] Sec. 42 of Civil Rights Act (1933).
[45] Sec. 43 of Civil Rights Act (1940).   [46] Sec. 220-e of Labor Law (1935).
[47] Ch. 118 of Laws of 1945. See Austin-Mahoney bill, A. 12501, S. 12187.
[48] Laws of 1945, ch. 169. See Appendix, no. 6.
[49] Ch. 235 of Laws of 1945. The law does not make unlawful discrimination in employment but authorizes the Indiana Commissioner of Labor to make studies of discrimination and its cure, to cooperate with employers and unions in programs to eliminate discrimination, and to investigate complaints. There is no power to issue orders or to compel obedience to recommendations.

The Law against Discrimination, as the statute is known, states that the act shall be deemed an exercise of the police power of the state, for the protection of the public welfare, health, and peace of the people of the state, and in fulfillment of the provision in the Constitution of 1938 concerning civil rights. It creates a State Commission against Discrimination, with power to eliminate and prevent discrimination in employment because of race, creed, color, or national origin, by employers, labor unions, and employment agencies. Opportunity for employment without discrimination is declared to be a civil right.

The Commission consists of five members, appointed by the governor, by and with the consent of the state Senate. Each commissioner receives an annual salary of $10,000.

A person claiming to be aggrieved is required to file a complaint. One of the commissioners is then appointed to make an investigation. If he determines that probable cause for the complaint exists, he is required to attempt to eliminate the practice through persuasion. If he fails, a formal hearing is held, at which he shall have no part. If the Commission finds that the respondent is guilty, it is to issue a cease and desist order. The law provides for judicial enforcement and review of the Commission's orders. Violation of such an order is a misdemeanor, punishable by imprisonment for not more than one year or by fine of not more than $500, or both.

The act does not apply to employers with fewer than six workers, nor to social, fraternal, religious, educational, and charitable organizations, if not organized for private profit.

The Commission is charged with the duty of creating advisory agencies, or conciliation councils, throughout the state, who are to study the problems of discrimination in specific fields or in specific instances, and to foster cooperation and good-will among the various groups in the state. Citizens serving on the councils shall not receive pay.

Article I, Section 11, of the New York Constitution provides that no person shall, because of race, color, creed, or religion, be subjected to any discrimination in his civil rights by any other person or by any firm, corporation, or institution, or by the state or any state agency. The Constitution does not define the term "civil rights"; but the Legislature has the right to declare what such rights are. No other state constitution has a declaration as broad as this one. But we have seen that under the Supreme Court decisions there can be no doubt but that any state, whether its constitution so provides or not, has the right and power to define the civil rights of its citizens.

As to the provision against discrimination by labor organizations, the recent decision of the Supreme Court in the *Railway Mail Association* case [50] leaves no doubt as to its constitutionality. Such a provision does not, said the court, offend the due process clause of the Fourteenth Amendment as an interference with the right of an organization to select its membership. It is no abridgment of the union's property rights or liberty of contract. A recent decision of the California Supreme Court [51] held that a union occupies a quasi-public position and has corresponding obligations. It may not exclude a Negro or place him in an auxiliary where he will have lesser rights than those enjoyed by white members. The court spoke of the "fundamental right to work for a living."

Nor can there be any doubt as to the constitutionality of the provision outlawing discrimination by employers, under the police power of the state or the power to declare and protect civil rights. While no decision for this proposition can be cited, there are no precedents against it, and considerable judicial *dicta* which point to its constitutionality.[52]

[50] 326 U.S. 88 (1945). See pp. 109, *supra.*
[51] James v. Marinship Corp., 155 P. (2d) 329 (1945). Cf. James v. Intern. Brotherhood of Boilermakers, 54 F. Supp. 94 (1944), in which a complaint filed by Negroes was dismissed because of lack of diversity of citizenship. As this is being written a case is pending in the Rhode Island Superior Court: Hill v. Intern. Brotherhood of Boilermakers.
[52] See "Fair Employment Practice Act," Hearings on S. 101 and S. 459, 79th Cong., 1st Sess. (1945), p. 184, where cases are cited; also opinion in Marinship case, cited in note 51, *supra;* Harold Dublirer, "Legislation Outlawing Racial Discrimination in Employment," 5 *Lawyers Guild Rev.* 101 (1945).

CHAPTER 8

Statutes Compelling or Allowing
Segregation or Discrimination

As we have seen, by the decision in the *Civil Rights Cases,* the Fourteenth Amendment gives no protection against discrimination by private persons; nor does it require states to prevent such discrimination. The matter of civil rights is left to the states. The states may act to prohibit discriminations; or they may take no action at all, in which case the owner of a place of public accommodation may do as he pleases; or they may act to compel discriminations. The only limitation, applicable in the latter instance, is that if the state compels segregation, provision must be made for equal facilities for the Negro. In brief, from the standpoint of the Constitution the situation is as follows:

1. States may *prohibit* discrimination. This has been done, in varying degree, by eighteen states.

2. States may *compel* discrimination (or segregation, which is not discrimination according to the United States Supreme Court). This has been done, in varying degree, by twenty states.

3. States may leave the matter to private discretion. This apparently has been done by ten states.

Here we propose to indicate the scope of the practice of segregration, constituting the fruit of the decision in the *Civil Rights Cases.*

Schools: In the following states segregation of pupils is mandatory or expressly permissive (though there are various shadings in the requirements): Alabama, Arizona, Delaware, Florida, Georgia, Indiana, Kansas, Kentucky, Louisiana, Maryland, Mississippi, Missouri, New Mexico, North Carolina, Oklahoma, South Carolina, Tennessee, Texas, Virginia, West Virginia. Delaware calls for three separate schools: for whites, for colored pupils, and for Moors or Indians. Maryland provides that the supervisor of colored schools shall be a white person. North Carolina calls for a separate school for certain Indians. Mississippi calls for separate schools for Indian children. The Kentucky and Oklahoma acts apply also to private schools.

In South Carolina, Texas, and Virginia the statutes require separate schools even for the deaf, dumb, and blind. In six states the statutes call for separate schools for the blind: Louisiana, North Carolina, Oklahoma, Tennessee, Virginia, and West Virginia. (In the following five states blind white and Negro pupils may attend the same schools: Alabama, Arkansas, Florida, Georgia, and Kentucky.) Deaf pupils are segregated by race in seven states: Kentucky, Louisiana, North Carolina, Oklahoma, Tennessee, Virginia, and West Virginia. (But in Alabama, Arkansas, Florida, and Georgia deaf pupils are not segregated by race.)

Sixteen states require segregation of Negro pupils in juvenile delinquent and reform schools: Alabama, Arkansas, Delaware, Florida, Georgia, Kentucky, Louisiana, Maryland, Mississippi, Missouri, North Carolina, Oklahoma, Tennessee, Texas, Virginia, and West Virginia.

Separate agricultural and trade schools are required in Alabama, Florida, Maryland, North Carolina, West Virginia, Kentucky, Missouri, Oklahoma, and South Carolina.

Separate school libraries are required in Missouri, North Carolina, and Texas. Florida stipulates that textbooks used by Negro pupils shall be stored separately.

Separate colleges are mandatory by statute in Alabama, Arkansas, Delaware, Florida, Georgia, Kentucky, Maryland, Missouri, North Carolina, Oklahoma, South Carolina, and Virginia. Separate teacher training schools are required in fourteen states: Alabama, Arkansas, Delaware, Georgia, Kentucky, Louisiana, Maryland, Mississippi, Missouri, North Carolina, Oklahoma, South Carolina, Texas, and West Virginia. North Carolina requires a separate normal school for Cherokee Indians.

In Florida, Kentucky, Tennessee, and West Virginia teachers

and pupils must belong to the same race. Tennessee provides that only white persons born in the United States, whose parents could speak English and who themselves have spoken English since childhood, may teach white pupils.

Transportation. In the following fourteen states statutes require separate railroad facilities: Alabama, Arkansas, Florida, Georgia, Kentucky, Louisiana, Maryland, Mississippi, North Carolina, Oklahoma, South Carolina, Tennessee, Texas, Virginia.

Arkansas, Georgia, and Texas statutes require separate sleeping compartments and bedding to be used by Negro train passengers. South Carolina and Virginia require separate dining-car and restaurant facilities. On the other hand, Maryland, North Carolina, Texas, and Virginia except Pullman sleeping cars from the strict Jim Crow regulations. Statutory exceptions relating to travel in freight car and caboose are found in Arkansas, Kentucky, Maryland, Oklahoma, South Carolina, Tennessee, Texas, and Virginia. In the following states various other exceptions are noted in the statutes (such as permission for an officer to travel together with his prisoner, though they are of different races, or for a nurse or servant to travel with her patient or. mistress): Alabama, Arkansas, Florida, Georgia, Kentucky, Louisiana, Maryland, North Carolina, Oklahoma, South Carolina, Tennessee, Texas, and Virginia.

Separate waiting rooms are required in Alabama, Arkansas, Florida, Louisiana, Mississippi, North Carolina, Oklahoma, and South Carolina.

Separation in buses is required by statute in Alabama, Arkansas, Florida, Georgia, Louisiana, Mississippi, North Carolina, Oklahoma, South Carolina, Texas, and Virginia.

Separation in street cars is required in Arkansas, Florida, Louisiana, Mississippi, North Carolina, Oklahoma, South Carolina, Tennessee, Texas, and Virginia.

Separation in steamships and ferries is required in North Carolina, South Carolina, and Maryland.

Amusements and Recreational Facilities. Louisiana and South

Carolina require separation of the races at circuses and tent shows. Tennessee and Virginia require separation at theaters and public halls. Missouri, Oklahoma, and South Carolina, require separation in parks, playgrounds, and on beaches. Arkansas requires separation at race tracks. Georgia, South Carolina, and West Virginia require separation in billiard and pool rooms.

Hospitals. Mississippi and South Carolina require separation in hospitals generally. In eleven states even mental defectives must be separated by race: Alabama, Georgia, Kentucky, Louisiana, Mississippi, Missouri, North Carolina, Oklahoma, Tennessee, Virginia, and West Virginia. North Carolina requires a separate hospital for insane Indians.

Separation in hospitals for tubercular patients is required in Alabama, Arkansas, Delaware, Maryland, Oklahoma, Texas, and West Virginia.

In Alabama a female white nurse is prohibited from taking care of a Negro male patient.

Penal and Correctional Institutions. Separation is required in eleven states: Alabama, Arkansas, Florida, Georgia, Louisiana, Mississippi, North Carolina, South Carolina, Tennessee, Virginia, and West Virginia. North Carolina requires also separate accommodations in jails for Indians. Separate bathing facilities in such institutions are required by the statutes of Alabama and Tennessee; separate beds, in Alabama and Arkansas; separate tables, in Arkansas.

The laws of five states—Alabama, Florida, Georgia, Arkansas, and South Carolina—provide that Negro and white prisoners may not be chained together.

Miscellaneous. In Alabama and Georgia paupers are required to be separated by race.

In Oklahoma, Tennessee, and West Virginia homes for orphans and the aged must separate their inmates.

The adoption laws of Louisiana, Montana, South Carolina, and Texas provide that foster parent and adopted child must belong to the same race.

Oklahoma requires separate telephone booths for Negroes.

A Texas statute prohibits whites and Negroes from engaging in boxing matches together.

North Carolina and Virginia prohibit Negroes and whites from forming fraternal benefit associations together.

Arkansas requires a separation of the races in voting or polling places.

Separate battalions or regiments are required in Indiana, West Virginia, and North Carolina. In the latter state Negro troops are required to be under the command of white officers.

In Georgia a Negro minister may marry only Negro couples.

In the labor laws of Oklahoma and Texas it is provided that there be separate bathing facilities in mines; separate toilets are required in North Carolina's labor laws. Such laws in South Carolina provide that in cotton textile factories, the races may not work together in the same room, nor may they use the same doors of entrance and exit at the same time, nor may they use the same pay windows or stairways at the same time, nor may they at any time use the same lavatory toilets, drinking buckets, pails, cups, dippers, or glasses.

If a state does not have an act calling for segregation with respect to a specific matter, it is not to be assumed that with respect to that matter there is no segregation. Many of the Border and Southern states do not have laws requiring segregation in theaters and other places of public amusement; but in such states custom takes the place of statutes and there is no mingling of the races in any place that might be described as a place of public accommodation. In addition to statutes and custom, municipal ordinances must also be considered, for in some places such ordinances require separation of the races.

Just as the civil rights laws tend to break up the pattern of segregation and other forms of race discrimination, so the Jim Crow laws tend to strengthen the local custom of segregation and the practices of race discrimination generally. "When the Supreme Court in 1883 declared the civil rights bill of 1875 unconstitutional in so far as it referred to acts of social discrimination by individuals," says Myrdal,

the way was left open for the Jim Crow legislation of the Southern states and municipalities. . . . We do not know much about the effects of the Jim Crow legislation. American sociologists, following the Sumner tradition of holding legislation to be inconsequential, are likely to underrate these effects. Southern Negroes tell quite a different story. From their own experience in different parts of the South they have told me how the Jim Crow statutes were effective means of tightening and freezing—in many cases of instigating—segregation and discrimination. . . . Before the Jim Crow legislation there is also said to have been a tendency on the part of white people to treat Negroes somewhat differently depending upon their class and education. This tendency was broken by the laws which applied to *all* Negroes. The legislation thus solidified the caste line and minimized the importance of class differences in the Negro group.[1]

Myrdal points out that the common opinion among Southern authors—and in most material on the South and the Negro problem, even when written by Northern authors—is that laws in the social field are almost insignificant. He believes this view to be exaggerated and to be an expression of the American bias toward minimizing the effects of formal legislation: a bias in the *laissez-faire* tradition.

Jim Crow laws and customs are based, says Myrdal, on the theory of color caste or of "no social equality," and this theory is the expression of the determination on the part of whites to preserve the "purity of the white race." There is the popular magical concept of "blood," to which the arguments in support of Jim Crowism are ultimately reducible. Civil rights equalities will lead to social equality, and social equality will lead to intermarriage. Inevitably the question is put, "Would you like to have your daughter marry a Negro?"

To uphold the ban on intermarriage, the white people have devised a definite order by rank of the various Jim Crow measures.

[1] *An American Dilemma*, I, 579–580.

Myrdal lists the measures in the order of importance as determined by white persons:[2]

1. The ban on intermarriage and other sex relations involving white women and colored men. This takes precedence over everything else. It is the end for which the other restrictions are arranged as means.

2. A strict etiquette, including all sorts of taboos, in personal contacts.

3. Segregation in schools and churches.

4. Segregation in hotels, restaurants, theaters, and other public places.

5. Segregation in public conveyances.

6. Discrimination in public services.

7. Inequality in politics.

8. Inequality in administration of justice.

9. Inequality in breadwinning and relief.

White liberals in the South today are willing to grant equality in breadwinning, relief, justice, and politics; and changes in these spheres are on the way. But when it comes to social relations in the narrow sense, the liberals are less prepared to split off from the majority. "Hardly anybody in the South is prepared to go the whole way and argue that even the ban on intermarriage should be lifted. . . . Even the one who has his philosophical doubts on the point must, if he is reasonable, abstain from ever voicing them."[3] T. J. Wootter, Jr., and Virginius Dabney, leading Southern liberals, are even willing to see Jim Crowism abolished, but would not touch items 1 and 2 in the measures set forth above.

But the "purity of the white race" principle, which is the bedrock on which the structure of race relations has been built in the South, is supported by reasoning which cannot withstand close examination.

Things are defended in the South as means of preserving racial purity which cannot possibly be defended in this way. To this extent we cannot avoid observing that *what white people really want is to keep*

[2] *Ibid.,* pp. 587–588.   [3] *Ibid.,* pp. 588–589.

the Negroes in a lower status. "Intermarriage" itself is resented because it would be a supreme indication of "social equality," while the rationalization is that "social equality" is opposed because it would bring "intermarriage." [4]

In the rationalization of segregation and discrimination against the Negroes, the persistent preoccupation with sex and marriage is, says Myrdal, an irrational escape on the part of the whites "from voicing an open demand for difference in social status between the two groups for its own sake." Were it not for the strength of the American creed of equality, the South would uphold the caste system "without this tense belief in sex and race dangers."

Legal segregation may be found in the North as well as in the South, and even in states which have civil rights acts. Thus, in New Jersey a statute requires separate Negro regiments in the state guard,[5] and, while segregation in the school system is illegal,[6] there is a state-supported industrial school for Negroes in Bordentown. Similarly, a California act empowers local school authorities to establish separate schools for children of Indian, Chinese, Japanese, or Mongolian parentage;[7] California also has an antimiscegenation act, and an alien-land law, under which Japanese aliens, because ineligible for American citizenship, may not own agricultural land.[8]

But such laws are admittedly rare; they are aberrations. Much discrimination exists, not because the law compels it, but rather despite the law.

The causes of segregation in the North, as set forth by Myrdal, are the following:

1. Residential segregation leads to institutional segregation. Schools, parks, playgrounds, stores, theaters, hospitals, clinics, relief agencies, and other institutions have a community or neighborhood basis; thus "Negro school districts" and "white school districts" are created.

2. Managerial refusal of services. While a manager may not,

---

[4] *Ibid.*, p. 591.   [5] 38:6–1.   [6] 18:14–2.
[7] Education Code 8003, 8004.   [8] Note in 30 *Calif. Law Rev.* 563, 564 (1942).

where there is a civil rights law, refuse to serve a Negro, actually many stores, hotels, and other establishments refuse service to Negroes. Even if the "law" catches up with such a manager or owner, he may go on refusing to serve Negroes because the probability of being called before a court a second time is rather small. There are also indirect devices for discouraging the Negro from seeking service in these establishments:

by letting him wait indefinitely for service, by telling him that there is no food left in the restaurant or rooms left in the hotel, by giving him dirty or inedible food, by charging him unconscionable prices, by insulting him verbally, and by dozens of other ways of keeping facilities from him.[9]

3. Voluntary organizations do not invite Negro participation or membership. Thus, the American Red Cross has refused to permit Negro women to assist in its civilian first-aid training program unless they form their own separate units on their own initiative.[10] At first the Red Cross also refused to accept Negro blood donors; later it changed its policy and segregated the blood from Negro donors and marked it to be used exclusively for Negroes in the armed forces. The United Service Organizations (USO) refused to let Negroes participate in many of its activities in several Northern states; and the Office of Civilian Defense has refused, in one Northern state, to permit Negroes to serve as volunteer airplane spotters.

4. A fourth device is for individual whites to insult or stare at Negroes in restaurants and other public places.

5. Voluntary withdrawal of Negroes into their own group. This is the result of the other causes of segregation.

How does the Negro react to the order by rank of discriminations set forth above? Does he, too, feel that first on the list is the bar against intermarriage and sex relations involving white women, and the lowest are the discriminations affecting his chance of earning a living or getting relief? On the contrary,[11] while the Negro's list parallels that of the whites, it is in inverse

9 *An American Dilemma*, I, 630–631.
10 *Ibid.*, II, 1367.   11 *Ibid.*, I, 60-61.

order. His resentment is deepest at discrimination on the employment level and is least on the sex and marriage level. The
Negroes are in desperate need of jobs and bread; next come justice in the courts, and the vote. Justice and the vote are more
urgently needed than better schools, because they may serve as
means to achieve the latter and other community facilities. These
are, in turn, more important than civil courtesies. The marriage
matter is of doubtful interest.

The question remains whether the white man is really prepared to stick to his own order of discriminations and give the
Negro a job, "rather than to allow him entrance to his front
door or to ride beside him in the street car." [12]

[12] *Ibid.*, p. 61.

Appendices

1. Civil Rights Bill for the District of Columbia

H.R. 1995

(*78th Congress, 1st Session*)

In the House of Representatives, February 25, 1943, Mr. Rowan introduced the following bill; which was referred to the Committee on the District of Columbia

A BILL To assure to all persons within the District of Columbia full and equal privileges of places of public accommodation, resort, entertainment, and amusement, and for other purposes.

Be it enacted by the Senate and House of Representatives of the United States of America in Congress assembled, That within the District of Columbia any person, natural or corporate, who shall make any distinction, discrimination, or restriction on account of race, color, or creed or for any reason not sanctioned by law and not applicable alike to persons generally, in the admission of any person to, or the accommodation or service of any person in any place of public accommodation, resort, entertainment, or amusement, whether licensed or not, or any public conveyance, or any public meeting or assemblage, or who shall aid, incite, or cause the making of any such distinction, discrimination, or restriction, shall for each such act or denial be liable to a penalty of not less than $100 or more than $500, to be recovered by the person aggrieved thereby, or by his assignee, in a civil action in the municipal court of the District of Columbia; and shall also for every such offense be deemed guilty of a misdemeanor, and upon conviction thereof in the police court of the District of Columbia shall be punished by a fine of not less than $10 or more than $100, or by imprisonment for not less than ten days or more than one hundred days, or by both such fine and such imprisonment.

Sec. 2. (a) Places of public accommodation, resort, entertainment, or amusement shall be deemed to include hotels, restaurants, stores, or shops where foodstuffs, drinks, goods, or wares are sold or offered, advertised, or displayed for sale to the public, hospitals, clinics, theaters, motion-picture houses, concert halls, amusement parks, and public parks and public buildings under the jurisdiction of the national or municipal government: *Provided,* That the foregoing enumeration shall not be construed as limiting in any way the meaning of the general phrase, "places of public accommodation, resort, entertainment, or amusement."

(b) The publication of any order, notice, or advertisement reasonably calculated to prevent or discourage the patronage or custom of persons of any race, color, or creed, as well as the actual exclusion or segregation of or discrimination against any person on account of race, color, or creed shall be deemed an unlawful distinction, discrimination, and restriction within the meaning of this Act. The production of any such order, notice, or advertisement purporting to be made by any person being the owner, lessee, operator, proprietor, manager, agent, or employee engaged in or exercising control over the operation of any public conveyance or any place of public accommodation, resort, entertainment, or amusement, shall be prima facie evidence in any civil or criminal action that the same was authorized and published by such person.

(c) The provisions and requirements of this Act shall bind and obligate every owner, lessee, operator, proprietor, manager, agent, and employee, whether natural person, corporation, or unincorporated association, engaged in or exercising control over the operation of any public conveyance or any place of public accommodation, resort, entertainment, or amusement: *Provided,* That whenever any agent or employee shall so exercise any function or employ any power with which he is charged or entrusted as to violate any provision of this Act, both he and his principal or employer shall be held equally responsible and liable: *Provided further,* That the provisions of section 251 of chapter 9 of title 24 of the Code of the District of Columbia shall be applicable to the enforcement of the civil penalty provided in section 1 of this Act wherever two or more persons shall be charged with legal responsibility for the act or denial complained of.

(d) Nothing in this Act shall be deemed to prohibit the providing of separate accommodations of facilities for persons of different sex.

Sec. 3. The Commissioners of the District of Columbia shall revoke any license issued pursuant to the provisions and requirements of part 9 of chapter 4 of title 20 of the Code of the District of Columbia whenever it shall have been judicially determined that the licensee or person operating or doing business under said license has violated this Act in the course of such operation or business two times or more within any twelve-month period. No similar license shall be issued to the offending person or for the use of the place where said violations shall have occurred for a period of sixty days following such revocation. The provisions of this section may be enforced by an action of mandamus filed against the said Commissioners by any citizen of the District of Columbia.

SEC. 4. The provisions of this Act are hereby declared to be separable. If any provision of this Act, or the application thereof to any person or circumstances, is held invalid, the remainder of the Act, and the application of such provision to other persons or circumstances, shall not be affected thereby.

SEC. 5. This Act may be cited as the "Equal Rights Law of the District of Columbia."

2. Model State Civil Rights Bill Proposed by the American Civil Liberties Union

A BILL To assure to all persons within the State of ———— full and equal privileges in places of public accommodation, resort, entertainment and amusement, and equal rights in employment and labor unions, and for other purposes.

SEC. 1. That within the jurisdiction of this State any person, natural or corporate, who shall make any distinction, discrimination, or restriction on account of race, color, creed, ancestry or national origin, or for any reason not sanctioned by law and not applicable alike to persons generally, in the admission of any person to, or the accommodation or service of any person in any place of public accommodation, resort, entertainment, or amusement, whether licensed or not, or any public conveyance, or any public meeting or assemblage, or who shall directly aid or cause the making of any such distinction, discrimination, or restriction, shall for each such act or denial be liable as hereinafter provided for in Sections 8 and 9.

SEC. 2. (a) Places of public accommodation, resort, entertainment, or amusement shall be deemed to include hotels, restaurants, stores, or shops where foodstuffs, drinks, goods, or wares are sold or offered, advertised, or displayed for sale to the public; hospitals, clinics, theaters, motion-picture houses, concert halls, amusement parks, public parks and public buildings under the jurisdiction of the national or municipal governments; buildings residential or otherwise enjoying eminent domain, or receiving any tax exemption from any source, or the construction of which was directly financed in whole or in part by any public funds or grants; public libraries, kindergartens, primary and secondary schools, high schools, academies, colleges and universities, extension courses, and all educational institutions under the supervision of the state authorities; and any such public library, kindergarten, primary and secondary school, academy, college, university, professional school, extension course or other educational facility, supported in whole or in part by public funds or by contributions solicited from the general public or obtaining any tax exemption from any source, except those institutions, admission to which is based on religious belief or affiliation: provided, that the foregoing enumeration shall not be construed as limiting in any way the meaning of the general phrase, "places of public accommodation, resort, entertainment, or amusement."

(b) The publication of any order, notice, or advertisement reasonably calculated to prevent or discourage the patronage or custom of persons of any race, color, creed, ancestry or national origin, as well as the actual exclusion or segregation of or discrimination against any person on account of race, color, creed, ancestry or national origin shall be deemed an unlawful distinction, discrimination, and restriction within the meaning of this Act. The production of any such order, notice, or advertisement purporting to be made by any person being the owner, lessee, operator, proprietor, manager, agent, or employee engaged in or exercising control over the operation of any public conveyance or any place of public accommodation, resort, entertainment, or amusement, shall be prima facie evidence in any civil or criminal action that the same was authorized and published by such person.

(c) The provisions and requirements of this Act shall bind and obligate every owner, lessee, operator, proprietor, manager, agent, and employee, whether natural person, corporation, or unincorporated association, engaged in or exercising control over the operation of any public conveyance or any place of public accommodation, resort, entertainment, or amusement: provided, that whenever any agent or employee shall so exercise any function or employ any power with which he is charged or entrusted as to violate any provision of this Act, both he and his principal or employer shall be held equally responsible and liable.

(d) Nothing in this Act shall be deemed to prohibit the providing of separate accommodations or facilities for persons of different sex.

SEC. 3. No person, agency, bureau, corporation or association, being the owner, lessee, proprietor, manager, superintendent, agent or employee of any place of public entertainment and amusement as hereinafter defined shall refuse to admit to any public performance held at such place any person over the age of twenty-one years who presents a ticket of admission to the performance a reasonable time before the commencement thereof, or shall eject or demand the departure of any such person from such place during the course of the performance, whether or not accompanied by an offer to refund the purchase price or value of the ticket of admission presented by such person; but nothing in this section contained shall be construed to prevent the refusal of admission to or the ejection of any person whose conduct or speech thereat or therein is abusive or offensive or of any person engaged in any activity which may tend to a breach of the peace.

The places of public entertainment and amusement within the meaning of this section shall include but not be limited to legitimate theatres, burlesque theatres, music halls, motion picture houses, opera houses, concert halls and circuses.

SEC. 4. No person, agency, bureau, corporation or association employed or maintained to obtain or aid in obtaining positions for teachers, principals, superintendents, clerks or other employees in the public schools of the State, and no individual or individuals conducting or employed by or interested directly or indirectly in such an agency, bureau, corporation or association, and no board of education, trustee of a school district, superintendent, principal or teacher of a public school or other official or employee of a board of education, shall refuse to employ or promote any person on account of race, color, creed, ancestry or national origin, or directly or indirectly ask, indicate or transmit orally or in writing the race, color, creed, ancestry or national origin of any person seeking employment or official position in the public schools of the State.

SEC. 5 It shall be unlawful for any public utility company, or a common carrier as defined by Sections ——— of the Statutes of ——— to refuse to employ or promote any person in any capacity in the operation or maintenance of a public service on account of the race, color, creed, ancestry or national origin of such person.

SEC. 6. It shall be unlawful for any person, firm or corporation engaged to any extent whatsoever in the production, manufacture or distribution of equipment or supplies for any public agency whether federal, state, or local to refuse to employ or promote any person in any capacity on account of the race, color, creed, ancestry or national origin of such person.

SEC. 7. As used in this section, the term "labor organization" means any organization which exists and is constituted for the purpose, in whole or in part, of collective bargaining, or of dealing with employers concerning grievances, terms or conditions of employment, or of other mutual aid or protection. No labor organization shall hereafter, directly or indirectly, by ritualistic practice, constitutional or by-law prescription, by tacit agreement among its members, or otherwise, deny a person or persons membership in its organization by reason of his race, color, creed, ancestry or national origin, or by regulations, practice or otherwise, segregate or deny to any of its members, by reason of race, color, creed, ancestry or national origin, equal treatment with all other members within such labor organization or in any designation of members to any employer for employment, promotion or dismissal by such employer.

SEC. 8. Any person who or any agency, bureau, corporation or association which shall violate any of the provisions of sections 1, 3, 4, 5, or 6 or who or which shall aid or cause the violation of any of said provisions, and any officer or member of a labor organization, as defined by section 7, or any person representing any organization or acting in its behalf who shall violate any of the provisions of section 7 or who shall aid or cause the violation of any of the provisions of such section shall for each and every violation thereof be liable to a penalty of not less than one hundred dollars nor more than five hundred dollars, to be recovered by the person aggrieved thereby or by any resident of this state, to whom such person shall assign his cause of action, in any court of competent jurisdiction in the county in which the plaintiff or the defendant shall reside.

SEC. 9. Any person who or any agency, bureau, corporation or association which shall violate any of the provisions of sections 1, 3, 4, 5, or 6 or who or which shall aid or cause the violation of any of said provisions, and any officer or member of a labor organization, as defined by section 7, or any person representing any organization or acting in its behalf who shall violate any of the provisions of section 7 or who shall aid or cause the violation of any of the provisions of such section shall be deemed guilty of a misdemeanor, and upon conviction thereof shall be fined not less than one hundred dollars nor more than five hundred dollars, or shall be imprisoned not less than thirty days nor more than ninety days, or both such fine and imprisonment.

SEC. 10. The Secretary of State shall revoke any license issued pursuant to the provisions and requirements of Section ——— of the Statutes of the State of ——— whenever it shall have been judicially determined that the licensee or person operating or doing business under said license has violated this Act in the course of such operation or business two times or more within any twelve-month period. No similar license shall be issued to the offending person or for the use of the place where said violations shall have occurred for a period of sixty days following such revocation. The provisions of this section may be enforced by an action of mandamus filed against the Secretary of State by any citizen of the State of ————.

SEC. 11. All persons within the jurisdiction of this state shall be entitled to the equal protection of the laws of this state or any subdivision thereof. No person shall, because of his race, color, creed, ancestry or national origin, be subjected to any discrimination in his civil rights by any other person or by any firm, corporation or institution, or by the state, or any agency or subdivision of the state. A person who shall violate this section is guilty of a misdemeanor punishable by a fine of not less than one hundred dollars or more than five hundred dollars.

SEC. 12. The provisions of this Act are hereby declared to be separable. If any provision of this Act, or the application thereof to any person or circumstances, is held invalid, the remainder of the Act, and the application of such provision to other persons or circumstances, shall not be affected thereby.

Memorandum in Support of Draft of a Model State Civil Rights Law

The object of the attached draft of a civil rights law is to prohibit discrimination on account of race, color, creed, ancestry or national origin, and the denial of equal rights to any person: (1) in admission to or in accommodation in places of public amusement or resort, (2) in employment in certain industries and businesses and (3) in labor unions.

Twenty-eight states have no civil rights laws whatsoever. Many of the other twenty-two states have laws which are inadequate and therefore largely inoperative. In those states which have some anti-discrimination legislation on the books, the bill is designed so that sections may be taken to supplement present legislation.

SEC. 1. This section is adapted from a bill introduced in Congress by the National Association for the Advancement of Colored People. It makes illegal not only active discrimination, but also punishes anyone who directly aids or causes it. The section is limited only to discrimination in admission or accommodation or service of any person in *places of public accommodation,* whether licensed by the state or not.

SEC. 2. (a) This section, adapted in part from the federal bill, is purposely not all-inclusive, since a bill enumerating a multitude of various places where equality is required would be strictly construed, and hence a failure to list certain other places would be held by the courts to be specifically excluded. Those provisions of the section referrable to educational institutions are adapted from the New York Civil Rights Law (Section 40) with the additional prohibition directed against institutions obtaining tax exemption. For obvious reasons, it does not cover educational institutions which limit admission on the basis of religious belief or affiliation.

(b) is designed to prohibit placing of signs or advertisements calling attention to the fact that the particular place of public accommodation or conveyance discourages or refuses patronage or service on the basis of race, color, creed, ancestry or national origin. Any such notice or advertisement is made prima facie evidence that the owner or manager of the particular place authorized publication.

(c) is designed to hold liable both the actual owner and his agent of any place practicing discrimination.

SEC. 3. This section is adapted from the New York Civil Rights Law, Section 40(b) and modifies the common law rule holding theater tickets to be a license revocable at the will of the theater owner. This law was recently held constitutional in *Christie* v. *46th St. Theater Corporation*, 1944. 292 N.Y. 520, 643, cert. den. 89 L. Ed. (Adv. Sheets) 35.

SEC. 4 is adapted from the New York Civil Rights Law, Section 40(a) and prohibits either the refusal to hire or the making of inquiries concerning the race, color, creed, ancestry or national origin of any person seeking employment in public schools.

SEC. 5 is adapted from the New York Civil Rights Law, Section 42 and prohibits public utility companies or common carriers from refusing to employ or promote employees on account of their race, color, creed, ancestry or national origin.

SEC. 6 is adapted from the New York Civil Rights Law, Section 44 and applies the same standard as in Section 5 to concerns doing business with federal, state or local agencies.

SEC. 7 is adapted from the New York Civil Rights Law, Section 43 and prohibits labor unions from discriminating or segregating on the basis of race, color, creed, ancestry or national origin either within the union or in employment opportunities. It extends the New York law by adding protection for union members after admission.

SEC. 8 is adapted from the New York Civil Rights Law, Section 41. This section provides a civil remedy for the violation of the prohibited discriminatory acts listed in previous sections.

SEC. 9 makes the unlawful discrimination a misdemeanor. It is desirable to provide both a civil and criminal remedy, and in terms not too severe to discourage enforcement. Where criminal penalties fail, civil damage suits can be used.

SEC. 10. This section empowers the Secretary of State to revoke the license of any person who has twice or more violated the act within a year. This section may be amended, however, to suit the particular instances, and it might be well to empower the Secretary of State, if it is within his jurisdiction, to revoke charters of incorporation or articles of partnership, etc. The revoking power, of course, may also be delegated to some other governmental agency.

SEC. 11 is adapted from the New York Penal Law, Section 700, and is a cover-all provision to punish discrimination.

SEC. 12. This is the usual separability clause which should be included wherever the proposed civil rights law is introduced as a whole.

3. Antilynching Bill

H.R. 51

(78th Congress, 1st Session)

In the House of Representatives, January 6, 1943, Mr. Gavagan introduced the following bill; which was referred to the Committee on the Judiciary

A BILL To assure to persons within the jurisdiction of every State due process of law and equal protection of the laws, and to prevent the crime of lynching.

Be it enacted by the Senate and House of Representatives of the United States of America in Congress assembled, That the provisions of this Act are enacted in exercise of the power of Congress to enforce, by appropriate legislation, the provisions of the fourteenth amendment to the Constitution of the United States and for the purpose of better assuring by the several States under said amendment equal protection and due process of law to all persons charged with or suspected or convicted of any offense within their jurisdiction.

Sec. 2. Any assemblage of three or more persons which exercises or attempts to exercise by physical violence and without authority of law any power of correction or punishment over any citizen or citizens or other person or persons in the custody of any peace officer or suspected of, charged with, or convicted of the commission of any offense, with the purpose or consequence of preventing the apprehension or trial or punishment by law of such citizen or citizens, person or persons, shall constitute a "mob" within the meaning of this Act. Any such violence by a mob which results in the death or maiming of the victim or victims thereof shall constitute "lynching" within the meaning of this Act.

Sec. 3. Whenever a lynching occurs, any officer or employee of a State or any governmental subdivision thereof who is charged with the duty or possesses the authority to protect such person or persons from lynching, and neglects or refuses to make all diligent efforts to protect such person or persons from lynching, or who has custody of the person or persons lynched and neglects or refuses to make all diligent efforts to protect such person or persons from lynching, or who is charged with the duty or possesses the authority to apprehend, keep in custody, or prosecute the members or any member of the lynching mob and neglects or refuses to make diligent efforts so to do, shall be guilty of a felony and upon conviction thereof shall be punished by a fine not exceeding $5,000 or by imprisonment not exceeding five years, or by both such fine and imprisonment.

SEC. 4. Whenever a lynching of any person or persons occurs and information on oath is submitted to the Attorney General of the United States that any officer or employee of a State or any governmental subdivision thereof who was charged with the duty or possessed the authority to protect such person or persons from lynching, or who had custody of the person or persons lynched, has neglected or refused to make all diligent efforts to protect such person or persons from lynching, or has neglected or refused to make all diligent efforts to apprehend, keep in custody, or prosecute the members or any member of the lynching mob, the Attorney General of the United States shall cause an investigation to be made to inquire whether there has been any violation of this Act.

SEC. 5. (a) Every governmental subdivision of a State to which the State shall have delegated functions of police shall be civilly liable for any lynching which occurs within its territorial jurisdiction or which follows upon seizure and abduction of the victim or victims by a mob within its territorial jurisdiction. In every case in which any officer (or officers) of that governmental subdivision charged with the duty or possessing the authority of preserving the peace, or citizens thereof when called upon by any such officer, have neglected or refused to use all diligence and all powers vested in them for the protection of the person or persons lynched. In every such case the culpable governmental subdivision shall be liable to each person injured, or to his or her next of kin if such injury results in death, for a sum not less than $2,000 and not more than $10,000 as monetary compensation for such injury or death: *Provided,* That the satisfaction of judgment against one governmental subdivision responsible for a lynching shall bar further proceedings against any other governmental subdivision which may also be responsible for that lynching.

(b) Liability arising under this section may be enforced and the compensation herein provided for may be recovered in a civil action in the United States district court for the judicial district of which the defendant governmental subdivision is a part. Such action shall be brought and prosecuted by the Attorney General of the United States or his duly authorized representative in the name of the United States for the use of the real party in interest, or, if the claimant or claimants shall so elect, by counsel employed by the claimant or claimants, but in any event without prepayment of costs. If the amount of any such judgment is not paid upon demand, payment thereof may be enforced by any process available under the State law for the enforcement of any other money judgment against such a governmental subdivision. Any officer of such governmental subdivision or any person who disobeys or fails to comply with any lawful order or decree of the court for the enforcement of the judgment shall be guilty of contempt of that court and punished accordingly. The cause of action accruing hereunder to a person injured by lynching shall not abate with the subsequent death of that person before final judgment but shall survive to his or her next of kin. For the purpose of this Act the next of kin of a deceased victim of lynching shall be determined according to the laws of intestate distribution in the State of domicile of the decedent. Any judgment or award under this Act shall be exempt from all claims of creditors.

(c) Any judge of the United States district court for the judicial district wherein any suit is instituted under the provisions of this Act may by order direct that such suit be tried in any division of such district as he may designate in such order.

(d) In any action instituted under this section, a showing either (1) that any peace officer or officers of the defendant governmental subdivision after timely notice of danger of mob violence failed to provide protection for the person subsequently lynched; or (2) that apprehension of danger of mob violence was general within the community where the abduction or lynching occurred; or (3) of any other circumstance or circumstances from which the trier of fact might reasonably conclude that the governmental subdivision had failed to use all diligence to protect the person or persons abducted or lynched, shall be prima facie evidence of liability.

SEC. 6. If any particular provision, sentence, or clause, or provisions, sentences, or clauses, of this Act, or the application thereof to any particular person or circumstance, is held invalid, the remainder of this Act, and the application of such provision to other persons or circumstances, shall not be affected thereby.

4. Federal Fair Employment Practice Bill

H.R. 2232

Union Calendar No. 49 [Report No. 187]

(79th Congress, 1st Session)

In the House of Representatives, February 16, 1945, MRS. NORTON introduced the following bill; which was referred to the Committee on Labor; February 20, 1945, Committed to the Committee of the Whole House on the state of the Union and ordered to be printed

A BILL To prohibit discrimination in employment because of race, creed, color, national origin, or ancestry.

Be it enacted by the Senate and House of Representatives of the United States of America in Congress assembled, That this Act may be cited as the "Fair Employment Practice Act."

FINDINGS AND DECLARATION OF POLICY

SEC. 2. (a) The Congress hereby finds—(1) that the practice of discriminating in the matter of employment, and in matters relating thereto, against properly qualified persons because of their race, creed, color, national origin, or ancestry leads to domestic and industrial strife and unrest and forces large segments of the population permanently into substandard conditions of living, thereby creating a drain upon the resources of the Nation and a constant threat to the maintenance of industrial peace and of the standard of living necessary to the health, efficiency, and well-being of workers; and

(2) that the existence of such practices in industries engaged in commerce or in the production of goods for commerce causes the means and instrumentalities of commerce to be used to spread and perpetuate such conditions throughout the several States and causes diminution of employment and wages in such volume as substantially to impair and disrupt the market for goods in commerce, and burdens, hinders, and obstructs commerce.

(b) Individuals shall have the right to work without discrimination against them because of their race, creed, color, national origin, or ancestry.

(c) It is hereby declared to be the policy of the Congress to protect such right and to eliminate all such discriminations to the fullest extent permitted by the Constitution. This act shall be construed to effectuate such policy.

DEFINITIONS

SEC. 3. As used in this Act—(a) The term "person" means an individual, partnership, association, corporation, legal representative, trustee, trustee in bankruptcy, receiver, or any organized group of persons, and includes any agency or instrumentality of the United States or of any Territory or possession thereof.

(b) The term "employer" means a person having in his employ six or more individuals, or any other person acting in the interest of such an employer, directly or indirectly.

(c) The term "labor union" means any organization, having six or more members, in which employees participate and which exists for the purpose, in whole or in part, of dealing with employers concerning grievances, or terms or conditions of employment.

(d) The term "commerce" means trade, traffic, commerce, transportation, or communication among the several States; or between any State or Territory, or the District of Columbia, and any place outside thereof; or within the District of Columbia or any Territory; or between points in the same State but through any point outside thereof.

(e) The term "affecting commerce" means in commerce, or burdening or obstructing commerce or the free flow of commerce, or having led or tending to lead to a labor dispute burdening or obstructing commerce or the free flow of commerce.

(f) The term "Commission" means the Fair Employment Practice Commission created by section 6.

RIGHT TO FREEDOM FROM DISCRIMINATION IN EMPLOYMENT

SEC. 4. The right to work and to seek work without discrimination because of race, creed, color, national origin, or ancestry is declared to be an immunity of all citizens of the United States, which shall not be abridged by any State or by an instrumentality or creature of the United States or of any State.

SEC. 5. (a) It shall be an unfair employment practice for the purposes of this Act for any employer—(1) to refuse to hire any individual because of such individual's race, creed, color, national origin, or ancestry; (2) to discharge any individual from employment because of such individual's race, creed, color, national origin, or ancestry; (3) to discriminate against any individual in the matter of compensation with respect to, or in other terms or conditions of, employment because of such individual's race, creed, color, national origin, or ancestry; or (4) to confine or limit recruitment or hiring of individuals for employment to any employment agency, placement service, training school or center, labor union or organization, or any other source that discriminates against individuals because of their race, color, creed, national origin, or ancestry.

(b) It shall be an unfair employment practice for the purposes of this Act for any labor union—(1) to deny full membership rights and privileges to any individual because of such individual's race, creed, color, national origin, or ancestry; (2) to expel from membership any individual because of such individual's race, creed, color, national origin, or ancestry; or (3) to discriminate against any member, employer, employee, or individual seeking employment, because of his race, creed, color, national origin, or ancestry.

(c) It shall be unfair employment practice for the purposes of this Act for any employer or labor union to discharge, expel, or otherwise discriminate against any person because such person has opposed any practice which constitutes an unfair employment practice under this Act or has filed a charge, testified, or assisted in any proceeding under this Act.

FAIR EMPLOYMENT PRACTICE COMMISSION

SEC. 6. (a) For the purpose of securing enforcement of the foregoing rights and preventing unfair employment practices, there is hereby created a commission to be known as the Fair Employment Practice Commission, which shall be composed of five members who shall be appointed by the President, by and with the advice and consent of the Senate. One of the original members shall be appointed for a term of one year, one for a term of two years, one for a term of three years, one for a term of four years, and one for a term of five years, but their successors shall be appointed for terms of five years each, except that any individual chosen to fill a vacancy shall be appointed only for the unexpired term of the member whom he shall succeed. The President shall designate one member to serve as chairman of the Commission. Any member of the Commission may be removed by the President upon notice and hearing for neglect of duty or malfeasance in office, but for no other cause.

(b) A vacancy in the Commission shall not impair the right of the remaining members to exercise all the powers of the Commission and three members of the Commission shall at all times constitute a quorum.

(c) The Commission shall have an official seal which shall be judicially noticed.

(d) The Commission shall at the close of each fiscal year report to the Congress and to the President concerning the cases it has heard, the decisions it has rendered, the names, salaries, and duties of all employees and officers in its employ or under its supervision, and an account of all moneys it has disbursed, and shall make such further reports on the cause of, and means of alleviating discrimination, and such recommendations for further legislation as may appear desirable.

(e) Each member of the Commission shall receive a salary at the rate of $10,000 a year, and shall not engage in any other business, vocation, or employment.

(f) When three members of the Commission have qualified and taken office, the Committee on Fair Employment Practice established by Executive Order Numbered 9346 of May 27, 1943, shall cease to exist. All employees of the said Committee shall then be transferred to and become employees of the Commission, and all records, papers, and property of the Committee shall then pass into the possession of the Commission.

(g) The principal office of the Commission shall be in the District of Columbia, but it may meet and exercise any or all of its powers at any other place and may establish such regional offices as it deems necessary. The Commission may, by one or more of its members or by such agents or agencies as it may designate, conduct any investigation, proceeding, or hearing necessary to its functions in any part of the United States.

(h) The Commission shall have power—(1) to appoint such officers and employees as it deems necessary to assist it in the performance of its functions; (2) to cooperate with or utilize regional, State, local, and other agencies and to utilize voluntary and uncompensated services; (3) to pay to witnesses whose depositions are taken or who are summoned before the Commission or any of its agents or agencies the same witness and mileage fees as are paid to witnesses in the courts of the United States; (4) to furnish to persons subject to this Act such technical assistance as they may request to further their compliance with this Act or any order issued thereunder; and (5) to make such technical studies as are appropriate to effectuate the purposes and policies of this Act and to make the results of such studies available to interested Government and nongovernmental agencies.

PREVENTION OF UNFAIR EMPLOYMENT PRACTICES

Sec. 7. (a) The Commission is empowered, as provided in this section—(1) to prevent unfair employment practices by employers affecting commerce; (2) to prevent unfair employment practices by employers who are parties to contracts with the United States or any Territory or possession thereof, or with any agency or instrumentality of any of the foregoing, and by employers performing, pursuant to subcontract or otherwise, any work required for the performance of any such contract; (3) to prevent unfair employment practices by agencies and instrumentalities of the United States, and of the Territories and possessions thereof; and (4) to prevent unfair employment practices by labor unions affecting commerce.

(b) Whenever it is alleged that any person has engaged in any such unfair employment practice, the Commission, or any referee, agent, or agency designated by the Commission for such purposes, shall have power to issue and cause to be served upon such person a complaint stating the charges in that respect and containing a notice of hearing before the Commission or a member thereof, or before a designated referee, agent, or agency at a place therein fixed not less than ten days after the serving of said complaint.

(c) The person so complained of shall have the right to file an answer to such complaint and to appear in person or otherwise, with or without counsel, and give testimony at the place and time fixed in the complaint.

(d) If upon the record, including all the testimony taken, the Commission shall find that any person named in the complaint has engaged in any such unfair employment practice, the Commission shall state its findings of fact and shall issue and cause to be served on such person an order requiring such person to cease and desist from such unfair employment practice and to take such affirmative action, including reinstatement or hiring of employees with or without back pay, as will effectuate the policies of this Act. If upon the record, including all the testimony taken, the Commission shall find that no person named in the complaint has engaged in any such unfair employment practice, the Commission shall state its findings of fact and shall issue an order dismissing the said complaint.

JUDICIAL REVIEW

SEC. 8. Except as provided in section 12 (relating to the enforcement of orders directed to Government agencies), orders of the Commission shall be subject to judicial enforcement and judicial review in the same manner, to the same extent, and subject to the same provisions of law, as in the case of orders of the National Labor Relations Board.

INVESTIGATORY POWERS

SEC. 9. (a) For the purpose of all investigations, proceedings, or hearings which the Commission deems necessary or proper for the exercise of the powers vested in it by this Act, the Commission, or its authorized agents or agencies, shall at all reasonable times have the right to examine or copy any evidence of any person being investigated or proceeded against relating to any such investigation, proceeding, or hearing.

(b) Any member of the Commission shall have power to issue subpoenas requiring the attendance and testimony of witnesses and the production of any evidence relating to any investigation, proceeding, or hearing before the Commission, its member, agent, or agency conducting such investigation, proceeding, or hearing.

(c) Any member of the Commission, or any agent or agency designated by the Commission for such purposes, may administer oaths, examine witnesses, and receive evidence.

(d) Such attendance of witnesses and the production of such evidence may be required, from any place in the United States or any Territory or possession thereof, at any designated place of hearing.

(e) In case of contumacy or refusal to obey a subpena issued to any person under this Act, any district court of the United States or the United States courts of any Territory or possession, or the District

Court of the United States for the District of Columbia, within the jurisdiction of which the investigation, proceeding, or hearing is carried on or within the jurisdiction of which said person guilty of contumacy or refusal to obey is found or resides or transacts business, upon application by the Commission shall have jurisdiction to issue to such person an order requiring such person to appear before the Commission, its member, agent, or agency, there to produce evidence if so ordered, or there to give testimony relating to the investigation, proceeding, or hearing; any failure to obey such order of the court may be punished by it as a contempt thereof.

(f) No person shall be excused from attending and testifying or from producing documentary or other evidence in obedience to the subpena of the Commission, on the ground that the testimony or evidence required of him may tend to incriminate him or subject him to a penalty or forfeiture; but no individual shall be prosecuted or subjected to any penalty or forfeiture for or on account of any transaction, matter, or thing concerning which he is compelled, after having claimed his privilege against self-incrimination, to testify or produce evidence, except that such individual so testifying shall not be exempt from prosecution and punishment for perjury committed in so testifying.

RULES AND REGULATIONS

SEC. 10. The Commission shall have authority from time to time to issue such regulations as it deems necessary to carry out the provisions of this Act, and to amend or rescind, from time to time, any such regulation whenever it deems such amendment or rescission necessary to carry out the provisions of this Act. If, within sixty days after the issuance of any such regulation or of an amendment to any such regulation, there is passed a concurrent resolution of the two Houses of the Congress stating in substance that Congress disapproves such regulation or amendment, as the case may be, such regulation or amendment, as the case may be, shall not be effective after the date of the passage of such concurrent resolution; and after the date of the passage of such concurrent resolution, no regulation or amendment having the same effect as that concerning which the concurrent resolution was passed shall be issued by the Commission.

Regulations issued under this section shall include the procedure for service and amendment of complaints, for intervention in proceedings before the Commission, for the taking of testimony and its reduction to writing, for the modification of the findings or orders prior to the filing of records in court, for the service and return of process, the qualification and disqualification of members and employees and any other matters appropriate in the execution of the provisions of this Act.

SEC. 11. (a) Every contract to which the United States, or any Territory or possession thereof, or any agency or instrumentality of any of the foregoing, is a party (except such classes of contracts as the Commission may by regulation issued under section 10 exempt from the scope of this section) shall contain a provision under which—(1) the contractor agrees that during the period required for the performance of the contract he will not engage in any unfair employment practices; and (2) the contractor agrees that he will include a provision in each subcontract made by him for the performance of any work required for the performance of his contract a provision under which the subcontractor agrees—(A) that during the period required for the performance of the subcontract, the subcontractor will not engage in any unfair employment practices; and (B) that the subcontractor will include in each subcontract made by him provisions corresponding to those required in subparagraph (A) and this subparagraph.

(b) Unless the Commission shall otherwise direct, no contract shall be made by the United States, or any Territory or possession thereof, or any agency or instrumentality of any of the foregoing, with any person found pursuant to this Act to have engaged in any unfair employment practice, or with any corporation, partnership, association, or other organization, in which such person owns a controlling interest, for a period (to be fixed by the Commission) not to exceed one year from the date on which such practice was so found to have been engaged in. The Commission may, by subsequent order, for good cause shown reduce any period so fixed. The Comptroller General of the United States shall distribute to all agencies and instrumentalities of the United States, and to the appropriate officials in the Territories and possessions of the United States, lists containing the names of such persons, corporations, partnerships, associations, and organizations.

ENFORCEMENT OF ORDERS DIRECTED TO GOVERNMENT AGENCIES

SEC. 12. The provisions of section 8 (providing for judicial enforcement and judicial review of orders of the Commission) shall not apply with respect to an order of the Commission under section 7 directed to any agency or instrumentality of the United States, or of any Territory or possession thereof. In the case of any such order, the Commission may request the President to take such action as he deems appropriate to secure compliance with such order, which may include the summary discharge of any officer or employee of any such agency or instrumentality who, in the opinion of the President or such person as the President may designate, has willfully failed to comply with such order.

WILLFUL INTERFERENCE WITH COMMISSION AGENTS

SEC. 13. Any person who shall willfully resist, prevent, impede, or interfere with any member of the Commission or any of its referees, agents, or agencies, in the performance of duties pursuant to this Act, shall be punished by a fine of not more than $5,000 or by imprisonment for not more than one year, or both.

SEPARABILITY CLAUSE

SEC. 14. If any provision of this Act or the application of such provision to any person or circumstance shall be held invalid, the remainder of such Act or the application of such provision to persons or circumstances other than those as to which it is held invalid shall not be affected thereby.

5. New York Law against Discrimination in Employment [1]

AN ACT To amend the executive law, in relation to prevention and elimination of practices of discrimination in employment and otherwise against persons because of race, creed, color or national origin, creating in the executive department a state commission against discrimination, defining its functions, powers and duties and providing for the appointment and compensation of its officers and employees

The People of the State of New York, represented in Senate and Assembly, do enact as follows:

SEC. 1. Chapter twenty-three of the laws of nineteen hundred nine, entitled "An act in relation to executive officers, constituting chapter eighteen of the consolidated laws," is hereby amended by inserting therein, after article eleven, a new article, to be article twelve, to read as follows:

ARTICLE 12, STATE COMMISSION AGAINST DISCRIMINATION

SEC. 125. Purposes of article. This article shall be known as the "Law Against Discrimination." It shall be deemed an exercise of the police power of the state for the protection of the public welfare, health and peace of the people of this state, and in fulfillment of the provisions of the constitution of this state concerning civil rights; and the legislature hereby finds and declares that practices of discrimination against any of its inhabitants because of race, creed, color or national origin are a matter of state concern, that such discrimination threatens not only the rights and proper privileges of its inhabitants but menaces the institutions and foundation of a free democratic state. A state agency is hereby created with power to eliminate and prevent discrimination in employment because of race, creed, color or national origin, either by employers, labor organizations, employment agencies or other persons, and to take other actions against discrimination because of race, creed, color or national origin, as herein pro-

[1] Became law March 12, 1945.

vided; and the commission established hereunder is hereby given general jurisdiction and power for such purposes.

SEC. 126. Opportunity for employment without discrimination a civil right. The opportunity to obtain employment without discrimination because of race, creed, color or national origin is hereby recognized as and declared to be a civil right.

SEC. 127. Definitions. When used in this article: 1. The term "person" includes one or more individuals, partnerships, associations, corporations, legal representatives, trustees, trustees in bankruptcy, or receivers.

2. The term "employment agency" includes any person undertaking to procure employees or opportunities to work.

3. The term "labor organization" includes any organization which exists and is constituted for the purpose, in whole or in part, of collective bargaining or of dealing with employers concerning grievances, terms or conditions of employment, or of other mutual aid or protection in connection with employment.

4. The term "unlawful employment practice" includes only those unlawful employment practices specified in section one hundred and thirty-one of this article.

5. The term "employer" does not include a club exclusively social or a fraternal, charitable, educational or religious association or corporation, if such club, association or corporation is not organized for private profit, nor does it include any employer with fewer than six persons in his employ.

6. The term "employee" and this article do not include any individual employed by his parents, spouse or child, or in the domestic service of any person.

7. The term "commission," unless a different meaning clearly appears from the context, means the state commission against discrimination created by this article.

8. The term "national origin" shall, for the purposes of this article, include "ancestry."

SEC. 128. State commission against discrimination. There is hereby created in the executive department a state commission against discrimination. Such commission shall consist of five members, to be known as commissioners, who shall be appointed by the governor, by and with the advice and consent of the senate, and one of whom shall be designated as chairman by the governor. The term of office of each member of the commission shall be for five years, provided, however, that of the commissioners first appointed, one shall be appointed for a term of one year, one for a term of two years, one for a term of three years, one for a term of four years, and one for a term of five years.

Any member chosen to fill a vacancy occurring otherwise than by expiration of term shall be appointed for the unexpired term of the member whom he is to succeed. Three members of the commission shall constitute a quorum for the purpose of conducting the business thereof. A vacancy in the commission shall not impair the right of the remaining members to exercise all the powers of the commission.

Each member of the commission shall receive a salary of ten thousand dollars a year and shall also be entitled to his expenses actually and necessarily incurred by him in the performance of his duties.

Any member of the commission may be removed by the governor for inefficiency, neglect of duty, misconduct or malfeasance in office, after being given a written statement of the charges and an opportunity to be heard thereon.

SEC. 129. General policies of commission. The commission shall formulate policies to effectuate the purposes of this article and may make recommendations to agencies and officers of the state or local subdivisions of government in aid of such policies and purposes.

SEC. 130. General powers and duties of commission. The commission shall have the following functions, powers and duties: 1. To establish and maintain its principal office in the city of Albany, and such other offices within the state as it may deem necessary.

2. To meet and function at any place within the state.

3. To appoint such attorneys, clerks, and other employees and agents as it may deem necessary, fix their compensation within the limitations provided by law, and prescribe their duties.

4. To obtain upon request and utilize the services of all governmental departments and agencies.

5. To adopt, promulgate, amend, and rescind suitable rules and regulations to carry out the provisions of this article, and the policies and practice of the commission in connection therewith.

6. To receive, investigate and pass upon complaints alleging discrimination in employment because of race, creed, color or national origin.

7. To hold hearings, subpoena witnesses, compel their attendance,

administer oaths, take the testimony of any person under oath, and in connection therewith, to require the production for examination of any books or papers relating to any matter under investigation or in question before the commission. The commission may make rules as to the issuance of subpoenas by individual commissioners.

No person shall be excused from attending and testifying or from producing records, correspondence, documents or other evidence in obedience to the subpoena of the commission or of any individual commissioner, on the ground that the testimony or evidence required of him may tend to incriminate him or subject him to a penalty or forfeiture, but no person shall be prosecuted or subjected to any penalty or forfeiture for or on account of any transaction, matter or thing concerning which he is compelled, after having claimed his privilege against self-incrimination, to testify or produce evidence, except that such person so testifying shall not be exempt from prosecution and punishment for perjury committed in so testifying. The immunity herein provided shall extend only to natural persons so compelled to testify.

8. To create such advisory agencies and conciliation councils, local, regional or state-wide, as in its judgment will aid in effectuating the purposes of this article and of section eleven of article one of the constitution of this state, and the commission may empower them to study the problem of discrimination in all or specific fields of human relationships or in specific instances of discrimination because of race, creed, color or national origin, and to foster through community effort or otherwise good-will, cooperation and conciliation among the groups and elements of the population of the state, and make recommendations to the commission for the development of policies and procedures in general and in specific instances, and for programs of formal and informal education which the commission may recommend to the appropriate state agency. Such advisory agencies and conciliation councils shall be composed of representative citizens, serving without pay, but with reimbursement for actual and necessary traveling expenses; and the commission may make provision for technical and clerical assistance to such agencies and councils and for the expenses of such assistance.

9. To issue such publications and such results of investigations and research as in its judgment will tend to promote good-will and mini-

mize or eliminate discrimination because of race, creed, color or national origin.

10. To render each year to the governor and to the legislature a full written report of all its activities and of its recommendations.

11. To adopt an official seal.

SEC. 131. Unlawful employment practices. It shall be an unlawful employment practice: 1. For an employer, because of the race, creed, color or national origin of any individual, to refuse to hire or employ or to bar or to discharge from employment such individual or to discriminate against such individual in compensation or in terms, conditions or privileges of employment.

2. For a labor organization, because of the race, creed, color or national origin of any individual, to exclude or to expel from its membership such individual or to discriminate in any way against any of its members or against any employer or any individual employed by an employer.

3. For any employer or employment agency to print or circulate or cause to be printed or circulated any statement, advertisement or publication, or to use any form of application for employment or to make any inquiry in connection with prospective employment, which expresses, directly or indirectly, any limitation, specification or discrimination as to race, creed, color or national origin, or any intent to make any such limitation, specification of discrimination, unless based upon a bona fide occupational qualification.

4. For any employer, labor organization or employment agency to discharge, expel or otherwise discriminate against any person because he has opposed any practices forbidden under this article or because he has filed a complaint, testified or assisted in any proceeding under this article.

5. For any person, whether an employer or an employee or not, to aid, abet, incite, compel or coerce the doing of any of the acts forbidden under this article, or to attempt to do so.

SEC. 132. Procedure. Any person claiming to be aggrieved by an alleged unlawful employment practice may, by himself or his attorney-at-law, make, sign and file with the commission a verified complaint in writing which shall state the name and address of the person, employer, labor organization or employment agency alleged to have committed the unlawful employment practice complained of and which shall set forth the particulars thereof and contain such other information as may be required by the commission. The industrial commissioner or attorney-general may, in like manner, make, sign and file such complaint. Any employer whose employees, or some of them, refuse or threaten to refuse to cooperate with the provisions of this article, may file with the commission a verified complaint asking for assistance by conciliation or other remedial action.

After the filing of any complaint, the chairman of the commission shall designate one of the commissioners to make, with the assistance of the commission's staff, prompt investigation in connection therewith; and if such commissioner shall determine after such investigation that probable cause exists for crediting the allegations of the complaint, he shall immediately endeavor to eliminate the unlawful employment practice complained of by conference, conciliation and persuasion. The members of the commission and its staff shall not disclose what has transpired in the course of such endeavors. In case of failure so to eliminate such practice, or in advance thereof if in his judgment circumstances so warrant, he shall cause to be issued and served in the name of the commission, a written notice, together with a copy of such complaint, as the same may have been amended, requiring the person, employer, labor organization or employment agency named in such complaint, hereinafter referred to as respondent, to answer the charges of such complaint at a hearing before three members of the commission, sitting as the commission, at a time and place to be specified in such notice. The place of any such hearing shall be the office of the commission or such other place as may be designated by it. The case in support of the complaint shall be presented before the commission by one of its attorneys or agents, and the commissioner who shall have previously made the investigation and caused the notice to be issued shall not participate in the hearing except as a witness, nor shall he participate in the deliberations of the commission in such case; and the aforesaid endeavors at conciliation shall not be received in evidence. The respondent may file a written verified answer to the complaint and appear at such hearing in person or otherwise, with or without counsel, and submit testimony. In the discretion of the commission, the complainant may be allowed to intervene and present testimony in person or by counsel. The commission or the complainant shall have the power reasonably and fairly to amend any complaint, and the respondent shall have like power to amend his answer. The commission shall not be bound by the strict rules of evidence prevailing in courts of law or equity. The testimony taken at the hearing shall be under oath and be transcribed. If, upon all the evidence at the hearing the commission shall find that a respondent has engaged in any unlawful employment practice as defined in this article, the commission shall state its findings of fact and shall issue and cause to be served on such respondent an order requiring such respondent to cease and desist from such unlawful employment practice and to take such affirmative action, including (but not limited to) hiring, reinstatement or upgrading of employees, with or without back pay, or restoration to membership in any respondent labor organization, as, in the judgment of the commission, will effectuate the purposes of this article, and including a requirement for report of the manner of compliance. If, upon all the evidence, the commission shall find that a respondent has not engaged in any such unlawful employment practice, the commission shall state its findings of fact and shall issue and cause to be served on the complainant an order dismissing the said complaint as to such respondent. A copy of its order shall be delivered in all cases to the industrial commissioner, the attorney-general, and such other public officers as the commission deems proper. The commission shall establish rules of practice to govern, expedite and effectuate the foregoing procedure and its own actions thereunder. Any complaint filed pursuant to this section must be so filed within ninety days after the alleged act of discrimination.

SEC. 133. Judicial review and enforcement. Any complainant, respondent or other person aggrieved by such order of the commission may obtain judicial review thereof, and the commission may obtain an order of court for its enforcement, in a proceeding as provided in this section. Such proceeding shall be brought in the supreme court of the state within any county wherein the unlawful employment practice which is the subject of the commission's order occurs or wherein any person required in the order to cease and desist from an unlawful employment practice or to take other affirmative action resides or transacts business. Such proceeding shall be initiated by the filing of a petition in such court, together with a written transcript of the record upon the hearing before the commission, and the issuance and service of a notice of motion returnable at a special term of such court. Thereupon the court shall have jurisdiction of the proceeding and of the questions determined therein, and shall have power to grant such temporary relief or restraining order as it deems just and proper, and to make and enter upon the pleadings, testimony, and proceedings set forth in such transcript an order enforcing, modifying, and enforcing as so modified, or setting aside in whole or in part the order of the commission. No objection that has not been urged before the commission shall be considered by the court, unless the failure or neglect to urge such objection shall be excused because of extraordinary circumstances. Any party may move the court to remit the case to the commission in the interests of justice for the purpose of adducing additional specified and material evidence and seeking findings thereon, provided he shows reasonable grounds for the failure to adduce such evidence before the commission. The findings of the commission as to the facts shall be conclusive if supported by sufficient evidence on the record considered as a whole. All such proceedings shall be heard and determined by the court and by any appellate court as expeditiously as possible and with lawful precedence over other matters. The jurisdiction of the supreme court shall be exclusive and its judgment and order shall be final, subject to review by the appellate division of the supreme court and the court of appeals in the same manner and form and with the same effect as provided in the civil practice act for appeals from a final order in a special proceeding. The commission's copy of the testimony shall be available at all reasonable times to all parties for examination without cost and for the purposes of judicial review of the order of the commission. The appeal shall be heard on the record without requirement of printing. The commission may appear in court by one of its attorneys. A proceeding under this section when instituted by any complainant, respondent or other person aggrieved must be instituted within thirty days after the service of the order of the commission.

SEC. 134. Penal provision. Any person, employer, labor organization or employment agency, who or which shall willfully resist, prevent, impede or interfere with the commission or any of its members or representatives in the performance of duty under this article, or shall willfully violate an order of the commission, shall be guilty of a misdemeanor and be punishable by imprisonment in a penitentiary, or county jail, for not more than one year, or by a fine of not more than five hundred dollars, or by both; but procedure for the review of the order shall not be deemed to be such willful conduct.

SEC. 135. Construction. The provisions of this article shall be construed liberally for the accomplishment of the purposes thereof. Nothing contained in this article shall be deemed to repeal any of the provisions of the civil rights law or of any other law of this state relating to discrimination because of race, creed, color or national origin; but, as to acts declared unlawful by section one hundred thirty-one of this article, the procedure herein provided shall, while pending, be exclusive; and the final determination therein shall exclude any other action, civil or criminal, based on the same grievance of the individual concerned. If such individual institutes any action based on such grievance without resorting to the procedure provided in this article, he may not subsequently resort to the procedure herein.

SEC. 136. Separability. If any clause, sentence, paragraph, or part of this article or the application thereof to any person or circumstances, shall, for any reason, be adjudged by a court of competent jurisdiction to be invalid, such judgment shall not affect, impair, or invalidate the remainder of this article.

SEC. 2. Existing article twelve of such chapter, as added by chapter eight hundred fifty-four of the laws of nineteen hundred forty-one and renumbered by chapter five of the laws of nineteen hundred forty-four, section one hundred forty-four have been amended by chapter two hundred sixteen of the laws of nineteen hundred forty-two, is hereby renumbered article twelve-a.

SEC. 3. This act shall take effect July first, nineteen hundred forty-five.

6. New Jersey Law against Discrimination in Employment

Chapter 169, P.L. 1945

AN ACT to prevent and eliminate practices of discrimination in employment and otherwise against persons because of race, creed, color, national origin or ancestry; to create a division in the Department of Education to effect such prevention and elimination; and making an appropriation therefor.

Be it enacted by the Senate and General Assembly of the State of New Jersey:

1. This act shall be known as "Law Against Discrimination."

2. The enactment hereof shall be deemed an exercise of the police power of the State for the protection of the public safety, health and morals and to promote the general welfare and in fulfillment of the provisions of the Constitution of this State guaranteeing civil rights.

3. The Legislature finds and declares that practices of discrimination against any of its inhabitants, because of race, creed, color, national origin or ancestry, are a matter of concern to the government of the State, and that such discrimination threatens not only the rights and proper privileges of the inhabitants of the State but menaces the institutions and foundation of a free democratic State.

4. The opportunity to obtain employment without discrimination because of race, creed, color, national origin or ancestry is recognized as and declared to be a civil right.

5. As used in this act, unless a different meaning clearly appears from the context: (a) "Person" includes one or more individuals, partnerships, associations, corporations, legal representatives, trustees, trustees in bankruptcy or receivers. (b) "Employment agency" includes any person undertaking to procure employees or opportunities to work. (c) "Labor organization" includes any organization which exists and is constituted for the purpose, in whole or in part, of collective bargaining or of dealing with employers concerning grievances, terms or conditions of employment, or of other mutual aid or protection in connection with employment. (d) "Unlawful employment practice" includes only those unlawful practices specified in section

eleven of this act. (e) "Employer" does not include a club exclusively social or a fraternal, charitable, educational or religious association or corporation, if such club, association or corporation is not organized for private profit nor does it include any employer with fewer than six persons in his employ. (f) "Employee" does not include any individual employed by his parents, spouse or child, or in the domestic service of any person. (g) "Division" means the State "Division against Discrimination" created by this act. (h) "Commissioner" means the State Commissioner of Education.

6. There is created in the State Department of Education a division to be known as "The Division against Discrimination" with power to prevent and eliminate discrimination in employment against persons because of race, creed, color, national origin or ancestry by employers, labor organizations, employment agencies or other persons and to take other actions against discrimination because of race, creed, color, national origin or ancestry, as herein provided; and the division created hereunder is given general jurisdiction and authority for such purposes.

7. The said division shall consist of the Commissioner of Education and a council. The council shall consist of seven members; each member shall be appointed by the Governor, with the advice and consent of the Senate, for a term of five years and until his successor is appointed and qualified, except that of those first appointed, one shall be appointed for a term of one year, one for a term of two years, one for a term of three years and two for a term of four years. Vacancies caused other than by expiration of term shall be filled in the same manner but for the unexpired term only. Members of the council shall serve without compensation but shall be reimbursed for necessary expenses incurred in the performance of their duties. The first chairman of the council shall be designated by the Governor and thereafter, the chairman shall be elected by the members, annually.

8. The commissioner shall (a) Exercise all powers of the division not vested in the council. (b) Administer the work of the division. (c) Prescribe the organization of the division and the duties of his subordinates and assistants. (d) Subject to the approval of the council and the Governor, appoint such other officers, employees and agents, and fix their compensation within the limits of available appropriations, except as may be otherwise provided by law. (e) Maintain liaison with local, State and Federal officials and agencies concerned with

matters related to the work of the division. (f) Subject to the approval of the council, adopt, promulgate, amend, and rescind suitable rules and regulations to carry out the provisions of this act. (g) Receive, investigate and pass upon complaints alleging discrimination in employment against persons because of race, creed, color, national origin or ancestry. (h) Hold hearings, subpoena witnesses, compel their attendance, administer oaths, take the testimony of any person, under oath, and in connection therewith, to require the production for examination of any books or papers relating to any matter under investigation or in question before the commissioner. The commissioner may make rules as to the issuance of subpoenas by the assistant commissioner. (i) Issue such publications and such results of investigations and research tending to promote good will and to minimize or eliminate discrimination because of race, creed, color, national origin or ancestry, as the council shall direct. (j) Render each year to the Governor and Legislature a full written report of all the activities of the division.

8A. An assistant commissioner of education, who shall be appointed by the Governor with the advice and consent of the Senate, shall be assigned to the division against discrimination. Such assistant commissioner shall act for the commissioner, in his place and with his power; he shall receive an annual salary of seven thousand dollars ($7,000.00); he shall hold office for five years and until his successor has qualified.

9. The council shall (a) Consult with and advise the commissioner with respect to the work of the division. (b) Approve or disapprove the appointment of officers, employees and agents, and the fixing of their compensation by the commissioner. (c) Survey and study the operations of the division. (d) Report to the Governor and the Legislature with respect to such matters relating to the work of the division and at such times as it may deem in the public interest. (e) Create such advisory agencies and conciliation councils, local, regional or State-wide, as in its judgment will aid in effectuating the purposes of this act, and the council may empower them to study the problems of discrimination in all or specific fields of human relationships or in specific instances of discrimination because of race, creed, color, national origin or ancestry and to foster through community effort or otherwise good will, co-operation and conciliation among the groups and elements of the population of the State, and make recommenda-

tions to the council for the development of policies and procedures in general and in specific instances and for programs of formal and informal education which the council may recommend to the appropriate State agency. Such advisory agencies and conciliation councils shall be composed of representative citizens, serving without pay, but with reimbursement for actual and necessary traveling expenses; and the council may make provision for technical and clerical assistance to such agencies and councils and for the expenses of such assistance.

10. No person shall be excused from attending and testifying or from producing records, correspondence, documents or other evidence in obedience to the subpoena of the commissioner or assistant commissioner, on the ground that the testimony or evidence required of him may tend to incriminate him or subject him to a penalty or forfeiture, but no person shall be prosecuted or subjected to any penalty or forfeiture for or on account of any transaction, matter or thing concerning which he is compelled, after having claimed his privilege against self-incrimination, to testify or produce evidence, except that such person so testifying shall not be exempt from prosecution and punishment for perjury committed in so testifying. The immunity herein provided shall extend only to natural persons so compelled to testify.

11. It shall be an unlawful employment practice: (a) For an employer, because of the race, creed, color, national origin or ancestry of any individual, to refuse to hire or employ or to bar or to discharge from employment such individual or to discriminate against such individual in compensation or in terms, conditions or privileges of employment. (b) For a labor organization, because of the race, creed, color, national origin or ancestry of any individual, to exclude or to expel from its membership such individual or to discriminate in any way against any of its members or against any employer or any individual employed by an employer. (c) For any employer or employment agency to print or circulate or cause to be printed or circulated any statement, advertisement or publication, or to use any form of application for employment, or to make any inquiry in connection with prospective employment, which expresses, directly or indirectly any limitation, specification or discrimination as to race, creed, color, national origin or ancestry or any intent to make any such limitation, specification or discrimination, unless based upon a bona fide occupational qualification. (d) For any employer, labor or-

ganization or employment agency to discharge, expel or otherwise discriminate against any person because he has opposed any practices forbidden under this act or because he has filed a complaint, testified or
assisted in any proceeding under this act. (e) For any person, whether
an employer or an employee or not, to aid, abet, incite, compel or coerce
the doing of any of the acts forbidden under this act, or to attempt to
do so.

12. Any person claiming to be aggrieved by an alleged unlawful
employment practice may, by himself or his attorney-at-law, make,
sign and file with the commissioner a verified complaint in writing
which shall state the name and address of the person, employer, labor
organization or employment agency alleged to have committed the
unlawful employment practice complained of and which shall set forth
the particulars thereof and contain such other information as may be
required by the commissioner. The Commissioner of Labor or Attorney-General may, in like manner, make, sign and file such complaint.
Any employer whose employees, or some of them, refuse or threaten
to refuse to co-operate with the provisions of this act, may file with
the commissioner a verified complaint asking for assistance by conciliation or other remedial action.

13. After the filing of any complaint, the commissioner shall cause
prompt investigation to be made in connection therewith; and if the
commissioner shall determine after such investigation that probable
cause exists for crediting the allegations of the complaint, he shall immediately endeavor to eliminate the unlawful employment practice
complained of by conference, conciliation and persuasion. Neither the
commissioner nor any officer or employee of the division shall disclose
what has transpired in the course of such endeavors.

14. In case of failure so to eliminate such practice, or in advance
thereof if in his judgment circumstances so warrant, he shall cause
to be issued and served in the name of the division, a written notice,
together with a copy of such complaint, as the same may have been
amended, requiring the person, employer, labor organization or employment agency named in such complaint, hereinafter referred to as
respondent, to answer the charges of such complaint at a hearing before the commissioner at a time and place to be specified in such
notice. The place of any such hearing shall be the office of the commissioner or such other place as may be designated by him.

15. The case in support of the complaint shall be presented before

the commissioner by the attorney for the division and evidence concerning attempted conciliation shall not be received. The respondent may file a written verified answer to the complaint and appear at such hearing in person or representative, with or without counsel, and submit testimony. In the discretion of the commissioner, the complainant may be allowed to intervene and present testimony in person or by counsel. The commissioner or the complainant shall have the power reasonably and fairly to amend any complaint, and the respondent shall have like power to amend his answer. The commissioner shall not be bound by the strict rules of evidence prevailing in courts of law or equity. The testimony taken at the hearing shall be under oath and be transcribed.

16. If, upon all the evidence at the hearing the commissioner shall find that the respondent has engaged in any unlawful employment practice as defined in this act, the commissioner shall state his findings of fact and shall issue and cause to be served on such respondent an order requiring such respondent to cease and desist from such unlawful employment practice and to take such affirmative action, including, but not limited to, hiring, reinstatement or upgrading of employees, with or without back pay, or restoration to membership in any respondent labor organization, as, in the judgment of the commissioner, will effectuate the purposes of this act, and including a requirement for report of the manner of compliance. If, upon all the evidence, the commissioner shall find that the respondent has not engaged in any such unlawful employment practice, the commissioner shall state his findings of fact and shall issue and cause to be served on the complainant an order dismissing the said complaint as to such respondent.

17. The commissioner shall establish rules of practice to govern, expedite and effectuate the foregoing procedure and his own actions thereunder. Any complaint filed pursuant to this section must be so filed within ninety days after the alleged act of discrimination.

18. Observance of the orders of the commissioner may be enforced by mandamus or injunction in appropriate cases, or by suit in equity to compel the specific performance of the order or of the duties imposed by law upon the respondent named in the order. Any order made by the commissioner may be reviewed upon certiorari by the Supreme Court. No certiorari shall be allowed unless application therefor be made within thirty days from the date of service of the order upon respondent nor unless notice in writing of the application shall have

been given to the commissioner with a copy of the affidavits or proof upon which the application is based. The notice shall be served upon the commissioner either personally or by leaving it at the office of the commissioner in Trenton. The evidence presented to the commissioner, together with his findings and the order issued thereon, shall be certified by the commissioner to the Supreme Court as his return.

19. The allowance of a writ of certiorari to review any order of the commissioner shall not supersede or stay such order unless the Supreme Court or a justice thereof shall so direct.

20. The Supreme Court is given jurisdiction to review any order of the commissioner and to set aside such order in whole or in part when it clearly appears that there was no evidence before the commissioner to support the same reasonably or that the same was without the jurisdiction of the commissioner.

21. No order of the commissioner shall be set aside in whole or in part for any irregularity or informality in the proceedings of the commissioner unless the irregularity or informality tends to defeat or impair the substantial right or interest of the prosecutor in certiorari.

22. Upon such review, the Supreme Court may affirm, reverse or modify any such order or may make such other order as shall appear equitable and just.

23. The commissioner's copy of the testimony shall be available at all reasonable times to all parties for examination without cost and for production upon an application for a writ of certiorari. The review upon certiorari shall be on the record without requirement of printing.

24. The Attorney-General shall be the attorney for the division.

25. Any person, employer, labor organization or employment agency, who or which shall willfully resist, prevent, impede or interfere with the commissioner or any representatives of the division in the performance of duty under this act, or shall willfully violate an order of the commissioner, shall be guilty of a misdemeanor and be punishable by imprisonment for not more than one year, or by a fine of not more than five hundred dollars ($500.00), or by both; but procedure for the review of the order shall not be deemed to be such willful conduct.

26. The provisions of this act shall be construed liberally for the accomplishment of the purposes thereof. Nothing contained in this act shall be deemed to repeal any of the provisions of the civil rights law or of any other law of this State relating to discrimination because

of race, creed, color, national origin or ancestry; but, as to acts declared unlawful by section eleven of this act, the procedure herein provided shall, while pending, be exclusive; and the final determination therein shall exclude any other action, civil or criminal, based on the same grievance of the individual concerned. If such individual institutes an action based on such grievance without resorting to the procedure provided in this act, he may not subsequently resort to the procedure herein.

27. If any clause, sentence, paragraph, or part of this act or the application thereof to any person or circumstances, shall, for any reason, be adjudged by a court of competent jurisdiction to be invalid, such judgment shall not affect, impair, or invalidate the remainder of this act.

28. There is appropriated to the Commissioner of Education the sum of forty-four thousand, three hundred fifty dollars ($44,350.00) for the fiscal year ending June thirtieth, one thousand nine hundred and forty-six, to carry out the purposes of this act.

29. This act shall take effect immediately.

Approved April 16, 1945.

7. Massachusetts Law against Discrimination in Employment [1]

AN ACT providing for a fair employment practice law and establishing a commission, to be known as the Massachusetts Fair Employment Practice Commission, and defining its powers and duties.

Be it enacted, etc., as follows:

SECTION 1. The right to work without discrimination because of race, color, religious creed, national origin or ancestry is hereby declared to be a right and privilege of the inhabitants of the commonwealth.

SECTION 2. Section seventeen of chapter six of the General Laws, as most recently amended by section one of chapter six hundred and nineteen of the acts of nineteen hundred and forty-five, is hereby further amended by inserting after the word "Authority" in the eleventh line the following:—, the Massachusetts fair employment practice commission,—so as to read as follows:—*Section 17.* The armory commission, the art commission, the commission on administration and finance, the commissioner of veterans' services, the commissioners on uniform state laws, the public bequest commission, the state ballot law commission, the board of trustees of the Soldiers' Home in Massachusetts, the milk regulation board, the alcoholic beverages control commission, the state planning board, the trustees of the state library, the state racing commission, the Greylock reservation commission, the Port of Boston Authority, the Massachusetts fair employment practice commission and the Massachusetts aeronautics commission shall serve under the governor and council, and shall be subject to such supervision as the governor and council deem necessary and proper.

SECTION 3. Said chapter six is hereby further amended by adding after section fifty-five, added by section two of chapter six hundred and nineteen of the acts of nineteen hundred and forty-five, under the caption Massachusetts Fair Employment Practice Commission, the following new section:—*Section 56.* There shall be a commission

[1] Approved May 23, 1946.

to be known as the Massachusetts Fair Employment Practice Commission.

Such commission shall consist of three members, to be known as commissioners, who shall be appointed by the governor, by and with the advice and consent of the council, and one of whom shall be designated as chairman by the governor. The term of office of each member of the commission shall be for three years, provided, however, that of the commissioners first appointed, one shall be appointed for a term of one year, one for a term of two years, one for a term of three years. Any member chosen to fill a vacancy occurring otherwise than by expiration of term shall be appointed for the unexpired term of the member whom he is to succeed. Two members of the commission shall constitute a quorum for the purpose of conducting the business thereof. A single vacancy in the commission shall not impair the right of the remaining members to exercise all the powers of the commission.

The chairman of the commission shall receive a salary of five thousand dollars per year, and each of the other members shall receive a salary of four thousand dollars per year, and each member shall also be entitled to his expenses actually and necessarily incurred by him in the performance of his duties, and shall be eligible for reappointment. Any member may be removed by the governor, with the consent of the council, for inefficiency, neglect of duty, misconduct or malfeasance in office, after being given a written statement of the charges and an opportunity to be heard thereon.

All employees of the commission, except an executive secretary, the heads of divisions, and attorneys, shall be subject to chapter thirty-one and the rules and regulations made thereunder.

SECTION 4. The General Laws are hereby amended by inserting after chapter one hundred and fifty-one A the following new chapter:—

CHAPTER 151B. UNLAWFUL DISCRIMINATION AGAINST RACE, COLOR, RELIGIOUS CREED, NATIONAL ORIGIN OR ANCESTRY.

Section 1. As used in this chapter

1. The term "person" includes one or more individuals, partnerships, associations, corporations, legal representatives, trustees, trustees in bankruptcy, receivers, and the commonwealth and all political subdivisions, boards, and commissions thereof.

2. The term "employment agency" includes any person undertaking to procure employees or opportunities to work.

3. The term "labor organization" includes any organization which exists and is constituted for the purpose, in whole or in part, of collective bargaining or of dealing with employers concerning grievances, terms or conditions of employment, or of other mutual aid or protection in connection with employment.

4. The term "unlawful employment practice" includes only those unlawful employment practices specified in section four.

5. The term "employer" does not include a club exclusively social, or a fraternal, charitable, educational or religious association or corporation, if such club, association or corporation is not organized for private profit, nor does it include any employer with fewer than six persons in his employ, but shall include the commonwealth and all political subdivisions, boards, departments, and commissions thereof.

6. The term "employee" does not include any individual employed by his parents, spouse or child, or in the domestic service of any person.

7. The term "commission," unless a different meaning clearly appears from the context, means the Massachusetts fair employment practice commission created by section fifty-six of chapter six.

Section 2. The commission, as established by section fifty-six of chapter six, shall formulate policies to effectuate the purposes of this chapter and may make recommendations to agencies and officers of the commonwealth or its political subdivisions in aid of such policies and purposes.

Section 3. The commission shall have the following functions, powers and duties:

1. To establish and maintain its principal office in the city of Boston, and such other offices within the commonwealth as it may deem necessary.

2. To meet and function at any place within the commonwealth.

3. To appoint such attorneys, clerks, and other employees and agents as it may deem necessary, fix their compensation within the limitations provided by law, and prescribe their duties.

4. To obtain upon request and utilize the services of all executive departments and agencies.

5. To adopt, promulgate, amend, and rescind rules and regulations

suitable to carry out the provisions of this chapter, and the policies and practice of the commission in connection therewith.

6. To receive, investigate and pass upon complaints alleging discrimination in employment because of race, color, religious creed, national origin, or ancestry.

7. To hold hearings, subpoena witnesses, compel their attendance, administer oaths, take the testimony of any person under oath, and in connection therewith, to require the production for examination of any books or papers relating to any matter under investigation or in question before the commission. The commission may make rules as to the issuance of subpoenas by individual commissioners.

No person shall be excused from attending and testifying or from producing books, records, correspondence, documents or other evidence in obedience to the subpoena of the commission, on the ground that the testimony or evidence required of him may tend to incriminate him or subject him to a penalty or forfeiture; but no individual shall be prosecuted or subjected to any penalty or forfeiture for or on account of any transaction, matter or thing concerning which he is compelled, after having claimed his privilege against self-incrimination, to testify or produce evidence, except that such individual so testifying shall not be exempt from prosecution and punishment for perjury committed in so testifying.

8. To create such advisory agencies and conciliation councils, local, regional or state-wide, as in its judgment will aid in effectuating the purposes of this chapter, and the commission may empower them to study the problems of discrimination in all or specific fields of human relationships or in specific instances of discrimination, because of race, color, religious creed, national origin, or ancestry, in order to foster, through community effort or otherwise, good will, co-operation and conciliation among the groups and elements of the population of the commonwealth, and make recommendations to the commission for the development of policies and procedures in general and in specific instances, and for programs of formal and informal education which the commission may recommend to the appropriate state agency. Such advisory agencies and conciliation councils shall be composed of representative citizens, serving without pay, but with reimbursement for actual and necessary traveling expenses; and the commission may make provision for technical and clerical assistance to such agencies and councils and for the expenses of such assistance.

9. To issue such publications and such results of investigations and research as in its judgment will tend to promote good will and minimize or eliminate discrimination because of race, color, religious creed, national origin or ancestry.

10. To render each year to the governor and to the general court a full written report of its activities and of its recommendations.

11. To adopt an official seal.

Section 4. It shall be an unlawful employment practice:

1. For an employer, by himself or his agent, because of the race, color, religious creed, national origin, or ancestry of any individual, to refuse to hire or employ or to bar or to discharge from employment such individual or to discriminate against such individual in compensation or in terms, conditions or privileges of employment, unless based upon a bona fide occupational qualification.

2. For a labor organization, because of the race, color, religious creed, national origin, or ancestry of any individual to exclude from full membership rights or to expel from its membership such individual or to discriminate in any way against any of its members or against any employer or any individual employed by an employer, unless based upon a bona fide occupational qualification.

3. For any employer or employment agency to print or circulate or cause to be printed or circulated any statement, advertisement or publication, or to use any form of application for employment or to make any inquiry or record in connection with employment, which expresses, directly or indirectly, any limitation, specification or discrimination as to race, color, religious creed, national origin or ancestry or any intent to make any such limitation, specification or discrimination, or to discriminate in any way on the ground of race, color, religious creed, national origin or ancestry, unless based upon a bona fide occupational qualification.

4. For any person, employer, labor organization or employment agency to discharge, expel or otherwise discriminate against any person because he has opposed any practices forbidden under this chapter or because he has filed a complaint, testified or assisted in any proceeding under section five.

5. For any person, whether an employer or an employee or not, to aid, abet, incite, compel or coerce the doing of any of the acts forbidden under this chapter or to attempt to do so.

Section 5. Any person claiming to be aggrieved by an alleged unlawful employment practice may, by himself or his attorney, make, sign and file with the commission a verified complaint in writing which shall state the name and address of the person, employer, labor organization or employment agency alleged to have committed the unlawful employment practice complained of and which shall set forth the particulars thereof and contain such other information as may be required by the commission. The attorney general may, in like manner, make, sign and file such complaint. The commission, whenever it has reason to believe that any person has been or is engaged in an unlawful employment practice, may issue such a complaint. Any employer whose employees, or some of them, refuse or threaten to refuse to co-operate with the provisions of this chapter, may file with the commission a verified complaint asking for assistance by conciliation or other remedial action.

After the filing of any complaint, the chairman of the commission shall designate one of the commissioners to make, with the assistance of the commission's staff, prompt investigation in connection therewith; and if such commissioner shall determine after such investigation that probable cause exists for crediting the allegations of the complaint, he shall immediately endeavor to eliminate the unlawful employment practice complained of by conference, conciliation and persuasion. The members of the commission and its staff shall not disclose what has occurred in the course of such endeavors, provided that the commission may publish the facts in the case of any complaint which has been dismissed, and the terms of conciliation when the complaint has been so disposed of. In case of failure so to eliminate such practice, or in advance thereof if in his judgment circumstances so warrant, he may cause to be issued and served in the name of the commission, a written notice, together with a copy of such complaint, as the same may have been amended, requiring the person, employer, labor organization or employment agency named in such complaint, hereinafter referred to as respondent, to answer the charges of such complaint at a hearing before the commission, at a time and place to be specified in such notice. The place of any such hearing shall be the office of the commission or such other place as may be designated by it. The case in support of the complaint shall be presented before the commission by one of its attorneys or agents, and the commissioner who shall have previously made the investigation and caused the notice to be issued shall not participate in the hearing except as a witness, nor shall he participate in the deliberations of the commission in such case; and the aforesaid endeavors at conciliation shall not be received in evidence. The respondent may file a written verified answer to the complaint and appear at such hearing in person or otherwise, with or without counsel, and submit testimony. In the discretion of the commission, the complainant may be allowed to intervene and present testimony in person or by counsel. The commission or the complainant shall have the power reasonably and fairly to amend any complaint, and the respondent shall have like power to amend his answer. The commission shall not be bound by the strict rules of evidence prevailing in courts of law or equity. The testimony taken at the hearing shall be under oath and be transcribed at the request of any party. If, upon all the evidence at the hearing the commission shall find that a respondent has engaged in any unlawful employment practice as defined in section four, the commission shall state its findings of fact and shall issue and cause to be served on such respondent an order requiring such respondent to cease and desist from such unlawful employment practice and to take such affirmative action, including (but not limited to) hiring, reinstatement or upgrading of employees, with or without back pay, or restoration to membership in any respondent labor organization, as, in the judgment of the commission, will effectuate the purposes of this chapter, and including a requirement for report of the manner of compliance. If, upon all the evidence, the commission shall find that a respondent has not engaged in any such unlawful employment practice, the commission shall state its findings of fact and shall issue and cause to be served on the complainant an order dismissing the said complaint as to such respondent. A copy of its order shall be delivered in all cases to the attorney general and such other public officers as the commission deems proper. The commission shall establish rules of practice to govern, expedite and effectuate the foregoing procedure and its own actions thereunder. Any complaint filed pursuant to this section must be so filed within six months after the alleged act of discrimination.

Section 6. Any complainant, respondent or other person aggrieved by such order of the commission may obtain judicial review thereof, and the commission may obtain an order of court for its enforcement, in a proceeding as provided in this section. Such proceeding shall be brought in the superior court of the commonwealth within any county wherein the unlawful employment practice which is the subject of the commission's order occurs or wherein any person required in the order to cease and desist from an unlawful employment practice or to take other affirmative action resides or transacts business. Such proceeding shall be initiated by the filing of a petition in such court, together with a written transcript of the record upon the hearing before the commission, and issuance and service of an order of notice as in proceedings in equity. The court shall have power to grant such temporary relief or restraining order as it deems just and proper, and to make and enter upon the pleadings, testimony and proceedings set forth in such transcript an order or decree enforcing, modifying, and enforcing as so modified, or setting aside in whole or in part the order of the commission with full power to issue injunctions against any respondent and to punish for contempt thereof. No objection that has not been urged before the commission shall be considered by the court, unless the failure or neglect to urge such objection shall be excused because of extraordinary circumstances. Any party may move the court to remit the case to the commission in the interests of justice for the purpose of adducing additional specified and material evidence and seeking findings thereon, provided he shows reasonable grounds for the failure to adduce such evidence before the commission. The findings of the commission as to the facts shall be conclusive if supported by sufficient evidence on the record considered as a whole. All such proceedings shall be heard and determined by the court as expeditiously as possible and shall take precedence over all other matters before it, except matters of like nature. The jurisdiction of the superior court shall be exclusive and its final order or decree shall be subject to review by the supreme judicial court in the same manner and form and with the same effect as in appeals from a final order or decree in proceedings in equity. The commission's copy of the testimony shall be available at all reasonable times to all parties for examination without cost and for the purposes of judicial review of the order of the commission. The review shall be heard on the record without requirement of printing. The commission may appear in court by one of its attorneys. A proceeding under this section when instituted by any complainant, respondent or other person aggrieved must be instituted within thirty days after the service of the order of the commission.

Section 7. Every employer, employment agency and labor union subject to this act, shall post in a conspicuous place or places on his premises a notice to be prepared or approved by the commission, which shall set forth excerpts of this chapter and such other relevant information which the commission deems necessary to explain the act. Any employer, employment agency or labor union refusing to comply with the provisions of this section shall be punished by a fine of not less than ten dollars nor more than one hundred dollars.

Section 8. Any person, employer, labor organization or employment agency, who or which shall willfully resist, prevent, impede or interfere with the commission or any of its members or representatives in the performance of duty under this chapter, or shall willfully violate a final order of the commission, or who shall willfully file a false complaint shall be punished for each offense by imprisonment for not more than one year, or by a fine of not more than five hundred dollars, or by both; but procedure for the review of the order shall not be deemed to be such willful conduct.

Section 9. The provisions of this chapter shall be construed liberally for the accomplishment of the purposes thereof, and any law inconsistent with any provision hereof shall not apply, but nothing contained in this chapter shall be deemed to repeal section ninety-eight of chapter two hundred and seventy-two or any other law of this commonwealth relating to discrimination because of race, color, religious creed, national origin, or ancestry; but, as to acts declared unlawful by section four, the procedure provided in this chapter shall, while pending, be exclusive; and the final determination therein shall exclude any other action, civil or criminal, based on the same grievance of the individual concerned. If such individual institutes any action based on such grievance without resorting to the procedure provided in this chapter, he may not subsequently resort to the procedure herein.

Section 10. If any provision of this chapter or the application thereof to any person or circumstance, shall, for any reason, be held invalid, the remainder of this chapter or the application of such provision to persons or circumstances other than those as to which it is held invalid shall not be affected thereby.

8. New York Civil Rights Acts

SEC. 13. *Right to serve on juries.* No citizen of the state possessing all other qualifications which are or may be required or prescribed by law, shall be disqualified to serve as a grand or petit juror in any court of this state on account of race, creed, color, national origin or sex, and any person charged with any duty in the selection or summoning of jurors who shall exclude or fail to summon any citizen for any of the causes aforesaid shall, on conviction thereof, be deemed guilty of a misdemeanor and be fined not less than one hundred dollars nor more than five hundred dollars, or imprisoned not less than thirty days, nor more than ninety days, or both such fine and imprisonment.

SEC. 40. *Equal rights in places of public accommodation, resort or amusement.* All persons within the jurisdiction of this state shall be entitled to the full and equal accommodations, advantages, facilities and privileges of any places of public accommodations, resort or amusement, subject only to the conditions and limitations established by law and applicable alike to all persons. No person, being the owner, lessee, proprietor, manager, superintendent, agent or employee of any such place shall directly or indirectly refuse, withhold from or deny to any person any of the accommodations, advantages, facilities or privileges thereof, or directly or indirectly publish, circulate, issue, display, post or mail any written or printed communication, notice or advertisement, to the effect that any of the accommodations, advantages, facilities and privileges of any such place shall be refused, withheld from or denied to any person on account of race, creed, or color or national origin or that the patronage or custom thereat, of any person belonging to or purporting to be of any particular race, creed or color or national origin is unwelcome, objectionable or not acceptable, desired or solicited. The production of any such written or printed communication, notice or advertisement, purporting to relate to any such place and to be made by any person being the owner, lessee, proprietor, superintendent or manager thereof, shall be presumptive evidence in any civil or criminal action that the same was authorized by such person. A place of public accommodation, resort or amusement within the meaning of this article, shall be deemed to include inns, taverns, road houses, hotels, whether conducted for the entertainment of transient guests or for the accommodation of those seeking health, recreation or rest, or restaurants, or eating houses, or any place where food is sold for consumption on the premises; buffets, saloons, barrooms, or any store, park or enclosure where spirituous or malt liquors are sold; ice cream parlors, confectioneries, soda fountains, and all stores where ice cream, ice and fruit preparations or their derivatives, or where beverages of any kind are retailed for consumption on the premises; retail stores and establishments, dispensaries, clinics, hospitals, bath-houses, barbershops, beauty parlors, theatres, motion picture houses, airdromes, roof gardens, music halls, race courses, skating rinks, amusement and recreation parks, fairs, bowling alleys, golf courses, gymnasiums, shooting galleries, billiard and pool parlors, public libraries, kindergartens, primary and secondary schools, high schools, academies, colleges and universities, extension courses, and all educational institutions under the supervision of the regents of the state of New York; and any such public library, kindergarten, primary and secondary school, academy, college, university, professional school, extension course, or other educational facility supported in whole or in part by public funds or by contributions solicited from the general public; garages, all public conveyances operated on land or water, as well as the stations and terminals thereof; public halls and public elevators of buildings and structures occupied by two or more tenants, or by the owner and one or more tenants. With regard to institutions for the care of neglected and/or delinquent children supported directly or indirectly, in whole or in part, by public funds, no accommodations, advantages, facilities and privileges of such institutions shall be refused, withheld from or denied to any person on account of race or color. Nothing herein contained shall be construed to modify or supersede any of the provisions of the children's court act, the social welfare law or the domestic relations court act of New York City in regard to religion of custodial persons or agencies or to include any institution, club, or place of accommodation which is in its nature distinctly private, or to prohibit the mailing of a private communication in writing sent in response to a specific written inquiry.

No institution, club, organization or place of accommodation which sponsors or conducts any amateur athletic contest or sparring exhibition and advertises or bills such contest or exhibition as a New York state championship contest or uses the words "New York state" in its announcements shall be deemed a private exhibition within the meaning of this section.

SEC. 40-a. *Inquiry concerning religion or religious affiliations of person seeking employment or official position in public schools prohibited.* No person, agency, bureau, corporation or association employed or maintained to obtain or aid in obtaining positions for teachers, principals, superintendents, clerks or other employees in the public schools of the state of New York, and no individual or individuals conducting or employed by or interested directly or indirectly in such an agency, bureau, corporation or association, and no board of education, trustee of a school district, superintendent, principal or teacher of a public school or other official or employee of a board of education, shall directly or indirectly ask, indicate or transmit orally or in writing the religion or religious affiliation of any person seeking employment or official position in the public schools of the state of New York.

SEC. 40-b. *Wrongful refusal of admission to and ejection from places of public entertainment and amusement.* No person, agency, bureau, corporation or association, being the owner, lessee, proprietor, manager, superintendent, agent or employee of any place of public entertainment and amusement as hereinafter defined shall refuse to admit to any public performance held at such place any person over the age of 21 years who presents a ticket of admission to the performance a reasonable time before the commencement thereof, or shall eject or demand the departure of any such person from such place during the course of the performance, whether or not accompanied by an offer to refund the purchase price or value of the ticket of admission presented by such person; but nothing in this section contained shall be construed to prevent the refusal of admission to or the ejection of any person whose conduct or speech thereat or therein is abusive or offensive or of any person engaged in any activity which may tend to a breach of the peace.

The places of public entertainment and amusement within the meaning of this section shall be legitimate theatres, burlesque theatres, music halls, opera houses, concert halls and circuses.

SEC. 41. *Penalty for violation.* Any person who or any agency, bureau, corporation or association which shall violate any of the provisions of sections 40, 40-a, 40-b, or 42 or who or which shall aid or incite the violation of any of said provisions and any officers or member of a labor organization as defined by sec. 43 of this chapter, or any person representing any organization or acting in its behalf who shall violate any of the provisions of sec. 43 of this chapter or who shall aid or incite the violation of any of the provisions of such section shall for each and every violation thereof be liable to a penalty of not less than $100 nor more than $500, to be recovered by the person aggrieved thereby or by any resident of this state, to whom such person shall assign his cause of action, in any court of competent jurisdiction in the county in which the plaintiff or the defendant shall reside; and such person and the manager or owner of or each officer of such agency, bureau, corporation or association, and such officers or member of a labor organization or person acting in his behalf, as the case may be shall, also, for every such offense be deemed guilty of a misdemeanor, and upon conviction thereof shall be fined not less than $100 nor more than $500, or shall be imprisoned not less than 30 days nor more than 90 days, or both such fine and imprisonment.

SEC. 42. *Discrimination by utility companies.* It shall be unlawful for any public utility company, as defined in the public service law, to refuse to employ any person in any capacity in the operation or maintenance of a public service on account of the race, creed, color or national origin of such person.

SEC. 43. *Discrimination by labor organizations prohibited.* As used in this section, the term "labor organization" means any organization which exists and is constituted for the purpose, in whole or in part, of collective bargaining, or of dealing with employers concerning grievances, terms or conditions of employment, or of other mutual aid or protection. No labor organization shall hereafter, directly or indirectly, by ritualistic practice, constitutional or by-law prescription, by tacit agreement among its members, or otherwise, deny a person or persons membership in its organization by reason of his race, creed, color or national origin or by regulations, practice or otherwise, deny to any of its members, by reason of race, creed, color or national origin equal treatment with all other members in any designation of members to any employer for employment, promotion or dismissal by such employer.

SEC. 44. *Discrimination by industries involved in defense contracts.* It shall be unlawful for any person, firm or corporation engaged to any extent whatsoever in the production, manufacture or distribution of military or naval material, equipment or supplies for the state of New

York or for the federal government to refuse to employ any person in any capacity on account of the race, color, creed or national origin of such person.

SEC. 45. *Powers of administration vested in industrial commissioner.* The industrial commissioner may enforce the provisions of sections 42, 43 and 44 of this chapter. For this purpose he may use the powers of administration, investigation, inquiry, subpoena, and hearing vested in him by the labor law; he may require submission at regular intervals or otherwise of information, records and reports pertinent to discriminatory practices in industries.

JUDICIARY LAW

SEC. 467. *Attorneys and Counsellors. Race or sex no bar to admission to practice.* Race, creed, color, national origin or sex shall constitute no cause for refusing any person examination or admission to practice.

PUBLIC SERVICE LAW

SEC. 79. *Adequate service; just and reasonable charges; unjust discrimination and unreasonable preferences.* . . . 3. No such corporation shall make or grant any undue or unreasonable preference or advantage to any person, corporation or locality, or to any particular description of service in any respect whatsoever, or subject any particular person, corporation or locality or any particular description of service to any undue or unreasonable prejudice or disadvantage in any respect whatsoever.

LABOR LAW

SEC. 220-e. *Provisions in contracts prohibiting discrimination on account of race or color in employment of citizens upon public works.* Every contract for or on behalf of the state or a municipality for the construction, alteration or repair of any public building or public work shall contain provisions by which the contractor with the state of municipality agrees: (a) That in the hiring of employees for the performance of work under this contract or any subcontract hereunder, no contractor, subcontractor, nor any person acting on behalf of such contractor or subcontractor, shall by reason of race, creed, color, or national origin discriminate against any citizen of the state of New York who is qualified and available to perform the work to which the employment relates; (b) That no contractor, subcontractor, nor any person on his behalf shall, in any manner, discriminate against or intimidate any employee hired for the performance of work under this contract on account of race, creed, color or national origin; (c) That there may be deducted from the amount payable to the contractor by the state or municipality under this contract a penalty of $5 for each person for each calendar day during which such person was discriminated against or intimidated in violation of the provisions of the contract; and (d) That this contract may be canceled or terminated by the state or municipality, and all moneys due or to become due hereunder may be forfeited, for a second or any subsequent violation of the terms or conditions of this section of the contract.

PENAL LAW

SEC. 514. *Protecting civil and public rights.* A person who: (1) Excludes a citizen of this state, by reason of race, color, creed, national origin or previous condition of servitude, from any public employment or employment in any capacity in industries engaged in defense contracts or from the equal enjoyment of any accommodation, facility or privilege furnished by innkeepers or common carriers, or by owners, managers or lessees of theatres or other places of amusement, or by teachers and officers of common schools and public institutions of learning; or, (2) Excludes a citizen of this state by reason of race, color, national origin or previous condition of servitude from the equal enjoyment of any accommodation, facility or privilege furnished by a cemetery association or associations; (3) Denies or aids or incites another to deny to any other person because of race, creed, color or national origin public employment or employment in any capacity in industries engaged in war contracts or the full enjoyment of any of the accommodations, advantages, facilities and privileges of any hotel, inn, tavern, restaurant, public conveyance on land or water, theatre or other place of public resort or amusement:

Is guilty of a misdemeanor, punishable by fine of not less than $50 nor more than $500. As amended L. 1918, c. 380; L. 1941, c. 478 Sec. 2; L. 1942, c. 438; L. 1942, c. 676, Sec. 2; L. 1943, c. 105, Sec. 5, eff. March 12, 1943.

SEC. 515. *Discrimination against person or class in price for admission.* If a person who owns, occupies, manages or controls a building, park, inclosure or other place, opens the same to the public generally at stated periods or otherwise, he shall not discriminate against any person or class of persons in the price charged for admission thereto. A person violating the provisions of this section is guilty of a misdemeanor.

SEC. 1191. *Discrimination and rebates by life insurance corporations prohibited.* Any life insurance corporation or corporation transacting the business of life insurance on the cooperative or assessment plan doing business in this state, or any officer or agent thereof, who:

1. Makes any discrimination in favor of individuals of the same class or of the same expectation of life either in the amount of the premium charged or in any return of premiums, dividends or other advantages; or,

4. Makes any distinction or discrimination between white persons and colored persons, wholly or partially of African descent, as to the premiums or rates charged for policies under the lives of such persons, or in any other manner whatever; or demands or requires a greater premium from such colored persons than is at that time required by such company from white persons of the same age, sex, general condition of health and prospect of longevity; or makes or requires any rebate, diminution or discount upon the amount to be paid on such policy in case of the death of such colored persons insured, or inserts in the policy any condition, or makes any stipulation whereby such person insured shall bind himself, or his heirs, executors, administrators and assigns to accept any sum less than the full value or amount of such policy in case of a claim accruing thereon by reason of the death of such person insured, other than such as are imposed upon white persons in similar cases, is guilty of a misdemeanor. Nothing in this section shall be construed to require any corporation doing business under articles 9-B or 14 of the insurance law, which limits and confines its business or membership to the members of a secret or fraternal order or body, to insure or accept any individual who is not a member of such secret or fraternal order or body.

As amended L. 1913, c. 180; L. 1940, c. 435, Sec. 3, eff. April 13, 1940.

PUBLIC HOUSING LAW

SEC. 223. *Prohibition against discrimination.* For all the purposes of this chapter, no person shall, because of race, color, creed, or national origin, be subjected to any discrimination.

EDUCATION LAW

ARTICLE 36: *Schools for Colored Children;* SEC. 920: *No exclusion on account of race or color.* No person shall be refused admission into or be excluded from any public school in the state of New York on account of race, creed, color or national origin.

INSURANCE LAW

SEC. 209. *Life, accident and health insurance; discrimination and rebating; prohibited inducements. . . .* 3. No life insurance company doing business in this state shall make any distinction or discrimination between white persons and colored persons, wholly or partially of African descent, as to the premiums or rates charged for policies upon the lives of such persons, or in any other manner whatever; nor shall any such company demand or require a greater premium from such colored persons than is at that time required by such company from white persons of the same age, sex, general condition of health and prospect of longevity, nor shall any such company make or require any rebate, diminution or discount upon the amount to be paid on such policy in case of the death of such colored persons insured, nor insert in the policy any condition, nor make any stipulation, whereby such person insured shall bind himself, or his heirs, executors, administrators or assigns, to accept any sum less than the full value or amount of such policy in case of a claim accruing thereon by reason of the death of such person insured, other than such as are imposed upon white persons in similar cases; and any such stipulation or condition so made or inserted shall be void. No life insurance company doing business in this state shall reject any application for a policy of life insurance issued and sold by it, or refuse to issue such policy after appropriate application therefor, nor shall any lower rate be fixed or discrimination be made by it in the fees or commissions of its agents for writing such a policy solely by reason of the applicant being wholly or partially of African descent.

SEC. 772-a. *Pernicious political activities.* It shall be unlawful for any person to: 3. Deprive, attempt to deprive or threaten to deprive, by any means, any person of any employment position, work, compensation or other benefit provided for or made possible in whole or in part by any act of congress or of the legislature appropriating funds for work relief or relief purposes, on account of race, creed, color, national origin or any political activity or on account of support for or opposition to any candidate or any political party in any nominating convention or election. . . .

MISCELLANEOUS

Alcoholic beverage control act, SEC. 65, prohibits refusal to serve beverage by licensee to a person on account of his race, creed, color or national origin.

Laws of 1945, ch. 813: provides for duties of Attorney General in connection with violations of a person's civil rights.

9. New Jersey Civil Rights Acts

Revised Statutes 10:1–2. Equal rights and privileges of all persons in public places. All persons within the jurisdiction of this state shall be entitled to the full and equal accommodations, advantages, facilities and privileges of any places of public accommodation, resort or amusement, subject only to the conditions and limitations established by law and applicable alike to all persons.

10:1–3. Exclusion because of race, creed or color unlawful. No owner, lessee, proprietor, manager, superintendent, agent or employee of any such place shall directly or indirectly refuse, withhold from, or deny to, any person any of the accommodations, advantages, facilities or privileges thereof, or directly or indirectly publish, circulate, issue, display, post, or mail any written or printed communication, notice or advertisement to the effect that any of the accommodations, advantages, facilities and privileges of any on account of race, creed or color, or that the patronage or custom thereat of any person belonging to or purporting to be of any particular race, creed or color is unwelcome, objectionable or not acceptable, desired or solicited.

10:1–4. Written announcement of discrimination; presumption. The production of any such written or printed communication, notice or advertisement, purporting to relate to any such place and to be made by any owner, lessee, proprietor, superintendent or manager thereof, shall be presumptive evidence in any civil or criminal action that the same was authorized by such person.

10:1–5. Place of public accommodation, resort or amusement defined. A place of public accommodation, resort or amusement within the meaning of this chapter shall be deemed to include any inn, tavern, road house or hotel, whether for entertainment of transient guests or accommodation of those seeking health, recreation or rest; any restaurant, eating house, or place where food is sold for consumption on the premises; any place maintained for sale of ice cream, ice and fruit preparations or their derivatives, soda water or confections, or where any beverages of any kind are retailed for consumption on the premises; any garage, any public conveyance operated on land or water, and stations and terminals thereof; any public bathhouse, public boardwalk, public seashore accommodation; any theater, or other place of public amusement, motion-picture house, airdrome, music hall, roof garden, skating rink, amusement and recreation park, fair, bowling alley, gymnasium, shooting gallery, billiard and pool parlor; any dispensary, clinic, hospital, public library, kindergarten, primary and secondary school, high school, academy, college and university, or any educational institution under the supervision of the regents of the state of New Jersey. Nothing contained in sections 10:1–2 to 10:1–7 of this title shall be construed to include, or to apply to, any institution, club, or place of accommodation which is in its nature distinctly private, or to prohibit the mailing of a private communication in writing sent in response to a specific written inquiry.

10:1–6. Penalty and punishment. Any person who shall violate any of the provisions of sections 10:1–2 to 10:1–5 of this title by denying to any citizen, except for reasons applicable alike to all citizens of every race, creed and color, and regardless of race, creed or color, or of previous condition of servitude, the full enjoyment of any of the accommodations, advantages, facilities or privileges in said sections enumerated, or by aiding or inciting such denial, or who shall aid, or incite the violation of any of the said provisions shall, for each and every violation thereof, forfeit and pay the sum of not less than one hundred dollars nor more than five hundred dollars, to the state, to be recovered in an action at law, with costs, and shall also, for every such violation, be deemed guilty of a misdemeanor, and upon conviction thereof, shall be subject to a fine of not more than five hundred dollars, or imprisonment of not more than ninety days, or both.

10:1–7. Action for penalty; costs and attorney's fee; taxation and determination; payment out of judgment. The aggrieved party or parties in any action authorized by section 10:1–6 of this title may institute said action in the name of the state of New Jersey. If judgment is awarded in favor of the plaintiff in such action, the aggrieved party shall be paid out of the judgment so recovered, the costs incurred in prosecuting such action, according to a bill of costs to be taxed as hereinafter provided, and also an attorney's fee of not less than twenty dollars nor more than one hundred dollars to be determined and fixed as hereinafter provided.

The bill of costs shall be taxed by the clerk of a district court if the action is brought in any district court of the state, or by the clerk of the court of common pleas if the action is brought in any civil action for tort within the jurisdiction of either of said courts. The amount of the attorney's fee shall be determined and fixed by an order of the judge of said district court or judge of the court of common pleas where such action is brought at the time of entry of said judgment.

10:1–8. Jurors not disqualified for race, color or previous condition of servitude. No citizen possessing all other qualifications prescribed by law shall be disqualified for service as a grand or petit juror in any court on account of race, color or previous condition of servitude, and any officer or other person charged with any duty in the selection or summoning of jurors who shall exclude or fail to summon any citizen for the cause aforesaid shall, on conviction thereof, be deemed guilty of a misdemeanor, and be fined not more than five thousand dollars.

LAWS 1941—CHAPTER 247

An act concerning civil rights, and amending section 10:1–1 of the revised statutes.

1. Section 10:1–1 of the Revised Statutes is amended to read as follows: *10:1–1.* The right of citizens of this state to hold office or employment shall be coextensive with their right to vote, shall be equal as to all citizens and shall not be denied or abridged on account of sex or marital status. Such equal rights and privileges shall extend to all offices, boards, commissions or other public service in the state and its political subdivisions of whatever nature or kind.

There shall be no discrimination based on sex or marital status in the compensation, appointment, assignment, promotion, transfer, dismissal or other matters pertaining to such office or employment of persons referred to in this section.

R.S. TITLE 11, CIVIL SERVICE

11:17–1. Political and religious discrimination prohibited. No person in or seeking admission to the classified service shall be appointed, demoted or removed or be favored or discriminated against because of his political or religious opinions or affiliations. No question in a test or contained in any form used in connection with the carrying out of the provisions of this subtitle shall relate to the political or religious opinions or affiliations of a competitor prospective competitor or eligible on an employment or reemployment list established and maintained by the Commission and chief examiner and secretary.

CHAPTER 114—LAWS 1942

An act prohibiting the discrimination by industries engaged in defense work in the employment of persons therein.

Whereas, during the present state of war it is essential to the interest and welfare of the people of the State of New Jersey that the utmost effort be expended in order to create the necessary war materials to carry said war to a successful conclusion; therefore, Be it enacted by the Senate and General Assembly of the State of New Jersey:

It is declared to be the public policy of the State of New Jersey that it opposes discrimination in the engagement of persons employed on defense contracts or public works, by reason of race, color or creed.

1. It shall be unlawful for any employer engaged to any extent whatsoever in the production, manufacture or distribution on military or naval material, equipment or supplies for the State of New Jersey, or for the Federal government, or for any subsidiary or agency of either the State or Federal government, or who is engaged on any defense contract whatsoever, to refuse to employ any person in any capacity on account of the race, color or creed of such person.

2. Any employer or person who (1) Excludes a citizen by reason of race, color or creed, or previous condition of servitude, from any public employment, or employment in any capacity, in industries engaged on defense contracts, (2) Denies, or aids or incites another to deny, to any person, because of race, color or creed, public employment or employment in any capacity, in industries engaged on defense contracts, shall be guilty of a misdemeanor and punishable by a fine of not less than one hundred dollars ($100.00), nor more than five hundred dollars ($500.00), or imprisonment for not more than six months, or both.

3. (a) "Employer" includes any individual, partnership, association, corporation, business trust, legal representative or any organized group of persons acting directly or indirectly in the interest of an employer in its relations to employees.

(b) "Industry" refers to any trade, business, industry or branch thereof, or group of industries, in which individuals are employed.

R.S. TITLE 18, EDUCATION

18:13–19. Nothing contained in Sections 18:13–16 to 18:13–18 of this title shall be held to limit the right of any school board to reduce the number of supervising principals, principals or teachers employed in the school district when the reduction is due to a natural diminution of the number of pupils in the district. Dismissals resulting from such reduction shall not be by reason of residence, age, sex, marriage, race, religion or political affiliation.

18:14–2. Exclusion on account of religion, nationality or color a misdemeanor. No child between the ages of four and twenty years shall be excluded from any public school on account of his religion, nationality or color. A member of any board of education who shall vote to exclude from any public school any child, on account of his religion, nationality or color shall be guilty of a misdemeanor and punished by a fine of not less than $50.00, no more than $250.00, or imprisonment in the county jail workhouse, or penitentiary of the country, for not less than 30 days nor more than 6 months, or by both such fine and imprisonment in the discretion of the court.

Article I, Rights and Privileges: 1. All men are by nature free and independent, and have certain natural and unalienable rights, among which are those of enjoying and defending life and liberty, acquiring, possessing, and protecting property, and of pursuing and obtaining safety and happiness.

4. There shall be no establishment of one religious sect in preference to another; no religious test shall be required as a qualification for any office or public trust; and no person shall be denied the enjoyment of any civil right merely on account of his religious principles.

DECISIONS OF N. J. SUPREME COURT

Bullock v. Wooding. In 1939, Supreme Court Justices Parker, Bodine and Perskie declared in their decision in *Bullock v. Wooding,* 123 N.J.L. 176: "It is, of course, settled that the dignities, equalities and rights of citizenship cannot be legally denied to members of the Negro race,"

N. J. Court of Errors and Appeals—*Patterson v. Board of Education,* Trenton, 112 N.J.L. 99.

AN ACT TO ESTABLISH A DEPARTMENT OF LAW IN THE STATE GOVERNMENT (Adopted March 6, 1944)

SEC. 4. The powers and duties of the Department of Law shall be the powers and duties now or hereafter conferred upon or required of the Attorney-General, either by the Constitution or by the common and statutory law of the State, and as specifically but not exclusively as detailed herein, to wit: . . . d. *Carry out and enforce the provisions of the New Jersey* securities law; *also the civil rights law.*

10. Civil Rights Acts of Sixteen States [1]

CALIFORNIA

1. Civil Rights Statutes

Sec. 51. *Rights of citizens in places of public accommodation or amusement.* All citizens within the jurisdiction of this state are entitled to the full and equal accommodation, advantages, facilities and privileges of inns, restaurants, hotels, eating-houses, places where ice cream or soft drinks of any kind are sold for consumption on the premises, barber shops, bath houses, theaters, skating rinks, public conveyances and all other places of public accommodation or amusement, subject only to the condition and limitations established by law, and applicable alike to all citizens.

Sec. 52. *Denial of accommodations: discrimination: liability in damages.* Whoever denies to any citizen, except for reasons applicable alike to every race or color, the full accommodations, advantages, facilities, and privileges enumerated in section fifty-one of this code, or who aids, or incites, such denial, or whoever makes any discrimination, distinction or restriction on account of color or race, or except for good cause, applicable alike to citizens of every color or race whatever, in respect to the admission of any citizen to, or his treatment in, any inn . . . , for each and every such offense is liable in damages in an amount not less than one hundred dollars, which may be recovered in an action at law brought for that purpose.

Sec. 53. *Admittance to place of amusement, etc. on presentation of ticket or price of tickets; exceptions.* It is unlawful for any corporation, person or association, or the proprietor, lessee, or the agents of either, of any opera-house, theater, melodeon, museum, circus, caravan, race-course, fair or other place of public amusement or entertainment, to refuse admittance to any person over the age of 21 years, who presents the ticket of admission . . . , or who tenders the price thereof for such ticket, and who demands admission to such place. Any person under the influence of liquor, or who is guilty of boisterous conduct or

---

[1] The author is grateful to Marie-Louise Nickerson for her contribution to this compilation of state civil rights acts.

any person of lewd or immoral character, may be excluded from any such place of amusement.

SEC. 54. *Violation of right of admission to places of amusement: damages.* A person refused admission contrary to the above provisions may recover his actual damages and $100.00 in addition thereto, from the proprietor, lessee, etc.

2. Employment Statutes

SEC. 1. Section 1735 is hereby added to the Labor Code, to read as follows: No discrimination shall be made in the employment of persons upon public works because of the race, color or religion of such persons and every contractor for public works violating this section is subject to all the penalties imposed for a violation of this chapter.[2] [The sanctions are not very clear. Sec. 1726 reads: "The body awarding the contract for public work shall take cognizance of violations of the provisions of this chapter . . ."[3] The only possible reference found is in Sec. 23.]

SEC. 23. Except in cases where a different punishment is prescribed, every offense declared by this code to be a misdemeanor is punishable by imprisonment in a county jail, not exceeding six months, or by a fine not exceeding $500. or both.[4]

ARTICLE 10, SEC. 201 [of the Civil Service Act provides that] In applying the provisions of this act or in doing any of the things provided for in this act, no person shall be discriminated against because of sex, race or marital status except that positions which in the opinion of the appointing power and the board require the services of a specific sex may be reserved to that sex.[5]

SEC. 1201.5 [makes it unlawful] to require, permit or suffer any notation or entry to be made upon or in any application, examination paper or other paper, book document or record indicating or in any wise suggesting or pertaining to race, color or religion of any person whomsoever.[6]

SCHOOL CODE, SEC. 5.798.[7] No questions relating to political or religious opinions, affiliations, race, color, or marital status shall be asked

[2] Calif. Civil Code (Deering, 1941), sec. 51–54. [3] Assembly Bill No. 31, ch. 643.
[4] Calif. Labor Code (Deering, 1937), ch. 643.   [5] *Ibid.*
[6] General Laws of Calif., Vol. I (Deering, 1937), State Civil Service Act. Act 1404, pp. 742 *et seq.* at p. 767.
[7] General Laws of Calif. (Deering, 1941 Supp., at p. 1918).

of any candidate whose name has been certified for appointment [as a member of the teaching forces], nor shall any discrimination be exercised therefor.[8]

3. General Legislation

SEC. 3.50. *Reflections on race, color or creed forbidden.* No teacher in giving instruction nor entertainments permitted in or about any school, shall reflect in any way upon citizens of the United States because of their race, color, or creed.

SEC. 3.51 [forbids use of textbooks, etc., reflecting upon race, color or creed].

SEC. 3.52 [forbids sectarian or partisan books and teachings.[9] Indian children for whom the Federal government has established schools may be excluded].[10]

SEC. 60. *Marriages of white and other persons.* All marriages of white persons with Negroes, Mongolians, members of the Malay race, or mulattoes are illegal and void.

SEC. 61. *Marriage license.* . . . and no license may be issued authorizing the marriage of a white person with a Negro, mulatto, Mongolian or member of the Malay race. . . .[11]

COLORADO

1. Civil Rights Statutes [1]

SEC. 1. *Equality of privileges to all persons.* All persons within the jurisdiction of said state shall be entitled to the full and equal enjoyment of the accommodations, advantages, facilities and privileges of inns, restaurants, eating houses, barber shops, public conveyances on land or water, theaters, and all other places of public accommodation and amusement, subject only to the conditions and limitations established by law and applicable alike to all citizens.

SEC. 2. Provides for penalty for violating this section and makes the violator civilly liable. Fine varies from $50. to $500. to be paid to person and from $10. to $300. or 1 year's imprisonment after conviction of misdemeanor.

SEC. 6. *Public accommodation, publishing of discriminative matter*

[8] Calif. School Code (Deering, 1937), pp. 385–386.
[9] Calif. School Code (Deering, 1937), pp. 184–185.
[10] *Ibid.*, at p. 4.   [11] Calif. Civil Code (Deering, 1937).
[1] Colo. Stats., 1935, ch. 35, Secs. 1–10.

forbidden. No person, being the owner, lessee, proprietor, manager, superintendent, agent or employee of any place of public accommodation, resort or amusement shall directly or indirectly, by himself or anybody else, publish, issue, circulate, send, distribute, give away or display in any way, manner, shape, means or method, except as hereinafter provided, any communication, paper, poster, folder, manuscript, book, pamphlet, writing, print, letter, notice or advertisement of any kind, nature or description, intended or calculated to discriminate or actually discriminating against any religious sect, creed, denomination or nationality, or against any of the members thereof in matter of furnishing or neglecting or refusing to furnish to them or any of them, any lodgings, housing, schooling, tuition, or any accommodations, right, privilege, advantage, or convenience offered to or enjoyed by the general public, or to the effect that any of the accommodations, rights, privileges, advantages, or conveniences of any such place of public accommodation, resort or amusement shall or will be refused, withheld from or denied to any person or persons or class of persons on account of race, sect, creed, denomination or nationality, or that the patronage, custom, presence, frequenting, dwelling, staying or lodging at such place of any person, persons, or class of persons belonging to or purporting to be of any particular race, sect, creed, denomination or nationality, is unwelcome, objectionable, or not acceptable, desired or solicited.

SEC. 8. *Places of public accommodation, resort or amusement.* A place of public accommodation, resort, or amusement within the meanings of sections 6–10 of this chapter, shall be deemed to include any inn, tavern or hotel, whether conducted for the entertainment, housing or lodging of transient guests, or for the benefit, use or accommodation of those seeking health, recreation or rest, any restaurant, eating house, public conveyance on land or water, bathhouse, barber shop, theater and music hall.

SEC. 9. [The exceptions do not prevent mailing a private communication in writing, in response to a specific written inquiry.]

SEC. 10 [provides for penalty for violation of Sec. 6, 8, and 9].[2]

2. General Legislation

Colorado Constitution, Article IX. Religious test and race discrimination forbidden; sectarian tenets. No religious test or qualification

[2] Colo. Stats. Annot. II (1935), 481–485.

shall ever be required of any person as a condition of admission into any public educational institution [3] of the state, either as a teacher or student; and no teacher or student of any such institution shall ever be required to attend or participate in any religious service whatever. No sectarian tenets or doctrines shall ever be taught in the public schools, nor shall any distinction [4] or classification of pupils be made [5] on account of race or color.

SEC. 5. *Race or sex not to disqualify.* No person shall be denied a license to practice as aforesaid on account of race or sex.[6]

SEC. 25. *Racial restrictions.* This article shall not be construed, in the case of any municipality, to confer or enlarge any authority or power to establish any restriction based upon race or color.[7]

An 1897 Act provides: all marriages between Negroes or mulattoes, of either sex, and white persons, are also declared to be absolutely void.[8]

CONNECTICUT

1. *Civil Rights Statutes* [1]

SEC. 6065. *Deprivation of rights on account of alienage, color or race.* Any person who shall subject, or cause to be subjected, any other person to the deprivation of any rights, privileges or immunities, secured or protected by the constitution or laws of this state or of the United States, on account of alienage, color or race, shall be fined not more than one thousand dollars or imprisoned not more than one year or both.

SEC. 6066. *Class discrimination.* Any person who shall, by his advertisement, ridicule or hold up to contempt any person or class of persons on account of the creed, religion, color, denomination, nationality or race of such person or class of persons, shall be fined not more than fifty dollars or imprisoned not more than thirty days or both.[2]

[3] People v. Higgins, 67 Colo. 441, 184, P. 365 (1919); "educational institution" means one of the so-called state institutions; e.g., University of Colorado, School of Mines.

[4] Jones v. Newlon, 81 Colo. 25, 253, P. 386, (1927). School official's order that separate social functions must be provided for white and colored pupils was held to violate this section.

[5] People v. Stanley, 81 Colo. 276, 255, P. 610 (1927); only the last sentence of this section refers to public schools.

[6] Colo. Stats. Annot. (1935), Vol. II, ch. 14, Atty's at Law.

[7] *Ibid.*, ch. 26, at p. 391.   [8] *Ibid.*, Vol. IV, ch. 107, at p. 57.

[1] Conn. Gen. Stats. (Supp. 1933), sec. 1160b.   [2] *Ibid.* (1930), p. 1887.

SEC. 1676c.[3] *Alienage, race or color discrimination.* All persons within the jurisdiction of this state shall be entitled to full and equal accommodations in every place of public accommodation, resort or amusement, subject only to the conditions and limitations established by law and applicable alike to all persons, and any denial of such accommodation by reason of the race, creed, or color of the applicant therefor shall be a violation of the provisions of this section. A place of public accommodation, resort or amusement within the meaning of this section shall include all inns, taverns, roadhouses, hotels, restaurants and eating houses or any place where food is sold for consumption on the premises; railroad cars and stations, street railway cars and stations, public service busses and taxicabs, and theaters, motion picture houses, music halls, amusement and recreation parks. Any person who shall violate any provision of this section shall be fined not more than one hundred dollars or imprisoned not more than thirty days or both. [Penalty changed by Sec. 860f. to read "Any person who shall violate any provision of this section shall be fined not less than twenty-five nor more than one hundred dollars or imprisoned not more than than thirty days or both."] [4]

2. General Legislation

SEC. 4183. *Discrimination against persons of African descent prohibited.* No life insurance company doing business in this state shall make any distinction or discrimination between white persons and colored persons wholly or partially of African descent, as to the premiums or rates charged for policies upon the lives of such persons; nor shall any such company demand or require greater premiums from such colored persons than such as are at that time required by such company from white persons of the same age, sex, general condition of health and hope of longevity; nor shall any such company make or require any rebate, diminution or discount upon the sum to be paid on any such policy in case of the death of any such colored person insured, nor insert in the policy any condition, nor make any stipulation whereby such person insured shall bind himself, his heirs, executors, administrators, or assigns to accept any sum less than the full value

[3] This section replaces Sec. 5985 of the General Statutes, enacted in 1918. The new section is the same as the old section except that in the new section the legislators have defined the specific places of public accommodation.
[4] Supp. to Conn. Gen. Stats., Jan. Sessions, 1, 31, 1933. 1935, ch. 319, p. 731.

or amount of such policy, in case of a claim accruing thereon by reason of the death of such person insured, other than such as are imposed upon white persons in so made or inserted shall be void.

Sec. 4184. *Affidavit of examining physician.* Each such company which shall refuse the application of any such colored person for insurance upon his life shall furnish him with the affidavit of some regular examining physician of such company, who has made the examination of such person, stating that the applicant has been refused, not because such person is a colored person, but solely upon such grounds as would be applicable to white persons of the same age and sex.

Section 4185. [Provides a fine of not more than one hundred dollars for violators of Sections 4183–84].[5]

Section 833. . . . The public schools of each town and district shall be open to children over six years of age without discrimination on account of race or color; . . .[6]

ILLINOIS

1. Civil Rights Statutes[1]

AN ACT To protect all citizens in their civil and legal rights and fixing a penalty for violation of the same.

Sec. 125. All persons entitled to equal enjoyment of accommodations —Discrimination in price on account of race or color prohibited.

Sec. 1. All persons within the jurisdiction of said state of Illinois shall be entitled to the full and equal enjoyment of the accommodations, advantages, facilities and privileges of inns, restaurants, eating houses, hotels, soda fountains, soft drink parlors, taverns, roadhouses, barber shops, department stores, clothing stores, hat stores, shoe stores, bathrooms, restrooms, theaters, skating rinks, concerts, cafes, bicycle rinks, elevators, ice cream parlors or rooms, railroads, omnibuses, busses, stages, aeroplanes, street cars, boats, funeral hearses and public conveyances on land, and amusement, subject only to the conditions and limitations established by laws and applicable alike to all citizens; nor shall there be any discrimination on account of race or color in the price to be charged and paid for lots or graves in any cemetery or places for burying the dead.

Sec. 128a. Sec. 5 . . . the owners, agents and occupants of any

[5] Conn. Gen. Stats. (1930), ch. 220, pp. 1344–45.   [6] *Ibid.*, ch. 45, p. 292.
[1] Ill. Rev. Stats. (1941), ch. 38, sec. 125.

such place [described in Sec. 125, found guilty of violating 125] shall be deemed guilty of maintaining a public nuisance, and may be enjoined. . . .

AN ACT To prohibit the publication and distribution of discriminating matter against any religious sect, creed, class, denomination, or nationality, and to punish the same. [The exemption allows mailing of a private communication in writing sent in response to a specific written or verbal inquiry.]

SEC. 129. That no person being the lessee, proprietor, manager, superintendent, agent or employee of any place of public accommodation, resort or amusement shall directly or indirectly by himself or anybody else publish, issue, circulate and distribute, give away or display in any way, manner, shape, means or method except as hereinafter provided, any communication, poster, folder, manuscript book, pamphlet, writing, print, letter, notice or advertisement of any kind, nature or description, intended or calculated to discriminate or actually discriminating against any religious sect, creed, class, denomination or nationality or against any of the members thereof in the matter of furnishing or neglecting or refusing to furnish to them or any of them lodgings, housing, schooling, tuition or any accommodations, rights, privileges, advantage or convenience offered to or enjoyed by the general public or to the effect that any of the accommodations, rights, privileges, advantages, or conveniences or any such place of public accommodation, resort or amusement shall or will be refused, withheld from or denied to any person or persons or class of persons on account of class, creed, religion, sect, denomination, nationality or that the patronage, custom, presence, frequenting, dwelling, staying or lodging at such place or any person, persons or class of persons belonging to or purporting to be of any particular religion, sect, creed, class, denomination or nationality is unwelcome, objectionable, or not acceptable, desired or solicited.

2. *Employment Statutes*

AN ACT in relation to civil and legal rights of persons in this state:

128h. SEC. 1. Discrimination in hiring persons for work relief. It shall be unlawful for any agent, appointee or employee of any State commission or governmental subdivision of this State or of any county, municipal, or political subdivision thereof or of any Park District or Forest Preserve District to either directly or indirectly discriminate or cause to be discriminated against any person or persons in this State on account of race, color or creed in the matter of hiring persons for work relief projects.

128k. *Denial of equal advantages by public officers.* SEC. 1. No officer or employee of the State of Illinois, or of any political subdivision thereof, or of any county, or of any Park District, or of any Forest Preserve District, or of any State University or subdivision thereof, or of any municipal corporation in the State of Illinois, shall deny or refuse to any person on account of race, color or religion the full and equal enjoyment of the accommodations, advantages, facilities or privileges of his office or services or of any property under his care.

17. *Race or color discrimination prohibited in contracts for public works.* SEC. 1. No person shall be refused or denied employment in any capacity on the ground of race or color, nor be discriminated against in any manner by reason thereof, in connection with the contracting for or the performance of any work or service of any kind, by, for, on behalf of, or for the benefit of this State, or of any department, bureau, commission, board, other political subdivision or agency, officer or agent thereof, providing for or relating to the performance of any of the said work or services or of any part thereof.

24a. SEC. 1. In the construction of this act the public policy of the State of Illinois is hereby declared as follows: To facilitate the rearmament and defense program of the Federal government by the integration into the war defense industries of the State of Illinois all available types of labor, skilled, semi-skilled and common, shall participate without discrimination as to race, color or creed, whatsoever.

24c. *Discrimination because of race or color in hiring or training employees prohibited.* SEC. 3. It shall be unlawful for any war defense contractor, its officers or agents or employees to discriminate against any citizen of the State of Illinois because of his race or color in the hiring of employees and training for skilled or semi-skilled employment, and every such discrimination shall be deemed violation of this act.

No housing corporation or contractor employed thereby shall deny employment to any person on account of race, creed or color.

INDIANA

1. Civil Rights Statutes

SEC. 10–901. *Persons entitled to equal accommodations.* All persons within the jurisdiction of said state shall be entitled to the full and equal enjoyments of the accommodations, advantages, facilities and privileges of inns, restaurants, eating houses, barber shops, public conveyances on land and water, theaters and all other places of public accommodations and amusement, subject only to the conditions and limitations established by law and applicable alike to all citizens.

SEC. 10–902 [provides for penalty up to $100. to aggrieved person and makes the violation a misdemeanor and the person so violating may be fined up to $100., or imprisoned for not more than 30 days or both].

SEC. 10–903 (4635). *Jurors, race or color no disqualification; penalty.* No citizen of the state of Indiana, possessing all other qualifications which are or may be prescribed by law, shall be disqualified to serve as (a) grand or petit juror in any court of said state on account of race or color, and any officer or other person charged with any duty in the selection or summoning of jurors who shall excuse or fail to summon any citizen for the cause aforesaid, shall on conviction thereof, be deemed guilty of a misdemeanor and be fined not more than one hundred dollars, or imprisoned not more than thirty days or both.[1]

IOWA

1. Civil Rights Statutes

SEC. 13251. *Civil rights defined.* All persons within this state shall be entitled to the full and equal enjoyment of the accommodations, advantages, facilities, and privileges of inns, restaurants, chop houses, eating houses, lunch counters, and all other places where refreshments are served, public conveyances, barber shops, bathhouses, theatres, and all other places of amusement.[2]

[Violation of this section is made a misdemeanor by section 13252, and the person so violating may be fined up to one hundred dollars or may be imprisoned for thirty days.]

[1] Ind. Stats. Annot. (Burns, 1933), 10–901, 10–902.
[2] Iowa Code (1939), sec. 13251.

KANSAS

1. Civil Rights Statutes

Chapter 21—Crimes and Punishments. SEC. 21–2424. *Denying civil rights on account of race or color; penalty.* That if any of the regents or trustees of any state university, college, or other school of public instruction or the state supervisor, or the owner or owners, agents, trustees, or managers in charge of any inn, hotel or boarding house, or any place of entertainment or amusement, for which a license is required by any of the municipal authorities of this state, or the owners or owner or person or persons in charge of any steamboat, railroad, stage coach, omnibus, streetcar, or any other means of public carriage for persons or freight within the state, shall make any discrimination on account of race, color, or previous condition of servitude, the person so offending shall be deemed guilty of a misdemeanor, and upon conviction thereof in any court of competent jurisdiction, shall be fined in any sum not less than ten nor more than one thousand dollars, and shall also be liable to damages in any court of competent jurisdiction to the person or persons injured thereby.[1]

2. Employment Statutes

21–2461. *Denying public work employment on account of race or color.* No person a citizen of the United States shall be refused or denied employment in any capacity on the ground of race or color, nor be discriminated against in any manner by reason thereof, in connection with any public work, or with the contracting for or the performance of any work, labor or service of any kind on any public work by or on behalf of the state of Kansas, or of any department, bureau, commission, board, or official thereof, or by or on behalf of any county, city, township, school district or other municipality of said state.

21–2462 [provides that the provision in 21–2461 shall become a part of contracts made by the state, or a department or municipality thereof and shall] apply to contractors, subcontractors or other persons doing or contracting to do the whole or a part of any public work contemplated by said contract.

21–2463 [provides a penalty for violation of the above section, the fine being not less than fifty dollars nor more than one thousand dol-

[1] Kans. Gen. Stats. Annot. (1935), 21- 2424.

lars, or by imprisonment of not more than six months or by both fine and imprisonment].[2]

75-2941. *Discrimination forbidden.* No discrimination shall be exercised, threatened or promised, by any person in the Civil Service against or in favor of any applicant, eligible, or employee in the Civil Service because of his political or religious opinions or affiliations, except that no person affiliated with a political movement advocating overthrow of government by force or violence shall be eligible to any appointment or employment under this act.[3]

44-801. *Certain labor organizations prohibited from being representative unit for the purpose of collective bargaining.* No labor organization of any kind, agency or representative committee or plan, in which employees participate and which sits for the purpose, in whole or in part, of dealing with employers concerning grievances, labor disputes, wages, rates of pay, hours of employment, or any other conditions of work, shall be the representative unit for the purpose of collective bargaining in the state of Kansas in any of the trades, crafts, schooled and unschooled, work, labor or employment of any kind or capacity, which in any manner discriminates against, or bars, or excludes from its membership any person because of his race or color: provided that the provisions of this act shall not apply to labor organizations within the provisions of 48 U.S. Sts. 1186 and 49 U.S. Sts. 1189. . . .[4]

MASSACHUSETTS

1. Civil Rights Statutes

92.A. *Places of accommodation or resort not to discriminate because of sect, creed, class, race, color or nationality.* No owner, lessee, proprietor, manager, superintendent, agent or employee of any place of public accommodation, resort or amusement shall, directly or indirectly, by himself or another, publish, issue, circulate, distribute, or display, or cause to be published, issued, circulated, distributed or displayed, in any way, any advertisement, circular, folder, book, pamphlet, written or painted or printed notice or sign, of any kind or description, intended to discriminate against or actually discriminating against persons of any religious sect, creed, class, race, color, denomi-

[2] Supp. to Kans. Gen. Stats. (1941), ch. 21, p. 239.
[3] *Ibid.*, ch. 75, p. 561. [4] *Ibid.*, ch. 44, p. 341.

nation or nationality, in the full enjoyment of the accommodations, advantages, facilities or privileges offered to the general public by such places of public accommodation, resort or amusement: provided, that nothing herein contained shall be construed to prohibit the mailing to any person of a private communication in writing, in response to his specific written inquiry.

A place of public accommodation, resort or amusement within the meaning hereof shall be defined as and shall be deemed to include any inn, whether conducted for the entertainment, housing or lodging of transient guests, or for the benefit, use or accommodation of those seeking health, recreation or rest, any restaurant, eating house, public conveyance on land or water or in the air, bathhouse, barber shop, theatre and music hall.

Any person who shall violate any provision of this section, or who shall aid in or incite, cause or bring about, in whole or in part, such a violation shall be punished by a fine of not more than one hundred dollars, or by imprisonment for not more than thirty days, or both.

SEC. 98. *Color or race discrimination.* Whoever makes any distinction, discrimination or restriction on account of color or race, except for good cause applicable alike to all persons of every color and race, relative to the admission of any person to, or his treatment in, a theatre, skating rink or other public place of amusement, licensed or unlicensed, or in a public conveyance or public meeting, or in an inn, barber shop or other public place kept for hire, gain or reward, lawful or unlawful, or whoever aids or incites such distinction, discrimination, or restriction, shall be punished by a fine of not more than three hundred dollars or by imprisonment for not more than one year, or both, and will pay to the aggrieved from twenty-five to three hundred dollars. [This last payment to the aggrieved has been changed in 1934 to read "not less than one hundred dollars nor more than five hundred dollars."] [1]

2. Employment Statutes

SEC. 98B. *Discrimination in employment on public works and in dispensing of public welfare because of race, color, religion or nationality.* Whoever, knowingly and willfully, employs discriminatory practices in the administration or giving of employment on public works or projects, or in the dispensing or giving of public relief or public welfare or

[1] Mass. Laws (Michie, 1933), ch. 272, sec. 98, amend. 1934.

any public benefit, because of race, color, religion or nationality, shall be punished by a fine of not more than one hundred dollars.[2]

MICHIGAN

1. Civil Rights Statutes [1]

Equal accommodations, etc. at restaurants, etc. All persons within the jurisdiction of this state shall be entitled to full and equal accommodations, advantages, facilities and privileges of inns, hotels, restaurants, eating houses, barber shops, billiard parlors, stores, public conveyances on land and water, theaters, motion picture houses, public educational institutions, in elevators, on escalators, in all methods of air transportation and all other places of public accommodation, amusement, and recreation, where refreshments are or may hereafter be served, subject only to the conditions and limitations established by law and applicable alike to all citizens and to all citizens alike, with uniform prices.

SEC. 2. *Denial of rights, notice of same; penalty.* Any person being an owner, lessee, proprietor, manager, superintendent, agent or employee of any such place, who shall directly or indirectly refuse, withhold from or deny to any person any of the accommodations, advantages, facilities and privileges thereof or directly or indirectly publish, circulate, issue, display, post or mail any written or printed communications, notice or advertisement to the effect that any of the accommodations, advantages, facilities and privileges of any such places shall be refused, withheld from or denied to any person on account of race, creed or color or that any particular race, creed or color is not welcome, objectionable or not acceptable, not desired or solicited, shall for every such offense be deemed guilty of a misdemeanor and upon conviction thereof shall be fined not less than fifteen (15) dollars nor more than one hundred (100) dollars or shall be imprisoned in the county jail for not less than ten (10) days nor more than ninety (90) days or both such fine and imprisonment in the discretion of the court.

2. Employment Legislation

1464–34. SEC. 24. *Discrimination prohibited.* No person in the classified civil service or seeking admission thereto, shall be appointed, re-

---

[2] 1942 Supp. to Mass. Laws, p. 77.
[1] Mich. Comp. Laws (Supp. 1933), secs. 17, 115–146.

duced or removed, or in any way favored or discriminated against because of his political, racial or religious opinions or affiliations, except for membership in any organization which has advocated or does advocate disloyalty to the government of the United States or any subdivision thereof.[2]

3. General Legislation

7368. *Persons attending school; discrimination* . . . SEC. 9. All persons residents of any school district, and five (5) years of age, shall have an equal right to attend any school therein; and no separate school or department shall be kept for any person or persons on account of race or color: Provided, That this shall not be construed to prevent the grading of schools according to the intellectual progress of the pupil, to be taught in separate places as may be deemed expedient.[3]

12457 [prohibits a life insurance corporation or company doing business in the state of Michigan from discriminating between white persons and colored persons, wholly or partially of African descent].[4]

MINNESOTA

1. Civil Rights Statutes [1]

Sec. 3?7.09. *Equal rights in hotels.* No person shall be excluded, on account of race or color, from full and equal enjoyment of any accommodation, advantage or privilege furnished by public conveyances, theaters, or other public places of amusement, or by hotels, barbershops, saloons, restaurants, or other places of refreshment, entertainment, or accommodation. Every person who violates any provision of this section, or aids or incites another to do so, shall be guilty of a gross misdemeanor, and, in addition to the penalty therefor, shall be liable in a civil action to the person aggrieved for damages not exceeding five hundred dollars.

SEC. 72.17 [forbids discrimination by insurance companies in policies or risks between persons of the same class and on account of race].

---

[2] Mich. Comp. Laws (1942 Supp.), p. 76.
[3] Mich. Comp. Laws (1929), p. 2687. This section is incorporated in Sec. 7156, at page 2623.
[4] *Ibid.,* p. 4432.   [1] Minn. Stats. (Mason, 1927), sec. 7321.

2. Employment Legislation

SEC. 181.59. *Discrimination on account of race, creed or color prohibited in contracts.* Every contract for or on behalf of the state of Minnesota, or any county, city, borough, town, township, school, school district, or any other district in the state, for materials, supplies, or construction shall contain provisions by which the contractor agrees: (1) That, in the hiring of common or skilled labor for the performance of any work under any contract, or any subcontract hereunder, no contractor, material supplier, or vendor, shall, by reason of race, creed, or color, discriminate against the person or persons who are citizens of the United States who are qualified and available to perform the work to which such employment relates; (2) That no contractor, material supplier, or vendor, shall, in any manner, discriminate against or intimidate, or prevent the employment of any such person or persons, or on being hired, prevent, or conspire to prevent, any such person or persons from the performance of work under any contract on account of race, creed or color; (3) [provides that violation is a misdemeanor]; and (4) [provides for cancellation of contract for violation].[2]

NEBRASKA

1. Civil Rights Statutes [1]

SEC. 101. *Civil rights of persons, enumerated.* All persons within this state shall be entitled to a full and equal enjoyment of the accommodations, advantages, facilities and privileges of inns, restaurants, public conveyances, barber shops, theaters and other places of amusement; subject only to the conditions and limitations established by law and applicable alike to every person.

SEC. 115. *Students, equal privileges, no distinction.* No person shall, because of age, sex, color or nationality, be deprived of the privileges of this institution [speaking of the state university].[2]

2. Employment Legislation

SEC. 801. *Collective bargaining, discrimination because of race or color prohibited, Department of Labor to enforce.* It is hereby declared to be the policy of this state that no representative agency of labor, in

[2] *Ibid.*, p. 1473.
[1] Nebr. Comp. Stats. (1929), ch. 23, art. 1.   [2] *Ibid.*, ch. 85, p. 1735.

collective bargaining with employers concerning grievances, labor disputes, wages, rates of pay, hours of employment or other conditions of
work, shall, in such collective bargaining, discriminate against any
person because of his race or color. The department of labor shall be
and hereby is charged with the duty of enforcement of this policy in
conformity with Article 2 of the Constitution of Nebraska and section
one of the 14th Amendment to the Constitution of the United States
of America.[3]

OHIO

1. Civil Rights Statutes

SEC. 12940. *Penalty for denial of privileges at inns and other places
by reason of color or race.* Whoever, being the proprietor or his employee, keeper or manager of an inn, restaurant, eating house, barber
shop, public conveyance by air, land or water, theater, store or other
place for the sale of merchandise, or any other place of public accommodation or amusement, denies to a citizen, except for reasons applicable alike to all citizens and regardless of color or race, the full enjoyment of the accommodations, advantages, facilities or privileges
thereof, or, being a person who aids or incites the denial thereof, shall
be fined not less than fifty dollars nor more than five hundred dollars
or imprisoned not less than thirty days nor more than ninety days,
or both.[1]

2. General Legislation

SEC. 12868. *Race or color shall not disqualify to act as juror.* Whoever, being an officer or other person charged with a duty in selecting
or summoning jurors, excludes or fails to summon a citizen as a grand
or petit juror on account of his race or color, provided such citizen
possesses all other qualifications required by law for jurors, shall be
fined not less than fifty dollars nor more than five hunded dollars, or
imprisoned not less than thirty days nor more than ninety days, or
both.[2]

SEC. 9401. *Discrimination against persons of African descent prohibited.* No life insurance company organized or doing business, or
that may be organized and do business within this state, shall make

[3] C.S. Supp. Nebr. (1941), ch. 48, p. 543.
[1] Ohio Code (Throckmorton, 1933), sec. 12940.   [2] *Ibid.,* p. 174.

any distinction or discrimination between white persons and colored, wholly or partially of African descent, or to premiums or rates charged for policies upon the lives of such persons than are at that time required by the company from white persons of the same age, sex, general condition of health and hope of longevity; nor make or require any rebate, diminution or discount upon the sum to be paid on such policy in case of the death of such colored person insured, nor insert in the policy any condition, nor make any stipulation whereby such person insured binds himself, his heirs, executors, administrators or assigns to accept any sum less than the full value or amount of such policy in case of a claim accruing thereon by reason of the death of the person insured, other than such as are imposed upon white persons in similar cases. Any such stipulation or condition so made or inserted shall be void.

SEC. 9402 [requires that when a company rejects a Negro such company shall furnish examining physician's certificate that rejection was because of health, etc. and not because of his color].[3]

PENNSYLVANIA

1. Civil Rights Statutes [1]

SEC. 4653. *Publishing matter discriminating against religious sect, creed, class, denomination, or nationality.* Whoever, being the owner, lessee, manager, superintendent, agent or employee of any place of public accommodation, resort or amusement, directly or indirectly, by himself or anybody else, publishes, issues, circulates, sends, distributes, gives away, or displays (except as hereinafter provided) any communication, paper, poster, folder, manuscript, book, pamphlet, writing, print, letter, notice or advertisement, of any kind, nature or description, intended or calculated to discriminate, or actually discriminating, against any religious sect, creed, class, denomination, or nationality, or against any of the members thereof, in the matter of furnishing, or neglecting or refusing to furnish, to them, or any one of them, any lodging, housing, schooling, tuition, or any accommodation, right, privilege, advantage, or convenience, offered to or enjoyed by the general public; or to the effect that any of the accommodations, rights, privileges, advantages, or conveniences of any such place of public accommodation, resort, or amusement, shall or will be refused,

[3] *Ibid.,* Div. III, p. 1174.   [1] Pa. Stats. (Purdon). Tit. 18, secs. 1211, 4653.

withheld from, or denied to any person or persons or class of persons, on account of religion, sect, creed, class, denomination, or nationality; or that the patronage, custom, presence, frequenting, dwelling, staying, or lodging at such place of any person, persons or class of persons, belonging to or purporting to be of any particular religion, sect, creed, denomination, or nationality is unwelcome, objectionable, or not acceptable, desired, or solicited, is guilty of a misdemeanor and upon conviction thereof, shall be sentenced to pay a fine of not more than one hundred dollars ($100.), or undergo imprisonment of not more than ninety (90) days, or both.

Places to which applicable: A place of public accommodation, resort or amusement, within the meaning of this act, shall be deemed to include any inn, tavern, or hotel, whether conducted for the entertainment, housing or lodging of transient guests, or for the benefit, use or accommodation of those seeking health, recreation or rest; any restaurant, eating-house, public conveyance, on land or water, bath-house, barber shop, theatre, and music hall.

SEC. 4654. *Discrimination on account of race and color.* (a) All persons within the jurisdiction of this commonwealth shall be entitled to the full and equal accommodations, advantages, facilities, and privileges of any place of public accommodation, resort or amusement, subject only to the conditions and limitations established by law and applicable alike to all persons. Whoever, being the owner, lessee, proprietor, manager, superintendent, agent or employee of any such place, directly or indirectly refuses, withholds from, or denies to any person, any of the accommodations, advantages, facilities, or privileges thereof, or directly or indirectly publishes, circulates, issues, displays, posts or mails any written or printed communication, notice or advertisement to the effect that any of the accommodations, advantages, facilities and privileges of any such places, shall be refused, withheld from or denied to, any person on account of race, creed, or color, or that the patronage or custom thereat of any person belonging to or purporting to be of any particular race, creed or color is unwelcome, objectionable or not acceptable, desired or solicited, is guilty of a misdemeanor, and upon conviction thereof, shall be sentenced to pay a fine of not more than one hundred (100) dollars, or shall undergo imprisonment for not more than ninety (90) days, or both. (b) [Any such letter or document] shall be presumptive evidence in any civil or criminal action that the same was authorized by such person. (c) [In-

cludes a comprehensive list of places deemed to be places of public
accommodation much like Sec. 1216 *supra*]. (d) Nothing contained
in this section shall be construed to include any institution, club or
place or places of public accommodation, resort or amusement, which
is or are in its or their nature distinctly private, or to prohibit the
mailing of a private communication in writing sent in response to a
specific written inquiry.

TITLE 18. SEC. 4655. *Discrimination by railroad and railway agents.*
Whoever, being an agent, conductor, or employee of any railroad or
railway corporation, excludes, allows to be excluded, or assists in the
exclusion, from any of their cars, set apart for the accommodation of
passengers, or refuses to carry thereon, any person on account of
race or color, or throws any car from the track, thereby preventing
such person from riding, is guilty of a misdemeanor, and upon conviction thereof shall be sentenced to pay a fine, not exceeding five hundred dollars, or undergo imprisonment for a term not exceeding three
months, or both.

2. Employment Legislation

SEC. 153. *Discrimination on account of race prohibited.* Every contract for, or on behalf of, the Commonwealth of Pennsylvania or of
any county, city, borough, town, township, school district, and poor
district, for the construction, alteration or repair of any public building
or public work, shall contain provisions by which the contractor agrees
(a) That, in the hiring of the employees for the performance of work
under this contract or any sub-contract hereunder, no contractor, subcontractor, nor any person acting on behalf of such contractor or
subcontractor, shall by reason of race, creed or color discriminate
against any citizen of the Commonwealth of Pennsylvania who is qualified and available to perform the work to which the employment relates. (b) That no contractor, subcontractor, nor any person on his
behalf, shall, in any manner, discriminate against or intimidate any
employee hired for the performance of work under his contract on
account of race, creed or color; (c) [Penalty for violation], (d) [con-
tract may be cancelled].[2]

SEC. 331.13. *Competitive examinations for positions.* . . . but no
applicant for appointment shall be excluded from the examinations

[2] *Ibid.*, Title 43, pp. 77–78.

conducted by the board for political, racial or religious reasons, or because of a lack of previous scholastic education. . . .[3]

SEC. 351.23 [forbids discrimination against or for any applicant or employee of the police forces in boroughs, incorporated towns and townships of the first class, because of political or religious opinions or affiliations or race].[4]

3. General Legislation

SEC. 1377. *Sub-division of districts; assignment of pupils to; distinction on account of race or color prohibited.* . . . Provided further, that hereafter it shall be unlawful for any school director, superintendent, or teacher to make any distinction whatever, on account of, or by reason of, the race or color of any pupil or scholar who may be in attendance upon, or seeking admission to, any public school maintained wholly or in part under the school laws of the Commonwealth.[5]

RHODE ISLAND

1. Civil Rights Statutes

SEC. 28. No person within the jurisdiction of this state shall be debarred from the full and equal enjoyment of the accommodations, advantages, facilities and privileges of any licensed inns, restaurants, eating houses, bath houses, music-halls, skating-rinks, theatres, public conveyances, on land or water, or from any licensed places of public accommodation or amusement, except upon conditions and limitations lawfully established and applicable alike to all citizens, or as provided by law.[1]

2. General Legislation

SEC. 1. No person shall be excluded from any public school on account of race or color, or for being over 15 years of age, nor except by force of some general regulation applicable to all persons under the same circumstances.[2]

WASHINGTON

1. Civil Rights Statutes

SEC. 2686. *Protecting civil public rights.* Every person who shall

[3] *Ibid.*, 1942, Supp. Title 61, p. 82.
[4] *Ibid.*, Title 53, p. 19.   [5] *Ibid.*, Title 24, p. 307.
[1] R.I. Gen. Laws (1938), ch. 606, sec. 27; ch. 612, sec. 47.   [2] *Ibid.*, ch. 198, p. 434.

deny to any other person because of race, creed or color, the full enjoyment of any of the accommodations, advantages, facilities or privileges of any place of public resort, accommodation, assemblage or amusement, shall be guilty of a misdemeanor.[1]

WISCONSIN

1. Civil Rights Statutes

SEC. 340.75. *Denial of rights.* Any person who shall deny to any other person, in whole or in part, the full and equal enjoyment of the accommodations, advantages, facilities and privileges of inns, restaurants, saloons, barber shops, eating houses, public conveyances on land or water, or any other place of public accommodation or amusement, except for reasons applicable alike to all persons of every race or color, or who shall aid or incite such denial, or require any person to pay a larger sum than the regular rate charged other persons for such accommodations, advantages, facilities, and privileges or any of them, or shall refuse to sell or furnish any type of automobile insurance or charge a higher rate for such insurance because of race or color, shall be liable to the person aggrieved thereby in damages not less than twenty-five dollars with costs, and shall also be punished for every such offense by fine of not more than one hundred dollars or be imprisoned in the county jail not exceeding six months, or by both such fine and imprisonment; provided, that a judgment in favor of the party aggrieved or the imposition of a fine or imprisonment shall bar any other proceeding.[2]

[1] Wash. Rev. Stats. (Remington, 1932), sec. 2686.
[2] Wis. Stats. (1941), sec. 34075.

11. State Laws Compelling or Permitting Segregation [1]

I. EDUCATION

General Segregation

ALABAMA: Const. art. 14, sec. 256; Code (1940) title 52, sec. 93.

ARIZONA: Code (1939) secs. 54–416, 430, 918.

ARKANSAS: (Pope, 1937) ch. 147, sec. 11535.

DELAWARE: Rev. Code (1935) ch. 71, art. 1, sec. 2631; art. 5, sec. 2684.

DISTRICT OF COLUMBIA: Code (1940) title 31, secs. 1110–1113.

FLORIDA: Const. art. 12, sec. 12; Fla. Stat. Annot. secs. 228.09; 242.25.

GEORGIA: Const. art. 8, sec. 1; Code (1933) Annot. secs. 2–6601; 32–909; 32–937, as amended Laws of 1945, p. 397.

INDIANA: Annot. Stat. (1933, Burns) as amended 1935, title 28, sec. 5104.

KANSAS: Gen. Stat. (1935) ch. 72, sec. 1724; amended 1937 (1943 Supp., Corrick) ch. 72, sec. 1744.

KENTUCKY: Const. sec. 187; Rev. Stat. (1944) sec. 158.020.

LOUISIANA: Const. 1921, amended 1944, art. 12, sec. 1.

MARYLAND: Annot. Code (1939) art. 77, secs. 111, 192.

MISSISSIPPI: Const. art. 8, sec. 207; Code (1942) Annot. sec. 6276; sec. 6632 (Indians).

MISSOURI: Const. art. 11, sec. 3; Rev. Stat. Annot. secs. 10349, 10488.

NEW MEXICO: Stat. Annot. (1941) sec. 55–1201.

NORTH CAROLINA: Const. art. 9, sec. 2; Gen. Stat. (1943) secs. 115–2, 115–30, 115–97, 115–66 (Indians).

OKLAHOMA: Const. art. 1, sec. 5; art. 13, sec. 3; Stat. (1941) title 70, secs. 451–460.

SOUTH CAROLINA: Const. art. 11, sec. 7; Code of Laws (1942) sec. 5377.

[1] The author is grateful to Samuel Tartalsky, Esq., for his contribution to this compilation of segregation acts.

TENNESSEE: Annot. Code (1934, Williams) secs. 2377, 2393.9, 11395.

TEXAS: Const. art. 7, sec. 7; Rev. Civil Stat. (1925, Vernon's Annot.) title 49, art. 2900.

VIRGINIA: Const. sec. 140; Code (1942) Annot. sec. 680.

WEST VIRGINIA: Code of 1943, sec. 1775.

Segregation among Deaf, Dumb, and Blind

KENTUCKY: Rev. Stat. (1944) secs. 167.080, 167.180.

LOUISIANA: Const. 1921, amended 1944, art. 12, sec. 9; Gen. Stat. 1939 (Dart) sec. 2498.

NORTH CAROLINA: Gen. Stat. (1943) secs. 116–84, 116–109, (Indians).

OKLAHOMA: Stat. (1941) title 10, sec. 201; Supp. (1945) title 10, sec. 206.1.

TEXAS: Rev. Civ. Stat. (Vernon) art. 3221.

VIRGINIA: Code (1942) Annot. sec. 979 ff.

Segregation among Blind

KENTUCKY: Rev. Stat. (1944) sec. 167.180.

LOUISIANA: Gen. Stat. 1939 (Dart) sec. 2476.

TENNESSEE: Annot. Code (1934, Williams) sec. 4545.

WEST VIRGINIA: Code of 1943, sec. 1904.

No Segregation of Blind White and Negro Pupils

ALABAMA: Code (1940) title 52, secs. 519–524.

ARKANSAS: (Pope, 1937) ch. 154, sec. 12879.

FLORIDA: Stat. Annot. sec. 242.33.

GEORGIA: Code (1933) Annot. sec. 35–703.

KANSAS: Laws of 1945, ch. 340, page 591.

NEW MEXICO: Stat. Annot. (1941) sec. 55–2203.

SOUTH CAROLINA: Code (1942) sec. 5494.

Segregation among Deaf Pupils

DISTRICT OF COLUMBIA: Code (1940) title 31, sec. 1011.

KENTUCKY: Rev. Stat. (1944) sec. 167.080.

LOUISIANA: Gen. Stat. (1939, Dart) sec. 2498.

TENNESSEE: Annot. Code 1934 (Williams) sec. 4561.

WEST VIRGINIA: Code of 1943, sec. 1904.

No Segregation among Deaf Pupils

ALABAMA: Code (1940) title 52, secs. 519–524.
ARKANSAS: (Pope, 1937) ch. 154, sec. 12827.
FLORIDA: Stat. Annot. sec. 242.33.
GEORGIA: Code (1933) Annot. sec. 35.805.
KANSAS: Laws of 1945, ch. 340, p. 591.
NEW MEXICO: Stat. Annot. (1941) sec. 55–2304.
SOUTH CAROLINA: Code (1942) sec. 5494.

Segregation in Juvenile Delinquent and Reform Schools

ALABAMA: Code (1940) title 52, secs. 603, 605, 609.
ARKANSAS: (Pope, 1937) ch. 154, secs. 12922–12929.
DISTRICT OF COLUMBIA: Code (1940) title 32, sec. 906 (girls).
DELAWARE: Rev. Code (1935) ch. 70, art. 3, secs. 2525–2531 (girls).
FLORIDA: Stat. Annot. secs. 955.12, 956.02.
GEORGIA: Code (1933) Annot. secs. 77–613.
KENTUCKY: Rev. Stat. (1944) secs. 198.030; 201.130.
LOUISIANA: Code of Crim. Law (Dart) sec. 1476.
MARYLAND: Annot. Code (1943 Supp., Flack) art. 78A, sec. 8A; art. 88A, sec. 17.
MISSISSIPPI: Code (1942) Annot. secs. 6803–6804.
MISSOURI: Rev. Stat. Annot, sec, 9021,
NORTH CAROLINA: Gen. Stat. (1943) secs. 134.82, 134.841.
OKLAHOMA: Stat. (1941) title 10, secs. 291–301; Supp. (1945), title 10, sec. 206.1.
SOUTH CAROLINA: Code (1942) secs. 2021, 2024.
TENNESSEE: Annot. Code (1934, Williams) secs. 4658, 4696, 4708.
TEXAS: Rev. Civ. Stat. (Vernon) art. 3259a, 3259b (1945 Supp., Vernon).
VIRGINIA: Code (1942) Annot. secs. 1961, 1961a, 5058 (10).
WEST VIRGINIA: Code (1943) secs. 2698, 2708, 2711, 2732.

Separate Agricultural and Trade Schools

ALABAMA: Code (1940) title 52, secs. 443, 454, 455.
FLORIDA: Stat. Annot. secs. 228.09; 241.41
KENTUCKY: Rev. Stat. (1944) sec. 166.030.
LOUISIANA: Gen. Stat. (1939, Dart) secs. 2420.32; 2465.
MARYLAND: Annot. Code (1939) art. 77, sec. 203.

MISSOURI: Rev. Stat. Annot. secs. 10773, 10779.
NORTH CAROLINA: Gen. Stat. (1943) sec. 116–92.
OKLAHOMA: Stat. (1941) title 70, sec. 1451.
SOUTH CAROLINA: Code (1942) sec. 5802.
TENNESSEE: Annot. Code (1934, Williams) sec. 2403.
TEXAS: Rev. Civ. Stat. (Vernon's Annot.) title 49, art. 2638 ff.; (1945 Supp.) title 49, sec. 2643a.
WEST VIRGINIA: Code (1943) sec. 1893.

Separate Libraries

MISSOURI: Rev. Stat. Annot. sec. 10474.
NORTH CAROLINA: Gen. Stat. (1943) sec. 125.10.
TEXAS: Rev. Civ. Stat. (Vernon's Annot.) art. 1688.

Separate Textbooks Used by Negro and White Pupils

FLORIDA: Stat. Annot. sec. 233.43(3).
NORTH CAROLINA: Gen. Stat. (1943) sec. 115–294.

Separate Colleges

ALABAMA: Code (1940) title 52, secs. 455, 456, 466, 486; ch. 23A, sec. 455(1).
ARKANSAS: (1937, Pope) sec. 13122–6.
DELAWARE: Rev. Code (1935) ch. 73, sec. 2793.
FLORIDA: Stat. Annot. sec. 241.39.
GEORGIA: Code (1933) Annot. secs. 32–101, 32–103, 32–123; Laws of 1943, p. 628.
KENTUCKY: Rev. Stat. (1944) sec. 166.010.
MARYLAND: Annot. Code (1939) art. 49B, sec. 4 ff.
MISSOURI: Rev. Stat. Annot. sec. 10773.
NORTH CAROLINA: Gen. Stat. (1943) sec. 116–99.
OKLAHOMA: Stat. (1941) title 70, secs. 455; 1451.
SOUTH CAROLINA: Const. Art. 11, sec. 8; Code (1942) secs. 5802–5803.
TENNESSEE: Annot. Code (1934, Williams) sec. 11395.
TEXAS: Rev. Civ. Stat. (Vernon's Annot.) title 49, art. 2638 ff.; (1945 Supp.) title 49, sec. 2642.
VIRGINIA: Code (1942) Annot. secs. 947; 1003l (b); (1944 Supp.) sec. 969a.
WEST VIRGINIA: Code (1943) sec. 1893.

Teacher Training Schools

ALABAMA: Code (1940) title 52, sec. 335.

ARKANSAS: (Pope, 1937) ch. 154, sec. 13063–13083.

DELAWARE: Rev. Code (1935) ch. 73, sec. 2801.

FLORIDA: Stat. Annot. secs. 241.39, 241.41.

GEORGIA: Code (1933) Annot. sec. 32–909; Laws of 1943, p. 628.

KENTUCKY: Rev. Stat. (1944) sec. 166.020.

LOUISIANA: Const. 1921, amended 1944, art. 12, sec. 9; Gen. Stat. (Dart) sec. 2421.

MARYLAND: Annot. Code (1939) art. 77, sec. 252.

MISSISSIPPI: Code (1942) Annot. sec. 6808; 1944 Supp. sec. 6808–01.

MISSOURI: Rev. Stat. Annot. sec. 10632.

NORTH CAROLINA: Gen. Stat. (1943) sec. 116.101.

OKLAHOMA: Stat. (1941) title 70, secs. 455; 1451.　.

SOUTH CAROLINA: Code (1942) sec. 5802.

TENNESSEE: Annot. Code (1934, Williams) sec. 2403.

TEXAS: Rev. Civ. Stat. (Vernon's Annot.) title 49, art. 2638; (1945 Supp.) title 49, sec. 2643a.

WEST VIRGINIA: Code (1943) sec. 1895.

Separate College for Indians

NORTH CAROLINA: Gen. Stat. (1943) sec. 116–79.

Teachers and Pupils of Same Race

TENNESSEE: Annot. Code (1934, Williams) sec. 2513.

WEST VIRGINIA: Code (1943) secs. 1775–1904.

2. TRANSPORTATION

Separate Railroad Facilities

ALABAMA: Code (1940) title 48, sec. 196.

ARKANSAS: (Pope, 1937) ch. 20, sec. 1190.

FLORIDA: Stat. Annot. sec. 352.04 ff.

GEORGIA: Code (1933) Annot. sec. 18.206 ff.

KENTUCKY: Rev. Stat. (1944) sec. 276.440.

LOUISIANA: Gen. Stat. (1939, Dart) sec. 8130.

MARYLAND: Annot. Code (1939) art. 27, sec. 510 ff.

MISSISSIPPI: Code (1942) Annot. secs. 2351–7784.

NORTH CAROLINA: Gen. Stat. (1943) secs. 60–94.

OKLAHOMA: Stat. (1941) title 13, sec. 181.

SOUTH CAROLINA: Code (1942) secs. 1269–8396.

TENNESSEE: Annot. Code (1934, Williams) secs. 5260, 5518.

TEXAS: Rev. Civ. Stat. (Vernon's Annot.) title 112, art. 6417; Penal Code (Vernon) art. 19, sec. 1659; 1945 Supp. *idem.*

VIRGINIA: Code (1942) Annot. sec. 3962.

Separate Sleeping Compartments and Bedding

ARKANSAS: (Pope, 1937) ch. 20, sec. 1193.

GEORGIA: Code (1933) Annot. sec. 18.210.

TEXAS: Rev. Civ. Stat. (Vernon) title 112, art. 6417; title 71, art. 4477, rules 71–72.

Separate Dining Car and Restaurant Facilities

SOUTH CAROLINA: Code (1942) sec. 8403.

No Separation in Pullman Sleeping Cars

MARYLAND: Annot. Code (1939) art. 27, sec. 516.

NORTH CAROLINA: Gen. Stat. (1943) secs. 60–94.

VIRGINIA: Code (1942) Annot. sec. 3968.

No Separation in Freight Cars and Caboose

ARKANSAS: (Pope, 1937) ch. 20, sec. 1201.

KENTUCKY: Rev. Stat. (1944) sec. 276.440.

MARYLAND: Annot. Code (1939) art. 27, sec. 516.

OKLAHOMA: Stat. (1941) title 13, sec. 187.

SOUTH CAROLINA: Code (1942) sec. 8399.

TENNESSEE: Annot. Code (1934, Williams) sec. 5518.

TEXAS: Rev. Civ. Stat. (Vernon) title 112, art. 6417.

VIRGINIA: Code (1942) Annot. sec. 3968.

Other Exceptions (as Sheriff with Prisoner, Nurse with Patient)

ALABAMA: Code (1940) title 48, sec. 196 ff.

ARKANSAS: (Pope, 1937) ch. 20, sec. 1192.

FLORIDA: Stat. Annot. sec. 352.10.
GEORGIA: Code (1933) Annot. sec. 18.209 ff.
KENTUCKY: Rev. Stat. (1944) sec. 276.440.
LOUISIANA: Gen. Stat. (1939, Dart) sec. 8132.
MARYLAND: Annot. Code (1939) art. 27, sec. 516.
NORTH CAROLINA: Gen. Stat. (1943) secs. 60–98.
OKLAHOMA: Stat. (1941) title 13, sec. 187 ff.
SOUTH CAROLINA: Code (1942) secs. 8396, 8398, 8399.
TENNESSEE: Annot. Code (1934, Williams) sec. 5518.
TEXAS: Rev. Civ. Stat. (Vernon) title 112, art. 6417.
VIRGINIA: Code (1942) Annot. secs. 3968–3982.

Separate Waiting Rooms

ALABAMA: Code (1940) title 48, secs. 186, 268.
ARKANSAS: (Pope, 1937) ch. 20, sec. 1190.
FLORIDA: Stat. Annot. secs. 350.21, 352.16.
LOUISIANA: Gen. Stat. (1939, Dart) sec. 8133.
MISSISSIPPI: Code (1942) Annot. sec. 7848
NORTH CAROLINA: Gen. Stat. (1943) secs .2–44.
OKLAHOMA: Stat. (1941) title 13, sec. 182.
SOUTH CAROLINA: Code (1942) sec. 8413.

Separation in Buses

ALABAMA: Code (1940) title 48, sec. 268.
ARKANSAS: (1944 Cum. Supp., 1937, Pope) secs. 6921–6927.
FLORIDA: Stat. Annot. sec. 352.04 (all common carriers).
GEORGIA: Code (1933) Annot. secs. 68.513–68.616.
LOUISIANA: Gen. Stat. (1939, Dart) sec. 5307.
MISSISSIPPI: 1944 Supp. to Code (1942) sec. 7785.
NORTH CAROLINA: Gen. Stat. (1943) sec. 62–109.
OKLAHOMA: Stat. (1941) title 47, secs. 201 ff.
SOUTH CAROLINA: Code (1942) secs. 8530–1.
TEXAS: Rev. Civ. Stat. (Vernon) title 112, art. 6417; Penal Code
    1661.1.
VIRGINIA: Code (1942) Annot. sec. 4097z.

Separation in Street Cars

ARKANSAS: (1937, Pope) ch. 20, sec. 1202.
FLORIDA: Stat. Annot. sec. 352.07.

LOUISIANA: Gen. Stat. (1939, Dart) sec. 8188.

MISSISSIPPI: 1944 Supp. to Code (1942) sec. 7785.

NORTH CAROLINA: Gen. Stat. (1943) secs. 60–135.

OKLAHOMA: Stat. (1941) title 13, sec. 181.

SOUTH CAROLINA: Code (1942) sec. 8490.

TENNESSEE: Annot. Code (1934, Williams) sec. 5527.

TEXAS: Rev. Civ. Stat. (Vernon) title 112, art. 6417; Penal Code 1659.

VIRGINIA: Code (1942) Annot. sec. 3978.

Separation in Steamboats and Ferries

MARYLAND: Annot. Code (1939) art. 27, secs. 517, 520.

NORTH CAROLINA: Gen. Stat. (1943) secs. 60–94.

SOUTH CAROLINA: Code (1942) sec. 8396.

VIRGINIA: Code (1942) sec. 4022.

3. AMUSEMENTS

Separation at Circuses

LOUISIANA: Gen. Stat. (1939, Dart) sec. 9791.

SOUTH CAROLINA: Code (1942) sec. 1271.

Separation in Theaters and Public Halls

TENNESSEE: Annot. Code (1934, Williams) sec. 5260.

VIRGINIA: Code (1942) Annot. secs. 1796a, 1796b.

Parks, Playgrounds, Beaches

MISSOURI: Rev. Stat. Annot. sec. 10474.

OKLAHOMA: Stat. (1941) title 82, sec. 489.

SOUTH CAROLINA: Code (1942) sec. 9316.

Racetracks

ARKANSAS: (1937, Pope) sec. 12473.

Billiard and Poolrooms

GEORGIA: Code (1933) Annot. sec. 84–1603.

SOUTH CAROLINA: Code (1942) sec. 6338.

WEST VIRGINIA: Code (1943) sec. 2830.

4. HOSPITALS

General

GEORGIA: Code (1933) Annot. sec. 35–225.
MISSISSIPPI: Code (1942) Annot. sec. 6927.
SOUTH CAROLINA: Code (1942) sec. 6223.

Separation of Mental Patients

ALABAMA: Code (1940) title 45, sec. 248.
GEORGIA: Code (1933) Annot. sec. 35–225.
KENTUCKY: Rev. Stat. (1944) sec. 203.180.
LOUISIANA: Gen. Stat. (1939, Dart) sec. 3896.
MISSISSIPPI: Code (1942) Annot. secs. 6766, 6882, 6883.
MISSOURI: Rev. Stat. Annot. sec. 9390.
NORTH CAROLINA: Gen. Stat. (1943) secs. 122.3, 122.83.
OKLAHOMA: Stat. (1941) title 35, sec. 251; 1945 Supp. title 10, sec. 206.1.
TENNESSEE: Annot. Code (1934, Williams) secs. 4434, 4523.
VIRGINIA: Code (1942) Annot. secs. 1004, 1005, 1092, 1093.
WEST VIRGINIA: Code (1943) sec. 2649.

Separation of Tubercular Patients

ALABAMA: Code (1940) title 45, sec. 4.
ARKANSAS: (Pope, 1937) ch. 154, secs. 12630, 12782.
DELAWARE: Rev. Code (1935) ch. 25, art. 5, sec. 820.
MARYLAND: Annot. Code (1939) art. 43, sec. 285.
OKLAHOMA: Stat. (1941) title 63, sec. 531.
TEXAS: Rev. Civ. Stat. (Vernon) title 51, art. 3254a.
WEST VIRGINIA: Code (1943) sec. 2637.

Nursing (female white nurse prohibited from nursing Negro male patient)

ALABAMA: Code (1940) title, sec. 188.

5. PENAL INSTITUTIONS

Separation

ALABAMA: Code (1940) title 12, sec. 188; title 45, secs. 52, 121, 183.

ARKANSAS: (1937, Pope) ch. 81, sec. 7125; ch. 154, secs. 12715, 12922.

DELAWARE: Rev. Code (1935) ch. 70, art. 3, sec. 2525.

FLORIDA: Stat. Annot. secs. 950.05, 950.06, 954.31.

GEORGIA: Code (1933) Annot. sec. 77.317.

LOUISIANA: Code Crim. Law (Dart) secs. 1432, 1475, 1476, 1495.

MISSISSIPPI: Code (1942) sec. 4259; 1944 Supp. to Code secs. 7950, 7956.

NORTH CAROLINA: Gen. Stat. (1943) secs. 148.43, 148.44, 153.51.

SOUTH CAROLINA: Code (1942) secs. 1035, 2021.

TENNESSEE: Annot. Code (1934, Williams) sec. 12119.

VIRGINIA: Code (1942) Annot. sec. 5048n.

WEST VIRGINIA: Code (1943) secs. 2708, 2732.

Separate Bathing Facilities

ALABAMA: Code (1940) title 45, secs. 172, 183.

TENNESSEE: Annot. Code (1934, Williams) sec. 12040.

Separate Beds

ALABAMA: Code (1940) title 45, secs. 52, 183.

ARKANSAS: (Pope, 1937) ch. 81, sec. 7125; ch. 154, secs. 12715, 12718.

MISSISSIPPI: Code (1942) sec. 7965; 1944 Supp. to Code secs. 7950, 7956.

White and Negroes Not to Be Chained Together

ALABAMA: Code (1940) title 45, sec. 52.

ARKANSAS: (1937, Pope) ch. 154, sec. 12716.

FLORIDA: Stat. Annot. sec. 952.15.

GEORGIA: Code (1933) Annot. sec. 77.9904.

NORTH CAROLINA: Gen. Stat. (1943) sec. 148.43.

SOUTH CAROLINA: Code (1942) sec. 1035.

6. WELFARE INSTITUTIONS

Paupers

ALABAMA: Code (1940) title 44, sec. 10.

GEORGIA: Code (1933) Annot. sec. 35.225.

Homes for Orphans and Aged

DELAWARE: Rev. Code (1935) ch. 70, art. 8, sec. 2590; art. 11, sec. 2598.
KENTUCKY: Rev. Stat. (1944) sec. 201.130.
NORTH CAROLINA: Gen. Stat. (1943) secs. 116–138.
OKLAHOMA: Stat. (1941) title 10, sec. 359; 1945 Supp. title 10, sec. 206.1.
TENNESSEE: Annot. Code (1934, Williams) sec. 4581.
WEST VIRGINIA: Code (1943) secs. 2627, 2630; 1945 Supp. sec. 2631(2).

7. MISCELLANEOUS

Adoption (By Persons of Same Race Only)

LOUISIANA: Gen. Stat. (1944 Supp. Dart) sec. 4839.43.
MONTANA: Rev. Code (1935) sec. 5856.
SOUTH CAROLINA: Code (1942) sec. 1446.
TEXAS: Rev. Civ. Stat. (Vernon) title 3, art. 46a(8).

Separate Telephone Booths

OKLAHOMA. Stat. (1941) title 17, sec. 135.

Boxing (White vs. Negro Prohibited)

TEXAS: Penal Code (Vernon) title 11, art. 614–11.

Fraternal Associations (Mixed Negro and White Prohibited)

NORTH CAROLINA: Gen. Stat. (1943) sec. 58.267.
VIRGINIA: Code (1942) Annot. sec. 4302a.

Army (Separate Battalions)

INDIANA: Annot. Stat. (1933, Burns) title 45, secs. 113, 114.
NEW JERSEY: Stat. Annot. 36:8–1.
NEW YORK: Consol. Laws (McKinney) Military Law, sec. 33.
NORTH CAROLINA: Gen. Stat. (1943) sec. 127.6.
WEST VIRGINIA: Code (1943) sec. 1152.

Clergy (Negro Minister May Marry Only Negro Couples)

GEORGIA: Code (1933) Annot. sec. 53–212.

Labor

ARKANSAS: (1937, Pope) ch. 111, sec. 9347.
NORTH CAROLINA: Gen. Stat. (1943) sec. 95.48.
OKLAHOMA: Stat. (1941) title 45, sec. 231.
SOUTH CAROLINA: Code (1942) sec. 1272.
TENNESSEE: Annot. Code (1934, Williams) sec. 5653.
TEXAS: Rev. Civ. Stat. (Vernon) title 95, art. 5920.

Index